Context in Action and How to Study It

Context in Action and How to Study It

Illustrations from Health Care

Edited by
Ninna Meier and Sue Dopson

UNIVERSITY PRESS

OXFORD
UNIVERSITY PRESS

Great Clarendon Street, Oxford, OX2 6DP,
United Kingdom

Oxford University Press is a department of the University of Oxford.
It furthers the University's objective of excellence in research, scholarship,
and education by publishing worldwide. Oxford is a registered trade mark of
Oxford University Press in the UK and in certain other countries

© Oxford University Press 2019

The moral rights of the authors have been asserted

First Edition published in 2019

Impression: 1

All rights reserved. No part of this publication may be reproduced, stored in
a retrieval system, or transmitted, in any form or by any means, without the
prior permission in writing of Oxford University Press, or as expressly permitted
by law, by licence or under terms agreed with the appropriate reprographics
rights organization. Enquiries concerning reproduction outside the scope of the
above should be sent to the Rights Department, Oxford University Press, at the
address above

You must not circulate this work in any other form
and you must impose this same condition on any acquirer

Published in the United States of America by Oxford University Press
198 Madison Avenue, New York, NY 10016, United States of America

British Library Cataloguing in Publication Data

Data available

Library of Congress Control Number: 2018967874

ISBN 978-0-19-880530-4

Printed and bound by
CPI Group (UK) Ltd, Croydon, CR0 4YY

Links to third party websites are provided by Oxford in good faith and
for information only. Oxford disclaims any responsibility for the materials
contained in any third party website referenced in this work.

For Troels
For John Paul, Robert, and David
Thank you

Acknowledgments

Several people have been crucial to the making of this book. First, we would like to thank our contributors, who accepted our invitation to share their experiences with and reflections on analyzing contexts in actions. Their interesting contributions plus their invaluable input to discussions helped us sharpen our ambitions for the book and our contributions to it. Second, we would like to thank Adam Swallow at Oxford University Press, for his dedication to the book from idea to finished product; Bethsheba McGill for her indispensable expertise with figures and tables; and the people who helped us to edit, proofread, and format the manuscript into the final book. Third, we are grateful for the constructive criticism provided by our three anonymous reviewers at OUP; their detailed feedback and questions inspired us to aim to provide "a milestone in the debate." Finally, we would like to thank our research communities and colleagues at Aalborg University, Department of Sociology and Social Work, Center for Organization and Management, and colleagues and cowriters in the Open Writing Community and Saïd Business School for lively debates about how to understand and operationalize the relationship between context and action.

Contents

List of Figures	xi
List of Tables	xiii
Notes on the Contributors	xv
1. Foregrounding Context in Action	1
2. Theoretical Lenses on Context	13
3. Methodological Challenges in Studying Context in Action	33

Part I. Context: What Constitutes the Context of a Situation/Event or Phenomenon?

4. Louise Fitzgerald: Enacted Context	71
5. David A. Chambers: Context of Health Policies and the Impact on Implementation of Health Care and Health Interventions	86
6. Kjell Tryggestad, Chris Harty, and Peter Holm Jacobsen: Bringing the Hospital Back In: Implications for Studying Organizations	104

Part II. Actors: How Do Actors Understand, Experience, and Engage with Context?

7. Maja Korica and Davide Nicolini: Tracing Context as Relational, Discursive Accomplishment: Analytical Lessons from a Shadowing-Based Study of Health Care Chief Executives	123
8. Helle Sofie Wentzer: Technology in Context: Exploring Vulnerability in Surgery	138
9. Louise Locock, Glenn Robert, and Ninna Meier: Patients, Families, and Care Settings	155
10. Ninna Meier: Place Matters in Context Analysis: Understanding Patients' Experiences of Context	166

Contents

11. Eleanor Murray: How Researchers Understand, Construct, and Bound Context: Liminality and the Integration Space   182

Part III. Change: How Do Contexts Change, and What Is the Role of Actors in Such Processes?

12. Ewan Ferlie: Analyzing Context in Health Care Organizations: Some Reflections on Past Work and Contemporary Research Challenges   197

13. Ian Kessler: Context and Work Organization in an Acute Health Care Setting   215

14. Carole A. Estabrooks and Stephanie A. Chamberlain: How Context Shapes the Experience of Staff and Residents in Residential Long-Term Care Settings   232

15. Ninna Meier and Sue Dopson: Context in Action: A Research Agenda   250

Index   257

List of Figures

1.1	Framework for Studying Context in Action	4
2.1	Framework for Studying Context in Action	23
3.1	GKP (Conception: 2001)	36
3.2	GKP (Formal early formation: 2002–3)	37
3.3	GKP (In practice mid 2003)	38
3.4	GKP (Pressure to deliver: end 2004)	39
3.5	GKP (end 2007)	40
5.1	Policies Can Affect Health and Health Care at Multiple Levels, and Can Be Targeted at One or More of Those Levels	88
8.1	Zones of Interaction, Communication, and Risk in Operation Rooms	141
8.2	Photographs of Practical, Low-Tech Solutions	148
8.3	Photographs of Removing a Blood Clot, by Image Technologies in Vascular Surgery	151
10.1	Continuity and Coherence in Patient Pathways	171
11.1	The Researcher's Bounding of Context through Transitioning Liminal Spaces	189
12.1	Model of Receptive and Non-receptive Contexts for Change, fromPettigrew Ferlie, and McKee (1992)	203
13.1	Distribution of Tasks Performed by Healthcare Support Workers by Clinical Area	227

List of Tables

2.1	Theoretical Lenses on Context	17
3.1	Examples of Contextual Forces in Health care Work	46
5.1	Summary of Selected Features of Health Policy and Their Influence on the Health care Context	94
13.1	The Pay Banding of Health Care Support Workers (%)	223
13.2	The Distribution and Performance of Tasks by Health Care Support Workers	225
13.3	Health Care Support Worker Type by Trust (%)	225

Notes on the Contributors

Stephanie A. Chamberlain is a doctoral candidate with Carole Estabrooks at the University of Alberta, Edmonton, Alberta, Canada. She is an Alzheimer Society of Canada Doctoral Fellow and a Revera Scholar. She is a trainee with the Translating Research in Elder Care (TREC) program, where she examines the relationship of organizational context to staff work life and quality of care. Before joining TREC, she was a research coordinator at the Bruyère Research Institute, Ottawa, Ontario, Canada, and a research assistant at the Nova Scotia Centre on Aging at Halifax, Nova Scotia, Canada. Her research focuses on care aides, quality of work life, and quality of care in long-term care homes. Her PhD work will document the prevalence, health outcomes, and potentially unmet care needs of nursing home residents who are under public guardianship in Alberta long-term care homes.

David A. Chambers is deputy director for Implementation Science Team in the Office of the Director in the Division of Cancer Control and Population Sciences at the National Cancer Institute, Bethesda, Maryland, USA, managing a team focusing on efforts to build and advance the field of Implementation Science. From 2008 to 2014, he served as chief of the Services Research and Clinical Epidemiology Branch (SRCEB) of the Division of Services and Intervention Research at the National Institute of Mental Health (NIMH). He first joined NIMH in 2001 to run the Dissemination and Implementation Research Program within SRCEB, where he managed a portfolio of grants to study the integration of scientific findings and effective clinical practices in mental health within real-world service settings. From 2006 to 2014, he also served as associate director for Dissemination and Implementation Research. He publishes on strategic research directions in implementation science and serves as a plenary speaker at numerous scientific conferences.

Sue Dopson is Rhodes Trust Professor of Organisational Behaviour at Saïd Business School; the academic director of the Oxford Diploma in Organisational Leadership, a Fellow of Green Templeton College, University of Oxford; and visiting professor at the University of Alberta, Canada. She is a noted specialist on the personal and organizational dimensions of leadership and transformational change. Her research centers on transformational change and knowledge exchange in the public and health care sectors. She has written and edited many major works on this topic, and her research has informed and influenced government bodies, such as the Department of Health and the National Institute for Health and Clinical Excellence, in their thinking on areas such as the dissemination of clinical evidence into practice, medical leadership, and the role of the support worker in the National Health Service (NHS). She currently

Notes on the Contributors

represents the University of Oxford as non-executive director of the Oxford Health NHS Foundation Trust.

Carole A. Estabrooks is a professor of the Faculty of Nursing at the University of Alberta, Edmonton, Alberta, Canada, and Tier 1 Canada Research Chair in Knowledge Translation. She is a Member of the Order of Canada and a Fellow in both the Canadian Academy of Health Sciences and the American Academy of Nursing. She is scientific director of the Knowledge Utilization Studies Program and the pan-Canadian Translating Research in Elder Care research program hosted at the University of Alberta. Her applied health services research program focuses on knowledge translation in the health sciences. She studies the influence of organizations on the use of knowledge and its effects on quality of care, quality of life/quality of end of life, and quality of work life outcomes. Her work is situated primarily in the residential long-term care sector, and she focuses increasingly on quality improvement and the spread and scaling-up of innovation. She is a coinvestigator on numerous national and international research projects, and was the 2014 recipient of the CIHR Institute of Aging's Betty Havens Prize in Knowledge Translation.

Ewan Ferlie is a professor of Public Management in King's Business School, King's College London. He previously worked at the Centre for Corporate Strategy and Change, Warwick Business School, where he was involved in a major study of strategic change processes in the UK National Health Service. He has published widely on themes of organizational change and restructuring in the health care and higher education sectors. He has undertaken mainly qualitative research, often involving the use of comparative case studies. He is coeditor of the recently published *Oxford Handbook of Health Care Management* (Oxford University Press, 2016). He was elected as a Fellow of the British Academy in 2016.

Louise Fitzgerald is a visiting professor (Organizational Change) at Saïd Business School, University of Oxford; Emeritus Professor at De Montfort University; and an elected Fellow of the Academy of Social Sciences. She has held management posts in human resource management and as an organizational development consultant in the private sector. In academia, she has worked at the Universities of Warwick, City, De Montfort, and Manchester. In her academic career, she has maintained a core focus on applied research and on the impact of academic work on practice and policy. She was a member of the pioneering Centre for Corporate Strategy and Change under the leadership of Professor Andrew Pettigrew, which was supported by a consortium of firms. From 2008 to 2016, she was a member of the Implementation Strategy Group of the National Institute for Health and Care Excellence, which guides strategy on the implementation of clinical guidelines in the UK. Currently, her research is focused on the implementation of organizational change in complex, professionalized organizations, in the health and social care sectors, and on innovation diffusion and knowledge mobilization across sectors. She has published widely: for example, in the *Leadership Quarterly* and *Academy of Management Journal*. Her most recent book is *Challenging Perspectives on Organizational Change in Health Care*, Routledge, 2017.

Chris Harty is a professor of Technology and Organization, and Head of the School of the Built Environment at the University of Reading. He has previously been the director of the Health and Care Infrastructure Research and Innovation Centre, and acting director of Design Innovation Research Centre at the University. He has been principal/lead investigator on over £3.5 million of research projects funded by the *Engineering and Physical Sciences Research Council*, TSB (bank), and Infrastructure UK. He was visiting professor in the Department of Organization at Copenhagen Business School, Denmark, 2013–16, and is currently visiting professor at Chalmers University of Technology, Gothenburg, Sweden. He has conducted ethnographic studies of the development and use of collaborative information systems in complex organizations, and undertaken video-ethnographic studies of the use of immersive virtual reality technologies in design processes and in user-centered design, notably in health care settings. He has also worked in the area of future studies and forecasting. His personal research contributions are in the areas of understanding innovation in the built environment and organizational processes, applying socio-technical systems-oriented approaches to organizations and projects, and the design, implementation, and use of information systems, and he has published widely in these areas.

Peter Holm Jacobsen is a postdoctoral fellow in the Department of Organization at Copenhagen Business School, Denmark. He received his PhD from Roskilde University, Denmark, in 2014. His work is mainly ethnographic; he has conducted ethnographic research in the design and construction of buildings, and in the energy sector. His research in construction and design focuses on organization and management in the early phases of large projects. More specifically, he has studied novel dialog-based interactions between client organizations, designers, and users as a part of architecture competitions. Within the area of architecture competitions, he has coauthored a book with Kristian Kreiner (in Danish, published in 2013) on the implications of introducing dialogs in architectural competitions in Denmark. He has also coauthored several journal articles and book chapters about new forms of architecture competitions. Currently, he is researching the market for flexibility in the energy sector. This work is a part of the postdoctoral project "Organizing Energy Consumption" that includes qualitative studies of how energy consumers and their households participate in the experimental market setup. His theoretical research interests include organization theory, actor–network theory, science and technology studies, project management, and economic sociology.

Ian Kessler is a professor of Public Policy and Management at King's College, University of London. He has been involved in a number of research projects on aspects of employment relations in the British public services, covering such topics as pay determination, strategic human resource management, and work organization. Over the last decade, he has been exploring nurse support roles in acute health care, and the more general restructuring of the nursing workforce. He has coauthored two books on aspects of public service employment relations. He was a commissioner on the Local Government Pay Commission in 2005, and has acted as adviser to the Royal College of Nursing, the Royal College of Midwives, the Police Federation, the Audit Commission, and the National Audit Office.

Maja Korica is an associate professor of Management and Organisation at Warwick Business School, University of Warwick. A qualitative researcher, her scholarly interests

Notes on the Contributors

mostly focus on the rarely seen "backstages" of organizations and organizing. This includes the work of senior executives and boards of directors, as well as mundane practices of leadership and governance and accountability. Her most recent work is on coordination in extreme settings.

Louise Locock is a professor of Health Services Research at the University of Aberdeen. Before that, she was director of Applied Research at the Health Experiences Research Group, University of Oxford. She is a qualitative social scientist with interests in personal experiences of health and illness; using patient-experience data to improve the quality of healthcare; people's experience of medical research participation; and patient and public involvement. Her recent grants have included awards from the National Health Service (NHS) National Institute for Health Research (NIHR), the Economic and Social Research Council, and a personal fellowship with the NIHR Oxford Biomedical Research Centre on patient and public involvement in health research. She is now working on a study with NHS Grampian and Care Opinion Scotland, on staff responses to online patient feedback. Louise holds a degree in French and German from the University of Oxford. She worked as a NHS senior manager for 9 years before returning to the University of Oxford to complete an M Phil in Comparative Social Policy, followed by a PhD at the London School of Economics on quasi-markets and rationing in healthcare.

Ninna Meier is an associate professor at the Department of Sociology and Social Work at Aalborg University, Denmark. Ninna is a qualitative researcher, focusing on micro-interactions and socio-material practices—specifically how work practices are organized and managed. Her PhD thesis examines similarities and differences in clinical managerial work carried out by health care professionals in managerial positions at the frontline of four different hospital units: internal medicine, elective surgery, radiology, and stroke. This work spurred her interest in the concept of context from a theoretical and methodological point of view, an interest she has carried with her ever since. Her latest research includes a 3-year process study of multilevel organizational change aimed at creating coherence, and she is currently working on a study of integrative mechanisms in cross-sectoral collaboration between primary and secondary health and social care systems. This research has deepened her interest in and knowledge of the link between context, action, and change. She is a visiting scholar at Saïd Business School, Oxford University, and a faculty member at the Relational Coordination Research Collaborative at Brandeis University, Waltham, Massachusetts, USA. She is the cofounder of the Open Writing Community, where she explores the link between how researchers write and the impact of their research.

Eleanor Murray is a Fellow in Management Practice at Saïd Business School, University of Oxford. Her area of expertise includes the emerging field of organizational and systems resilience, with a focus on identifying and enhancing the capacity and capabilities of organizations and systems in conditions of uncertainty. Her research examines how resilience can be understood, assessed, and applied in a range of sectors. Her concurrent interest is systems change, with a research program that reevaluates large-scale systems change theory and reinterprets the role of systems leaders undertaking complex change both in the UK and internationally. Eleanor has extensive experience in the health sector: a 20-year career, including 10 years in senior manager and executive director roles in the National Health Service, and, since 2008, she has expanded her reach to other sectors as director of her own consulting company, advising and delivering on health, education, and government projects. Previously, she held the role of Senior Research Fellow at Saïd Business School, supported by a 3-year improvement science fellowship with the Health Foundation. Before joining Oxford, Eleanor was an Honorary Lecturer, research fellow, and postdoctoral researcher in the Faculty of Medicine at Imperial College London. Her PhD examines organizational resilience in the UK health sector.

Davide Nicolini is a professor of Organization Studies at Warwick Business School, UK, where he co-directs the Innovation, Knowledge & Organizational Networks Research Centre. In the past, he has held positions and visiting appointments at the University of Oslo, The Tavistock Institute of Human Relations in London, ESADE Business School in Barcelona, and the Universities of Trento and Bergamo in Italy. His current research focuses on the development of the practice-based approach and its application to phenomena such as knowing, collaboration, safety, and technological innovation in organizations. While at present, most of his empirical work is carried out in health care organizations, he has also studied construction sites, factories, public organizations, cybersecurity, pharmacies, scientific laboratories, and the work of chief executive officers.

Glenn Robert is a professor of Healthcare Quality and Innovation at King's College London. His research interests include identifying, adapting, and implementing interventions that might have value in addressing the organizational development and change challenges facing health care organizations; developing and evaluating innovations in quality improvement and service delivery; and design thinking.

Kjell Tryggestad is a full professor at Inland Norway University of Applied Sciences, Department of Business Administration, Norway, and associate professor at Copenhagen Business School, Department of Accounting and Auditing, Denmark. His research interests span the role of management technologies in strategic and organizational change, and the design and delivery of sustainable innovations in health and care, and the built environment. He has published on these topics in books and journals within the fields of accounting, construction and project management, organization studies, sociology, and marketing. In his research, he adopts a constructivist approach informed by the symmetrical socio-material perspective of actor–network theory, supplemented with fieldwork and case studies of the unfolding empirical processes and practices.

Helle Sofie Wentzer is an adjunct professor, Senior Research Associate at KORA, the Danish Institute for Local and Regional Government Research, Copenhagen/Aarhus, Denmark. Her main research interests include organizational innovation of health care practices, and patient care paths, especially in relation to knowledge sharing, information, coordination, and documentation practices. She has a special interest in the role of digitalization in interaction and communication.

1

Foregrounding Context in Action

Ninna Meier and Sue Dopson

Why Study Context in Action?

The purpose of this book is to provide an exploration of the role of context and action in the broader field of organization and management theory, illustrated by examples from health care research. The book is based primarily on research carried out in health care organizations, but the overall points are relevant for organization and management researchers in other fields.

Etymologically, the term *context* means weaving or knitting together, to make a connection (Rousseau & Fried, 2001 p. 1) between a phenomenon and what is relevant for understanding it. The philosopher Hannah Arendt (1958) discusses *action* as a core element of the human conditions and defines it as the human capacity to begin a new series of events; the potential for bringing something new into the world, through words or deeds: "In this sense of initiative, an element of action, and therefore of natality, is inherent in all human activities" (p. 9). Actions are "embedded in interactions – past, present, and imagined future... actions may generate further meanings, both with regard to further actions and the interactions in which they are embedded" (Strauss, 1993 p. 24). Elias (1994) notes that actions are affected by the activities of past generations, not only in terms of material things such as buildings, but also in terms of language, educational systems, and so on. A key point for Elias is, therefore, that we cannot understand people's actions outside of their social and historical context. In their own right, both context and action are essential theoretical concepts rooted in philosophical reflections. Moreover, they pose potential methodological challenges to research in the fields of organization and management. Our contributors have generously offered to share their own challenges in undertaking research where context and action are central to their scholarly endeavors. These examples also relate to the health sector, but reflect theoretical issues and practical concerns relevant to organization and management scholars in general. After all, the context–action relationship deals with issues relating to questions such as what *is* organizational change, and how can we study it empirically? How are macro- and microlevel events or actions connected, and how do they influence and co-constitute each other through their relationships across analytical levels (Clarke, Friese, & Washburn, 2015; Knorr-Centina & Cicourel, 1981)? These are challenging questions that organization and management researchers—also in health care—still debate, and we hope this book can contribute here.

Analyses of context are made particularly difficult by the unbounded nature of the concept: "To understand anything well we must grasp it in its context. However, the attempt to be thorough in understanding context leads to a total contextualization, in which everything becomes the context of everything else" (Scharfstein, 1989 p. xii). It is not difficult to use the concept of context in practice—we do it all the time—but this tendency to use context in a generalized manner has spilled over into the broad field of organization and management research, making it complicated to use the concept theoretically. This produces a paradoxical problem: the very concept that is central to producing research, which provides meaning or pays attention to a specific situation in which the social phenomena unfolds in practice, is in itself used in an unspecific, general way or is underappreciated (Johns, 2017). This is more so for context than for action (see, for example, the work of Strauss,1993; Shove et al., 2012; Nicolini, 2012), and it hampers our ability to produce research that furthers nuanced understandings of key issues in organization and management.

So what is it about the concept that makes it complex to grasp and is yet so central to social sciences in general? First, contexts are mediated through language, and represent an integral part of the way we construct and make sense of our lives, deliberately or as unarticulated background assumptions (Edmonds, 2002). Key elements of thinking–acting processes—making distinctions and classifications, framing situations, and drawing boundaries of identity/difference—are both cognitive and social actions that are always carried out in and have meaning attributed to them within a context (Zerubavel, 1999). We carry out these iterations of actions continuously in order to make sense of the world and our experiences, and for the most part, we do not pay any particular attention to them; they fade into the background and become taken for granted (Zerubavel, 1991). It is precisely this "taken for granted" aspect that spills over into the concept of context as theoretical construct and methodological approach, with potential problematic consequences for research. From earlier work proposing a more nuanced approach to context, we know that contexts in action are dynamic, changing, and potentially overlapping (Dopson & Fitzgerald, 2005), and they are produced, altered, and reproduced by actors in the continuous flow of open-ended interactions that constitute social worlds. This makes the analysis of context complex, but important in understanding the very nature of the relationship between the two: "the dynamic, socially constitutive properties of context are inescapable since each additional move within the interaction modifies the existing context while creating a new arena for subsequent interaction" (Duranti & Goodwin, 1992). As long as scholars do not reflect systematically on their approach to context and in their research, our understanding of *action* and related concepts such as *change, innovation, leadership*, and *strategy* will suffer.

In this book, we distinguish between context as a theoretical construct, on the one hand, and context as methodological approach—how we operationalize and use the concept in the research process—on the other. We suggest the following definition:

> Context *is a relational construct that specifies what is at any given point considered the background for understanding a phenomenon or event. This background/foreground relationship is continually constructed by people, as they make sense of their experiences and the social worlds in which they engage.*

Understood in this way, *context* and *phenomenon/event* mutually constitute each other. In other words, what we construct as context in our research and otherwise will always depend on the phenomenon or event we are trying to understand and give meaning to. We refer to contextualization as "construction" or "enactment" to highlight its close relationship to sensemaking processes: a point we unfold in the theoretical chapter Theoretical Lenses on Context, by Meier and Dopson. When we explore context as a methodological concept, we refer to contexts as bounded, to highlight "bounding" as a result of the researcher's own contextualization process. Research can be understood as "world-making"; we produce very specific and often important consequential accounts of the world based on our engagement with it. Thus, when researchers bound certain "contexts" analytically as phenomena or events, they can increase the transparency of their efforts by reflecting critically on their own approach, the vantage point from which context is viewed, and whose context they aim to represent in their work. We focus our contribution on context and how context relates to action and change. In doing so, we acknowledge the legacy of process researchers who furthered studies of phenomena that are characterized by a fundamental processual nature (Langley et al., 2013; Langley, 1999; Pettigrew, 1990; Van de Ven & Huber, 1990).

Contribution of the Book

In this book, we seek to contribute to improving contextual analyses in organization and management research in general and in health care research in particular. We offer a theory–method package (Clarke, 2005) illustrated by our Framework for Studying Context in Action, see Figure 1.1. In our view, contexts in action *are* the raw material that change processes are mediated by, and the framework should be understood as a model for thoughtfully exploring this further. The framework demonstrates the analytical consequences that arise from the choices we must make, when we study, analyze, and theorize about context and action. Moreover, it shows how analytical and methodological reflections on vantage point and representation are linked to these.

The framework will be discussed in more detail in Chapters 2 and 3, the theoretical and methodological chapters, where we show how the collection of Chapters 4 through 14 by our contributors illustrate different elements of the framework. Each of these chapters focuses on one or more of the elements *context*, *actors*, and *change*. These chapters contain theoretical, analytical, and methodological reflections, and they can be read as standalone contributions or as in-depth discussions of the overall theme of the book. For example,

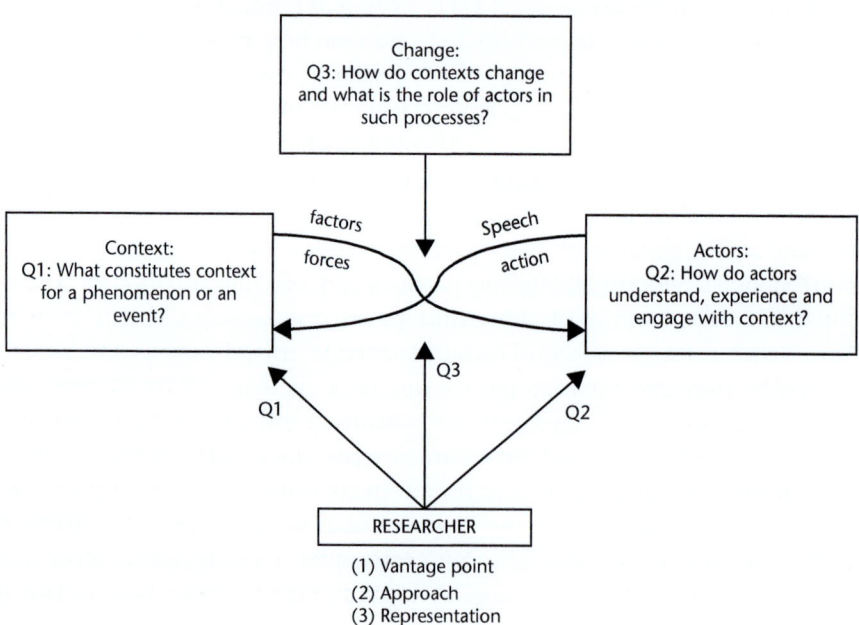

Figure 1.1 Framework for Studying Context in Action

Chapters 4 and 12 contribute with broader, more theoretical discussions of context and change, whereas Chapters 5, 6, 8, 13, and 14 (with different methods, approaches, and levels of analysis) illustrate how elements of what is constructed as context actively shapes and is shaped by actors. Moreover, discussions of vantage point, researcher approach, and representation can be found across Chapters 7 and 11, which discuss methodological and analytical lessons to be drawn from reflection on and specifying the approach to the study of context taken in a piece of research, whereas, for example, Chapter 10 focuses on the analytical insights a researcher may gain from paying attention to vantage point. Questions of representation are discussed throughout the book; however, Chapters 9 and 10 suggest avenues for further research into illuminating the less researched experiences of patients and their families.

In this book, we propose an analytical distinction between context as a theoretical construct and context as a methodological approach, although a basic premise of the book is that questions of theory and method are equally linked to questions of contexts in action. This distinction between context as theoretical construct and context as methodological approach is important because questions of context matter in different ways for theory and method. For example, context as theoretical construct specifies how *context* is defined, as well as the basic assumptions that definition rests on, and the scope conditions for its use. This is discussed in Chapter 2. How we define and understand *context* theoretically is in turn important for how we can operationalize, study, and analyze context in our work: how we "bound" context in our empirical investigations. This is discussed in Chapter 3. The analytical distinction is important because of the current overwhelming variety and simultaneous lack of specificity in how the concept of *context* is used in the majority of the literature. To further a more productive understanding of the role of context in mediating action, a first step is that researchers need to specify how they understand and use context.

In addition to proposing this distinction, we also offer a definition of *context* as theoretical construct, as presented above. This definition, and our discussion of the key elements in it, offers a starting point for other researchers to engage with context as a theoretical construct: to critically debate the aspects we suggest, to add their own nuances, and, in doing this, to move the concept of *context* forward as a useful theoretical construct. Finally, we make a process-oriented methodological contribution, as the book presents a variety of approaches to study "how both individual actors and social structure contribute to the course and outcome of a process, and how the process contributes to the continuity and change of actors and structure" (Sminia, 2016 p. 127).

The book, in short, discusses the referential relationship between context and action: specifically, how they are related, and what that means for how we might study and analyze context and action as they unfold, change and are experienced in time and place. The theoretical and methodological Chapters 2 and 3 integrate lessons derived from the research experiences showcased by our contributors. These contributions are contained in a range of shorter thematic chapters exemplifying how such a nuanced approach to context might unfold in different fields, through different designs, methods, and analytical lenses. In these chapters, the reader can find both conceptual and methodological inspiration from our contributors' contextual analysis, as well as several topic-specific analyses based on examples from health care. Our ambition for this book is to provide readers with a reflective, nuanced, and yet practical framework from which to carry out contextual analysis. Chapter 15 sums up the main points and propose directions for future research.

Outline of the Book: A Guide to Reading

Chapter 2 presents a focused theoretical discussion of the concept of *context*. Here we discuss context as a construct having a relationship to action at multiple analytical levels. We examine construct clarity in context along four dimensions: definition, scope conditions, semantic relationship to other constructs, and coherence, i.e., the way that context—as a theoretical construct—is connected to the overall theoretical argument. The construct clarity of context is important for several reasons, as Suddaby argues, "First, clear constructs facilitate communication between scholars. Second, improved clarity of constructs enhances researchers' ability to explore phenomena empirically. Third, clear constructs allow for greater creativity and innovation in research" (2010, p. 352). Hence, we argue that a systematic approach to studying and analyzing context and its relationship to action can lead to better theories, more robust and nuanced interpretations of empirical results, and improved foundations for comparative studies. As a crucial aspect of any research endeavor, the concept of *context* must be addressed explicitly and presented as a central part of the theory–method approach, and not serve only as a nonspecific background. These arguments have been made before, along with a call for more process methodologies that aim to take the important questions of context into account (Sminia, 2016). Our point is that there is no such thing as "the" context, unless you specify what this entails. What constitutes context for a phenomenon or an event is formed by the perspective we take on a given phenomenon in relation to the frame that we understand when we make sense of something, as Weick and others have demonstrated (Maitlis & Christianson, 2014; Sandberg & Tsoukas, 2015; Weick, 1995; Weick, Sutcliffe, & Obstfeld, 2005). Based on a brief discussion of how context has been understood theoretically in different fields of research, we focus our attention on research that furthers our understanding of the context–action relationship.

In Chapter 3, we discuss the methodological implications of the definition and approach to context we set down in this book. As social scientists, context is the way we first frame the phenomenon we wish to study. This frame is *not* out there or fixed by the start of our endeavor; as our understanding of the phenomenon develops, we shall most likely adjust our framing to zoom in on, include, or downplay aspects along the way. To illustrate this, we share examples from our own work in two vignettes presented and discussed in the chapter. Here, we draw on a study of the dynamics of a complex network in health care and a recent 3-year multicase study of organizational change processes in hospitals. The first vignette illuminates the complexity of the stakeholders and subcultures that often exist in health care "change contexts," as well as the impact of the interdependences on action. It also demonstrates the importance of understanding the wider policy context and the formation of the network locally. The second vignette displays the process of operationalizing the concept of context into a configuration of contextual factors influencing, and influenced by, the organizational change processes in the three cases. Based on these and the insights from our contributors, we provide a methodological approach to the study of contexts in action. Thus, the chapter offers practical insights into the process of *how* to study context, and it relates these to the theoretical foundation of the book.

The majority of the book (Chapters 4–14) showcases our contributors' empirical and theoretical analyses of specific topics in which context in health care plays a crucial role. These chapters are organized according to the framework we have developed (Figure 1.1). We have chosen to focus Chapters 4 through 14 in one organizational field (health care) to underscore the many different ways in which contextual analyses can be made within what is often referred to as a single context: "the health care context." The authors contributing to this book represent a range of sub-fields in health care and carry out context-sensitive research in a variety of ways and with very different foci. The contributors are primarily qualitative researchers and thus trained in carrying out research in which the concept of *context* is expected to play a significant role. In their contributions, they reflect on how they have thought about context and action in their research. These chapters show how context, action, and change can be studied at multiple analytical levels, from different theoretical perspectives and by adopting a range of designs and methods, thus contributing to their individual fields of research, as well as to the book. However, they also demonstrate what can be gained from reflecting on and specifying the *approach* taken to context: how we understand and define *context*, and how we operationalize and study it.

In Chapter 15, we seek to sum up the points made throughout the book and discuss them in relation to the framework we have presented. We argue why the concept of *context* deserves a stringent and analytical approach in organization research, and what is to be gained from this.

What Can We Learn About Context from Health Care Research?

The concept of *context* is a particularly important in research into the complex and dynamic field of health care (Dopson, Fitzgerald, & Ferlie, 2008; Dopson & Fitzgerald, 2005). Interestingly, there seems to be a scholarly focus on some elements of context at the expense of others. When examining empirical studies of health care organization in context, *specific* aspects of this "field" appear to be paid more attention than others are, for example, institutional norms and logics, New Public Management, evidence-based medicine, and patient safety culture, to name just a few. In Chapters 4 to 14, we have chosen to include elements of context that are essential but in some cases, less well-researched or understood. These chapters focus on patients and their relatives; care for elderly people; or patients' perspectives on context, buildings, and technologies; service assistants and top executives; and policy implementation work, and all display the complexity that can easily be experienced in practice. These aspects are central when we explore health care systems and how they are developing in the UK, the USA, Canada, and Scandinavia.[1] Moreover, each of these aspects is changing and thus potentially impacting both the larger system and each other in complex ways. We have asked our contributors to reflect on context and action in relation to these aspects in detail, based on their work and research experiences in different national settings.

Health Care as "Context"

The areas analyzed as macrolevels of context have received the majority of scholarly attention, often through studies of national setting, governance, system structures, and the relationship between health care professions and the state, primarily through documentary analyses, historic analysis, surveys, or interviews. From the field-level perspective, researchers have looked at the political, historic developments specific to a national health care sector (Jespersen, Nielsen, & Sognstrup, 2002); on government structures and forms of governance (Kirkpatrick, et al., 2009; Kitchener, 2002); and on changes in field-level structures (Scott et al., 2000). Generally, health care can be understood as an institutional field, governed by strong professional norms and divided into areas of medical specialties with their own body of knowledge and work practices (Dacin, Goodstein, & Scott, 2002; Freidson, 1984; Strauss, 2001). The right to practice as a physician or nurse is state sanctioned, and the quality of health care service is increasingly standardized, monitored, and benchmarked, either by central governance agencies or international accreditation organizations (Berg, 1997; Kuhlmann & Saks, 2008a, 2008b). These aspects are generally shared, with national and international variations, and are essential aspects of understanding health care. When researchers bound elements of context as institutional forces or specific policies, what we may understand as macrolayers of context can be subject to national comparison and further our knowledge of *similarities* and differences across countries or sectors.

Health care is also a field of professional practice, characterized by high degrees of specialization, variation, unpredictability, and change (Berg & Mol, 1998; Bohmer, 2009; Strauss et al., 1997; Timmermans & Angell, 2001). In health care, the institution of medicine prescribes a certain set of rules and norms for action, which actors are expected to follow and thus reproduce. However, medical professionals can act as institutional agents (Scott, 2008) and engage in reconstruction, and negotiations and transformations, of the institution of medicine itself. While the institutional field of medicine is often researched as a macrocontext for action, Mouzelis (1992) suggests that we think about institutions and interactions not as belonging to two different levels (macro and micro) of reality, but as two perspectives that should be studied to mutually inform one other. Institutions are not macroentities that act on their own; rather, they are inhabited by people (Hallett & Ventresca, 2006) who interact, and through this, people enact, reconstruct, maintain, and change the institutions they are influenced by, often without giving such actions any deliberate reflection. Actions can be connected across time and space (Czarniawska, 2004; Shove et al., 2012), for example, through practices of translating an idea, enacting certain norms, or abiding by a set of regulations.

When we refer to the health care field and health care systems throughout the book, we acknowledge that the framing of this is analytical. In practice, demarcations around what is included and excluded as part of a given health care system vary and may be blurred and often overlapping, or even drawn very differently, depending on perspective and engagement with the field, just as any contextualization will be. In fact, this overlapping is one of the aspects we have chosen to explore because integration and coherence of work processes across individuals, subunits, organizations, and sectors seems to be a recurring theme of the political and administrative governance agenda across modern health care sectors as services are increasingly moving from hospital admissions to outpatient services and home care. When we refer to "the health care system," we focus primarily on the national settings of the UK, the USA, Canada, and Denmark, the national systems on which the contributors to the book have focused. Reflecting on context and its relationship to action from a theoretical and methodological standpoint, all of the contributors share the ambition of furthering what we know about context and action, and how to study such complex social processes of which they are a part.

Note

1. The empirical national settings we focus on are included because they represent national settings where editors or contributors have done empirical work. In chapters where research from a specific national setting provides an example or the empirical material of the text, the given role and significance of the national health care system in question will be explained.

References

Arendt, H. (1958). *The human condition*. Chicago: University of Chicago Press.

Berg, M. (1997). *Rationalizing medical work: Decision-support techniques and medical practices*. Cambridge, MA: The MIT Press.

Berg, M. & Mol, A. (eds.). (1998). *Differences in medicine—unraveling practices, techniques and bodies*. Durham and London: Duke University Press.

Bohmer, R. M. J. (2009). *Designing care: Aligning the nature and management of health care*. Boston: Harvard Business Press.

Clarke, A. (2005). *Situational analysis: Grounded theory after the postmodern turn*. Thousand Oaks, CA: Sage.

Clarke, A., Friese, C., & Washburn, R. (2015). *Situational analysis in practice: Mapping research with grounded theory*. Walnut Creek, CA: Left Coast Press.

Czarniawska, B. (2004). On time, space, and action nets. *Organization, 11*(6), 773–91.

Dacin, T. M., Goodstein, J., & Scott, R. W. (2002). Institutional theory and institutional change: Introduction to the special research forum. *Academy of Management Journal, 45*(1), 43–56.

Dopson, S., & Fitzgerald, L. (2005). *Knowledge to action? Evidence based health care in context*. New York: Oxford University Press.

Dopson, S., Fitzgerald, L., & Ferlie, E. (2008). Understanding change and innovation in health care settings: Reconceptualizing the active role of context. *Journal of Change Management, 8*(3–4), 213–31.

Duranti, A. & Goodwin, C. (eds.). (1992). *Rethinking context: Language as an interactive phenomenon*. Cambridge: Cambridge University Press.

Edmonds, B. (2002). Editorial: Context in context. *Foundations of Science, 7*(3), 233–8.

Elias, N. (1994). *The civilizing process*. Oxford: Blackwells Publishers Ltd.

Freidson, E. (1984). The changing nature of professional control. *Annual Review of Sociology, 10*, 1–20.

Hallett, T. & Ventresca, M. J. (2006). Inhabited institutions: Social interactions and organizational forms in Gouldner's patterns of industrial bureaucracy. *Theory and Society, 35*, 213–36.

Jespersen, P. K., Nielsen, L. M., & Sognstrup, H. (2002). Professions, institutional dynamics, and new public management in the Danish hospital field. *International Journal of Public Administration, 25*(12), 1555–74.

Johns, G. (2017). Incorporating context in organizational research: Reflections on the 2016 AMR decade award. *Academy of Management Review, 42* (4) 577–95.

Kirkpatrick, I., Jespersen, P. K., Dent, M., & Neogy, I. (2009). Medicine and management in a comparative perspective: The case of Denmark and England. *Sociology of Health & Illness, 31*, 642–58.

Kitchener, M. (2002). Mobilizing the logic of managerialism in professional fields: The case of academic health centre mergers. *Organization Studies, 23*(3), 391–420.

Knorr-Centina, K. &Cicourel, V. A. (eds.) (1981). *Advances in social theory and methodology. Toward an integration of micro-and macro-sociologies*. Boston: Routledge and Kegan Paul.

Kuhlmann, E. & Saks, M. (2008a). Changing patterns of health professional governance. In E. Kuhlmann & M. Saks (eds.), *Rethinking professional governance*. Bristol: The Policy Press, University of Bristol, pp. 1–11.

Kuhlmann, E. & Saks, M. (eds.). (2008b). *Rethinking professional governance: International directions in healthcare*. Bristol: The Policy Press.

Langley, A. (1999). Strategies for theorizing from process data. *Academy of Management Review, 24*(4), 691–710.

Langley, A., Smallman, C., Tsoukas, H., & Van, d. V. (2013). Process studies of change in organization and management: Unveiling temporality, activity, and flow. *Academy of Management Journal, 56*(1), 1–13.

Maitlis, S. & Christianson, M. (2014). Sensemaking in organizations: Taking stock and moving forward. *The Academy of Management Annals, 8*(1), 57–125.

Mouzelis, N. (1992). The interaction order and the micro-macro distinction. *Sociological Theory, 10*(1), 122–8.

Nicolini, D. (2012). *Practice theory, work, and organization: An introduction*. Oxford: Oxford University Press.

Pettigrew, A. M. (1990). Longitudinal field research on change: Theory and practice. *Organization Science, 1*(3), 267–92.

Rousseau, M. D. & Fried, Y. (2001). Location, location, location: Contextualizing organizational research. *Journal of Organizational Behavior, 22*(1), 1–13.

Sandberg, J. & Tsoukas, H. (2015). Making sense of the sensemaking perspective: Its constituents, limitations, and opportunities for further development. *Journal of Organizational Behavior, 36*(S1), S6–S32.

Scharfstein, B. A. (1989). *The dilemma of context*. New York: New York University Press.

Scott, W. R. (2008). Lords of the dance: Professionals as institutional agents. *Organization Studies, 29*, 219–38.

Scott, W. R., Ruef, M., Mendel, P., & Caronna, C. A. (2000). *Institutional change and healthcare organizations: From professional dominance to managed care*. Chicago: University of Chicago Press.

Shove, E., Pantzar, M., & Watson, M. (2012). *The dynamics of social practice: Everyday life and how it changes*. London: Sage.

Sminia, H. (2016). Pioneering process research: Andrew Pettigrew's contribution to management scholarship, 1962–2014. *International Journal of Management Reviews, 18*(2), 111–32.

Strauss, A. (1993). *Continual permutations of action* (3rd ed.). New York: Transaction Publishers.

Strauss, A. (2001). *Professions, work and careers*. Somerset, NJ: Transaction Publishers.

Strauss, A., Fagerhaugh, S., Suczek, B., & Weiner, C. (1997). *Social organization of medical work* (2nd ed.). New Brunswick: Transaction Publishers, Rutgers.

Suddaby, R. (2010). Editor's comments: Construct clarity in theories of management and organization. *Academy of Management Review, 35*(3), 346–57.

Timmermans, S. & Angell, A. (2001). Evidence-based medicine, clinical uncertainty, and learning to doctor. *Journal of Health and Social Behavior, 42*(4), 342–59.

Van de Ven, A. H., & Huber, G. P. (1990). Longitudinal field research methods for studying processes of organizational change. *Organization Science, 1*(3), 213–19.

Weick, K. E. (1995). *Sensemaking in organizations* Thousand Oaks, CA: Sage.

Weick, K. E., Sutcliffe, K. M., & Obstfeld, D. (2005). Organizing and the process of sensemaking. *Organization Science, 16*(4), 409–21.

Zerubavel, E. (1991). *The fine line: Making distinctions in everyday life*. Chicago: University of Chicago Press.

Zerubavel, E. (1999). *Social mindscapes: An invitation to cognitive sociology*. Cambridge, MA: Harvard University Press.

2

Theoretical Lenses on Context

Ninna Meier and Sue Dopson

Introduction

In this chapter, *Theoretical Lenses on Context*, we define and discuss *context* as a theoretical construct, we relate these discussions to our Framework for Studying Context in Action, and we reflect upon the analytical consequences of the choices this approach entails. The concept of context is central to many fields and streams of research. It therefore becomes impossible to present an exhaustive review within this book; indeed, the impossibility of such an enterprise has been demonstrated elsewhere (Akman & Bazzanella, 2003). Instead, we present an overview of where we believe readers can find further discussions of context, as well as debates on how best to analyses and study context empirically within specific scholarly fields. In the first chapter, *Foregrounding Context*, we put forward a definition of context and discussed how the current and even more general conceptualizations of context draw on discussions of context, which can be found in the fields of philosophy and linguistic theory. In these fields, the concept of context is discussed in relation to language and social interaction (see, e.g., Duranti & Goodwin, 1992; Fetzer & Akman, 2002; Pomerantz, 1998) from a pragmatist viewpoint (see, e.g., Akman & Bazzanella, 2003; Givón, 1989), and the central, yet challenging, concept of context in social science, in general, and anthropological disciplines, in particular, is explored (Dilley, 1999; Scharfstein, 1989). In Chapter 3 we present the methodological aspects of our approach and discuss the analytical consequences hereof. Furthermore, we share examples from our own work on context and highlight key lessons and reflections shared by our contributors.

Theoretical Discussions of Context

The concept of context is often found in discussions of generalizability (Edmonds, 2002), comparability, or scope conditions, where it is used to specify "the context" in which a construct applies (Suddaby, 2010). While linguistic accounts of context have focused on context in relation to language and speech situations (Fetzer & Akman, 2002), less attention has been paid to the dynamic, multidirectional interactions between actors and dimensions of context: "Existing studies seem not to effectively address what we believe to be the major lacuna in discussions of the role of context, that is the way in which individuals can influence context and bring aspects of context into change initiatives, thus shaping action" (Dopson, Fitzgerald, & Ferlie, 2008 p. 217). With a few exceptions, the current use of the concept of context in organization and management, in particular, and social science research, in general, is detached from its theoretical foundation in philosophy, practice theory, and linguistic theory.[1] This is problematic because the concept of context has traveled far beyond these foundations, having acquired additional shades of meaning and/or edits with each transfer into a new field of research. To contribute here, we discuss context as a theoretical construct, and show how the current lack of construct clarity in the general use of the term *concept* may hamper both theoretical and empirical analysis of important organizational phenomena in health care and beyond.

How we understand and define context as a theoretical concept matters in relation to our research questions, design, approach to the philosophy of science, and thus our results. As researchers, we obviously privilege some aspects of a context while minimizing or ignoring others. The observer is obligated to justify what has been included and what has been excluded, according to stated theoretical goals, methodological strategies employed, and the consistency and convincingness of an argument or analysis (Cicourel, 1992 p. 309). However, a nuanced approach to context is not only a matter of listing all included and excluded elements related to the respective theoretical and methodological goals. In short, how we understand and operationalize context theoretically and methodologically is relevant for more than one reason. As we shall demonstrate, this is because dimensions of context as theoretical construct are relevant for different *aspects* of research, and we shall discuss these in this chapter.

Previously published nuanced discussions of the relationship between context and action are available, and we seek to build on these here (Dopson & Fitzgerald, 2005; Fitzgerald & McDermott, 2017; Johns, 2017). In relation to the challenges tied to the implementation of evidence-based health care into practice, Dopson and Fitzgerald (2005) discuss the different ways in which context has been understood and studied in various branches of organizational studies, from contingency theory to the more interpretative social-psychological perspectives, such as sensemaking theory. In their book *Knowledge to Action? Evidence-based Health Care in Context*, these authors dedicate a chapter to discussing context, and they point to the importance of adopting an approach to context appropriate to the phenomenon studied. However, they also critically engage with conceptualization of contexts as presented in macro-, meso-, and microlayers or "inner" and "outer" layers. Such understandings might provide an analytical overview, but this comes at the expense of dynamic, multidimensional understandings, which explain the context–action relationship: actions are interpreted and given meaning in context. Dopson and Fitzgerald end their discussion of the active role of context by suggesting that we think of local contexts as multidimensional, multifaceted configurations of forces that influence and in turn, are influenced in complex ways by individuals and/or groups of actors, and that in this, the way actors make sense of and enact contexts must be taken into account.

Johns (2017) makes a convincing argument that the importance of contextual analysis is increasingly recognized across the social and behavioral sciences, but he also shows what still needs to be done. For example, he reviews how different fields have approached context, provides an overview of scholarly fields in which context is particularly relevant, and argues for why attention to context should be a "core competence of the management discipline" (p. 581). In terms of theory, he argues, "a useful theory incorporating context provides an *orderly* way to proceed with research. This is especially important in the case of context because situations or environments have a plethora of distinctive features, and they are in principle all open to scrutiny" (2017 p. 583). Moreover, we might add, such features might be experienced differently by actors (including the researcher), and this understanding can be influenced by the relationships between actors and thus change dynamically over time. Indeed, Johns acknowledges that there is a tendency to understand and represent context in our research as being stable, "in part because context is a background factor in much research" (2017 p. 588). Perhaps this is because the dynamism introduced by a more nuanced approach to context is difficult to handle theoretically, as well as methodologically by nonprocessual research designs This is particularly relevant in questions of emerging organizational change: "natural, ambient change that occurs gradually has been treated haphazardly, despite its potential importance" (Johns, 2017 p. 589). As March (1981 p. 564) puts it, "Change takes place because most of the time most people in an organization do more or less what they are supposed to do; that is, they are intelligently attentive to their environments and their jobs." For an early discussion of different approaches to the classic organization–environment' relationship, see Smircich & Stubbart (1985).

Fitzgerald and McDermott (2017) review the way in which organization scholars have understood and researched context as a central part of studies of organizational change. Early contributions conceptualized contexts as organizations' external environments, and demonstrated the potential diversity inherent within them. Later contributions highlight the importance of including cultural and/or historical events in contexts for change. The authors also point to the contributions made by researchers studying change processes in public sector health care organizations, specifically the attempts made to explore why change initiatives, such as national policies and/or evidence-based medicine guidelines, were implemented so differently across the sector. The role of context in organizational change processes is still under-researched. Here, the authors stress that context needs to be understood as multifactorial and be analyzed across multiple levels to capture fully the dynamic and interactionist aspects of the concept. They draw out actors and their enactment or construction of context and change as central, as well as temporal aspects: change processes unfold dynamically over time. These theoretical points are further developed in Chapters 4 and 12.

Multiple Approaches to Context Calls for Multiple Theoretical Perspectives

We have produced a table containing an overview of the different theoretical fields that have informed our thinking and the production of this book (Table 2.1).

Its detail is not meant to be exhaustive, but rather it is meant to illustrate the different debates from which we have drawn contributions during the making of this book. The table should be seen in relation to our Framework for Studying Context in Action, which presents the three main questions in contextual analysis. Our Question 1 is *What constitutes the context of a situation/event or phenomenon?* Question 2 is *How do actors understand, experience, and engage with context in a given situation or phenomenon?* Question 3 is twofold: *How do contexts change, and what is the role of actors in such processes?* The framework illustrates how each question is *one potential avenue* in exploring context and action, and we argue that this is tied to a specific approach, vantage point, and issue of representation: *Whose* context is analyzed? The researcher's? The actors' in a given setting? As Table 2.1 illustrates, there is a wide range of theoretical lenses to draw from, depending on one's focus, research question, unit of analysis, and level of analysis. Additionally, the table can work as a guide to the two additional key concepts of the book, e.g., *action* and *change*, as it displays the central works from which we have drawn.

Table 2.1 Theoretical Lenses on Context

Theoretical perspective	Focus	Level of analysis	Unit of analysis	Methods	Central works we are inspired by
Sensemaking	How actors make sense of their world and themselves	Group Individual	Sensemaking processes Actors' experience	Interviews Narrative methods	(Rousseau & Fried, 2001; Sandberg & Tsoukas, 2015; Smircich & Stubbart, 1985; Weick, 2012, 2001)
Institutional theory	How institutions shape and are shaped by organizations/actors over time	Organization Group	Institutions Organizations Institutionalization processes	Archival analysis Document analysis Interviews	(Hallett & Ventresca, 2006; Scott, Ruef, Mendel, & Caronna, 2000; Scott & Meyer, 1994)
Organizational change theory, organizational behavior	How organizations change/ organizational change processes unfold	Organization Group	Change processes Actors' agency Actors' experience	Archival analysis Document analysis Interviews observations	(Dopson et al., 2008; Fitzgerald & McDermott, 2017; Pettigrew, 1987)
Sociology	The relationship between structure and agency Cognition, action, and interaction	Society Group Individual	Structuration processes Actions and interactions Structures	Interviews Observations Archival analysis	(Barley & Tolbert, 1997; Elias, 1978; Scheff, 1997; Strauss, 1993; Zerubavel, 1991, 1999)
Practice Theory/ Philosophy	The relationship between focal event and context Practices and interactions The social, social interactions	Group Individual	Practices Actions and interactions Situations Concepts	Interviews Ethnography Ethno-methodology	(Nicolini, 2012; Scharfstein, 1989; Schatzki, Cetina-Knorr, & Savigny, 2001; Schatzki, 1996; Shove, Pantzar, & Watson, 2012)
Social and cultural linguistic theory Social anthropology	The relationship between language, mind, and context Between phenomenon and context	Group Individual	Language in use Meaning systems	Discourse analysis Conversation analysis Ethno-methodology	(Akman & Bazzanella, 2003; Dilley, 1999; Duranti & Goodwin, 1992; Fetzer & Akman, 2002; Fetzer, 2004; Givón, 1989)
Activity theory Social learning theory Organizational learning	The relationship between mind, culture, and activity	Individual Group Society	Activities Activity system Cognition and learning	Observation Interviews Discourse analysis Experiments	(Blackler, 1995; Brown & Duguid, 1991; Brown & Duguid, 2001; Cole & Engeström, 1993; Wenger, 2000)

Theoretical Perspectives on Contexts in Action

The concepts of context and action, and the way in which they interrelate, are essential for contextualized research of social phenomena, because at its base, this is also research of human actions and interactions as they unfold, unpredictably, in time and space. Thus the material and embodied aspects of human experience, the notion and role of time, and the relationship between individual actors and social structures/institutions are all potentially relevant elements to include in an analysis of context, depending on the researcher's approach to context and the vantage point from which s/he investigates his/her research question. Thus, context is tied to meaning and to people's understandings, in other words, how they make sense of their world and the events that occur, to paraphrase Weick (2006), and to their actions, that is, the human capacity to begin a new series of events or the potential for bringing something new into the world through words or deeds (Arendt 1958). These two core elements of the social world (understanding and action) are interdependent and mutually constituting.

As is evident from our definition of context, we focus on contextualization as something we all *do* as we go about our lives. Perhaps, for this reason, the term *context* is often used indiscriminately and in a generalized manner. "In the local context" or "in a social context" are examples of recurring phrases in qualitative research, phrases that carry a broad range of meanings and can refer to everything from a geographical location to a particular situation experienced from a variety of angles. Thus, it is up to the reader of the text to understand what the author's reference to context might mean. More troubling, often the text does not even specify from which perspective the reference to context is made. Is it the researcher's evaluation of what might be the most influential contextual forces in a given setting? Is it the shared perspective of a certain group or organization? In both cases, the way in which the researcher determines what were the most significant aspects of context is often not made explicit, and, thus, it not open to evaluation and discussion. This is problematic, because context used in this manner leaves the very foundations of the analysis out of the reader's reach. A possible reason for this can be found in the many shades of meaning in the concept itself: *context* refers simultaneously to a part of how we make meaning in everyday life, and it is a central part of systematic research activities.

As contexts are an integral part of social cognition and interaction, and sensemaking, they have the potential to shape actions in powerful ways: what can be "true" or recognized as "facts" by different people or groups depends heavily on the context in which such judgments are made. These processes are social: "A major set of conditions for actors' perspectives, and thus their interactions, is their membership in social worlds and subworlds. In contemporary societies, these memberships are often complex, overlapping, contrasting, conflicting, and not always apparent to other interactants" (Strauss, 1993 p. 41). Weick's (2006) example of pediatricians' initial inability to "see" and diagnose child abuse reminds us of the potentially powerful interplay between context and action, and how the way in which individuals understand, make sense of, and, thus, act varies among actors, develops over time, and, in turn, reshapes the context for action for oneself and others. Weick explains:

> The big change was the addition of social workers. Once social workers joined the team, there was no need for the other members to feel helpless in the face of manifest signs of child abuse because now there was a way to deal with it. Physicians didn't know what to do with abusing parents but social workers did. They were familiar with protective services and how to separate abusing parents from the children that pediatricians kept handing back to them. (2006 p. 1723)

Here, the introduction of social workers markedly changed the actions available in relation to child abuse, and, in this process, naming or labeling the phenomenon differently was key. Weick shows us that depending on what actors decide to forefront as the focus or center of attention, the perspective and vocabulary—and, thus, the actions made possible—shift with consequences for actions:

> The story of discovering child abuse is also a story of labels that make a difference (multiple trauma, brittle bones, battered child, child abuse, protective services). What becomes clear in the story is that vocabularies are tools for coping rather than tools for representation [...] The question then becomes what is the object that is at the focus of the coping? In the case of child abuse, is it a child, parents, fellow pediatricians, medical teams, a reputation, symptoms, diagnosis, or getting through the day? (2006 p. 1725)

In the sensemaking processes that go into organizing, whether such organizing is directed at the prevention of child abuse or a research project, something needs to be "the object" of attention: a part of the process of sensemaking itself: where do I direct my attention? What is most important to focus on here? This in turn assigns other elements to the, albeit temporary, role of "background" or "the context." Thus, *contextualizing*, we shall argue, refers to processes similar to those labeled *sensemaking* (Weick, 2012; Sandberg & Tsoukas, 2015), with at least two specific different nuances. First, where sensemaking activities are aimed at understanding and making sense of an (unexpected) event or situation, contextualizing is the process of drawing the boundaries "around" the event or situation, and, thus, of deciding what should count as relevant and what should not. These processes are fast faced, embodied, and often emotional, and participants in the same situations or interactions might experience and make sense of the event or situation and its elements differently (Clarke, 2005; Strauss, 1993).

The processes by which we contextualize a situation or a phenomenon is tied to the ways in which we make distinctions and draw cognitive and social boundaries in our everyday lives (Zerubavel, 1991, 1999). Second, contextualizing may have a significant nonverbal, embodied element because it is not in the same as sensemaking tied to identity, experiences, and stories, but rather is understanding and action in relation to a phenomena, situation, or event. Contextualizing, just as sensemaking, may be fast paced and may happen several times within the same situation (for example, the context for a meeting may change in an instant if a manager announces cutbacks as the last item on the agenda). Here, if, analytically, we were to separate the processes by which a participating employee might contextualize and make sense of the meeting—specifically how this changes with the manager's announcement of cutbacks—we would argue that contextualization and sensemaking are mutually constitutive. As an employee, you hear the announcement of cutbacks; your experience of what is the focal event is changes (from routine briefing to cutbacks) and you must now make sense of this new situation and decide how it might influence you and your colleagues. In short, contextualization is directed at situations and events, and sensemaking is directed at how the individual makes sense of these in relation to past, present, and future—individually and socially.

A Framework for Contextual Analysis

In our discussions, we found that studies of context, broadly speaking, can be divided into three overall bodies of work, each focused on contributing to the answer of a different question, which we have included into our Framework for Studying Context in Action.

Figure 2.1 displays how the book's three questions relate to different approaches and conceptualizations of context. Each question represents a specific framing of and focus on context, which comes with a series of choices concerning the unit of analysis, research design, and methods.

Context: What Constitutes the Context of an Event, Situation, or Phenomenon?

Our Question 1 (What constitutes an event, situation, or phenomenon?) has received much attention from the field of organization and management scholarship and from social science in general. Research contributing to Question 1 typically focuses on elements of context, often separated analytically into "macro-," "meso-," and "micro-layers." Here, context is understood as a relatively stable "background" that gives meaning to a "foreground." Often, actors and organizations are seen to explore their surroundings or external environment in order to navigate these waters in the best way possible. Research here may be comparative across, for example, national or organizational contexts. These kinds of comparative analyses require systematic constructions of what is meant by "relevant context" and how this is operationalized and investigated empirically. Context as analytical construct must be held stable to analyze change over time or to compare phenomena or events across what the researcher frames as the relevant contexts. This research can be carried out with quantitative or qualitative methods and can be focused on different analytical levels. Often elements of context are referred to as "factors" or "forces," whose influence is studied and compared. Researchers pursuing such lines of inquiry often focus on macrolevel analysis, traditionally working with quantitative methods, although the question lends itself equally to microlevel or multilevel analysis, and both quantitative and qualitative methods.

Actors and Change

Research contributing to our Question 2 (How do actors understand, experience, and engage with context?) typically focuses on microlevel analysis, predominantly carried out using qualitative methods. Although, here, the focus is on actors' experiences and engagement with context, it is often operationalized as specific elements; for example, how actors talk and act in implementation of policies or standards in different settings (Meier, 2015; Timmermans & Berg, 1997; Timmermans & Epstein, 2010; Wentzer & Bygholm, 2007), or influence of a clinical setting on the delegation and distribution of decisions and responsibility (Currie & Lockett, 2011; Klein et al., 2006).

Researchers contributing to Question 3 (How do contexts change, and what is the role of actors in such processes?) focus on how actors and patterns of action are significant in changing contexts over time. In our view, this is the least researched and most complex area of inquiry regarding context. Often, the contributions to this body of work are processual studies that focus on multilevel analysis, and to them, time or temporal aspects are essential. Units of time can be brief (contexts for action can change in an instant) or longitudinal, depending on the research question, design, and methods used.

However, regardless of research question, unit of analysis, and choice of methods, contextualized research entails a systematic approach. This is particularly relevant in terms of reflection and transparency concerning the *approach* one takes to studying and analyzing context, what *vantage point* the analysis is made from, and *whose context* is represented. Figure 2.1 shows how the vantage point from which a study is carried out can differ. In this example, the vantage point is the traditional "outsider position," but, as we shall demonstrate in this book, it does not need to be. A researcher can aim to study how context is made to matter by certain people, for specific social groups, or how this happens through continuous processes of contextualization: for example, through studying how relatives, as informal caregivers, may come to play increasingly important roles as health systems reorganize toward outpatient treatment. In such a study, we might find the actions of many people and at multiple levels of analysis relevant for changes in "the context for illness." What is important is the researcher's reflections and transparency regarding the vantage point from which the research is carried out. Additionally, the approach to context that the researcher brings to the work is also important. How is context understood and thus operationalized in the work: As relatively stable factors or as dynamic multidirectional forces?

Finally, the framework illustrates how the questions of focus, approach, and vantage point are interconnected and supplement each other. Research from one body of work can help to illuminate aspects relevant, but not essential to, research contributing to other bodies of work. For example, health care researchers might study what constitutes the context for the use of telemedicine in the treatment of patients with chronic pulmonary obstructive disease (COPD) in different countries. Here, an argument can be made for including macro elements such as health policies, increasing demands for efficiency in public health care, or institutional changes in the field and practice of pulmonary medicine. However, a contextual analysis of the use of telemedicine in the treatment of patients with COPD could also be framed as a study of where and how different actors (patients, informal caregivers, and health care professionals) understand, experience, and engage with telemedicine. Finally, such a study could also be designed to explore how "the context" for the use of telemedicine changes over time, and what the role of actors such as patients or home care nurses play in such processes.

It is our view that the research into how contexts change and the role of actors in such processes could be further developed, and, therefore, in this book, we seek to contribute by exploring how we study context and action in "a world on the move" (Hernes, 2014 p. 1). This means that we view contexts as constructed and enacted by people as part of the way they experience, make sense of, and engage with the world in which they live. Importantly, this also applies to researchers, *their* understanding of the world, and their definitions of knowledge and truth. Their understanding and the processes by which their knowledge is produced are important parts of all research processes and should be explicated. Usually, researchers write about these topics under the headline "philosophy of science," and they believe they need to specify their positions on these matters in their research texts to increase

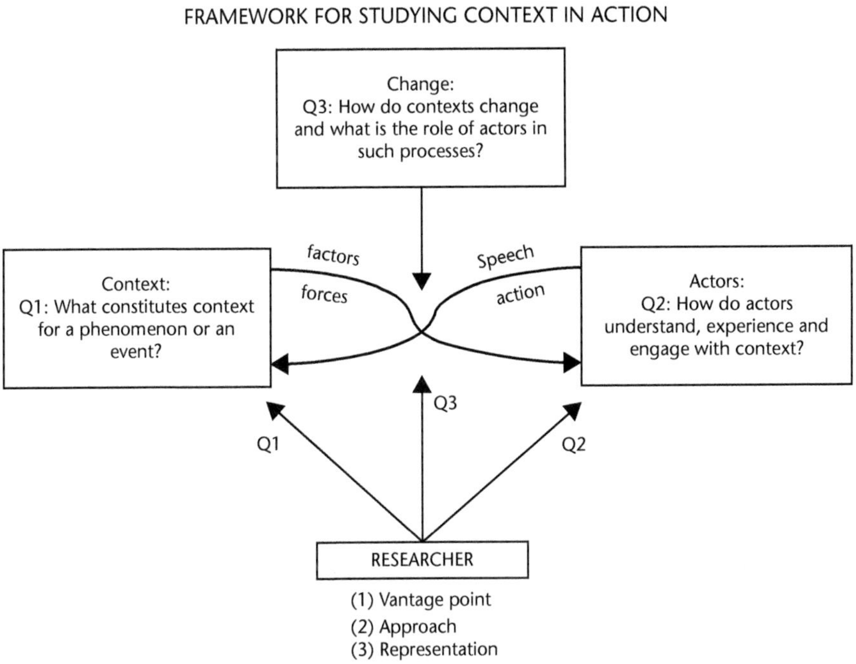

Theoretical Lenses on Context

FRAMEWORK FOR STUDYING CONTEXT IN ACTION

```
                    ┌─────────────────────────┐
                    │        Change:          │
                    │ Q3: How do contexts     │
                    │ change and what is the  │
                    │ role of actors in       │
                    │ such processes?         │
                    └─────────────────────────┘
                               │
              factors          ▼         speech
┌──────────────────┐    forces      action    ┌──────────────────┐
│    Context:      │         ╲    ╱           │     Actors:      │
│ Q1: What         │          ╲  ╱            │ Q2: How do       │
│ constitutes      │◄─────────►╳◄────────────►│ actors           │
│ context for a    │          ╱  ╲            │ understand,      │
│ phenomenon or    │         ╱    ╲           │ experience and   │
│ an event?        │                          │ engage with      │
│                  │                          │ context?         │
└──────────────────┘         ▲                └──────────────────┘
              ▲              │ Q3                    ▲
               ╲             │                      ╱
                ╲  Q1        │                 Q2  ╱
                 ╲           │                    ╱
                  ┌──────────────────┐
                  │    RESEARCHER    │
                  └──────────────────┘
```

(1) Vantage point
(2) Approach
(3) Representation

Figure 2.1 Framework for Studying Context in Action

transparency and enable their peers to evaluate their work and results. Researchers acknowledge that such transparency is always bounded, because every effort to make certain choices and assumptions visible will make other choices and assumptions inherently invisible. In terms of context and its relation to action, the researcher's worldview might make certain research questions, theoretical concepts, designs, and methods a more obvious choice. As such, there is nothing new in this call, but the variety and extent of the use of context make transparency essential. As editors of this book, we position ourselves within the field of research on context that favors interpretive, interactionist approaches. Thus, we understand contexts as being constructed and enacted by actors, as they make sense of and act in their world, and, in this process, contexts and actions are mutually constitutive. This runs counter to most traditional approaches to contextual analysis, where contexts are perceived as the setting or environment "out there," often underappreciated or ignored (Härtel & O'Connor, 2014; Johns, 2001, 2006; Rousseau & Fried, 2001). A notable exception can be found in the works of Johns (2006, 2017), who encourages cross-level and comparative designs, as well as research that is more qualitative, specifically studies of processes and events to contextualize organizational research.

Furthering Context as Theoretical Construct

In our theoretical discussion of context, we have focused on the referential relationship between context and action, because constructs are "suspended in a complex web of references to and relationships with other constructs" (Suddaby, 2010 p. 350). Suddaby argues that construct clarity is essential to theory building, particularly in the social sciences, where constructs are rarely universally applicable. Because clearly defined and delineated constructs are the building blocks of strong theory, and because context has such a prominent role in both variance and process theories, we propose that social science, in general, and organization and management theories, in particular, will benefit from a thorough discussion of what defines *context*, under which scope conditions this definition applies, how this definition of semantically and referentially relates to other concepts, and how this definition of context coheres with the overall arguments we introduce in this book. Next, we discuss context in relation to dimensions.

Definition

Traditionally, the word *context* has a double meaning: it is a word used to help explain the meaning of other words, and it is a concept that refers to the conditions or circumstances in which an event takes place (Akman, 2000). Both aspects of context are related to both meaning and how we understand and make sense of things. In this sense, the concept of context resembles Goffman's (1974) concept of "frames," because both frames and contexts are constructs that refer to key elements in the processes by which we try to understand what is happening in situations, what phenomena mean, and how other people are involved (Akman, 2000). In our definition of *context*, we integrate the two elements, because they are interrelated:

> *Context* is a relational construct, which specifies what, at any given point, is considered the background for understanding a phenomena or event. The background/foreground relationship is continually constructed by people, as they make sense of their experiences in the social worlds they are part of.

The essential characteristics of context as a theoretical construct are relational, interactional, constructed, and tied to meaning. By *relational construct*, we mean that *context* is always a context in relation to the phenomenon or event of which it helps to explain the meaning. Context as a theoretical construct might differ depending on the kind of research it is being used in because:

> constructs in process theory are qualitatively different from constructs derived from variance theory [...] constructs derived from processes, therefore, tend to be

relational inasmuch as they focus on events that are multidimensional, temporally embedded and often spanning multiple levels of analysis. (Suddaby, 2010 p. 351)

By *interactional*, we mean that to understand something in its context is the act of constructing meaning from the interaction between "background" and "foreground." The meaning of a phenomenon or an event is not in the background: it is produced by considering the interaction between a phenomenon or an event and the background. Importantly, this means that in our use of the word pair, *context–event* does not refer to relatively stable opposites. Rather, we focus on how context and event interact, as well as the role of action within them.

By *constructed*, we mean that contextualization is the process with which we make sense of and give meaning to our lived experiences and the social worlds of which we are a part. This construction is simultaneously individual and social; individuals construct contexts for making sense of phenomena or events *in interaction* with other people and the world around them, and these processes are social, just as sensemaking processes are social. At the same time, contexts cannot be regarded as given or as a "shared background" just because they are social (Fetzer & Akman, 2002).

By *tied to meaning*, we understand that context, as a theoretical construct, is essential to linguistics, philosophy, and studies of language use in practice: it is crucial to understand how language and cognition works, i.e., how human beings make meaning in and of their world. Moreover, meaning is also something we *do:* cognitive phenomena are accomplished interactionally: "what is background at one moment can be made focal event at the next" (Pomerantz, 1998 p. 129). Context changes meanings: depending on what is foregrounded and what is bounded as the context, events or phenomena might mean different things to different people, in different places, or at different times. Moreover, these meanings are shaped by the interdependencies and changing relationships between people over time.

Scope Conditions

The scope conditions for the concept of context are hard to specify because this term usually refers to "the contextual circumstances under which a construct will or will not apply" (Suddaby, 2010 p. 347). Our definition of *context* draws on theories from a broad range of fields, and on empirical work carried out in public sector health care organizations, as the thematic chapters illustrate. Because we define *context* as a processual concept in a referential relationship to action that covers activities resembling sensemaking, the scope conditions for our theoretical construct are relatively broad, and they include social science, in general, and organization and management studies, in particular, because these are the theoretical and empirical resources we draw on. However, we invite researchers to "pick up" our definition of context and refine or expand it, for example, with studies of such processes carried out under different conditions. An example of this could be to study how actors understand, experience, and engage with context in situations with unusually high levels of uncertainty or pressure to act, in emotionally charged situations, or in individuals or groups who suffer physical impairments (loss of hearing, loss of sight), which might provide them with markedly different processes of contextualization.

We are conscious of the fact that the chapters in this book do not display studies of how actors experience contextualization processes in and of themselves, even though health care offers ample opportunities for such work. Paget's (1988) analysis of how doctors experience the fundamentally "error-proned" nature of their work, the temporal displacement of errors, which always start out as actions (it is only in retrospect an action reveals itself to be an error), is an example of the "complex sorrow" that accompanies doctors as they make decisions that can turn out to be wrong. Exploring how emotions affect doctors' well-being and clinical practice, Ofri (2013) shows how disregard of doctors' emotions is harmful not only to the people working in medicine, but also to the quality and safety of the practice of medicine. Furthering Paget's and Ofri's work, researchers could examine the effects of emotions on how people engage in and experience contextualization processes: for example, under what circumstances experiences or expectations for the future influence what we construct as context for actions or events.

With the definition we present, context is a theoretical construct relevant across multiple analytical levels: individual/group, organization, and wider system. In some cases, the relevant context for a phenomenon might be multilevel and multiorganizational and thus distributed across space: for example, in a network or system. Are we in such cases talking about the same theoretical construct of context if we compare context across levels or organizations? Also, is this construct of context the same as when we talk about individuals' experiences in specific situations? Configurational analysis (Meyer, Tsui, & Hinings, 1993) is one way to handle the complexity and multilayered nature of context analytically, as, for example, in studies of health care (Dopson & Fitzgerald, 2005; Meier, 2015). Practice theories, particularly with their focus on the interconnectedness of practices across space (Nicolini, 2009, 2011, 2012; Shove et al., 2012), can provide a different theoretical and analytical framework for studying the potentially distributed nature of a certain (constructed) context.

In our definition of context, it is essential to specify *time* and the temporal boundaries a researcher constructs for his/her usage of context as theoretical construct. The meaning of context might vary in settings with different temporal orderings or over different time scales: snapshots, short time spans, or long time spans. The temporal scope conditions must be related to the level of analysis, so it is clear how the construct of context might be operationalized and studied differently. Typically, units of time differ across analytical levels, so that analyses of context for phenomena on a national or systems level work with longer time spans, whereas studies at the individual or group level work with very brief or shorter units of time, as, for example, in conversational analysis, and longer units of time, as, for example, in process studies (see, e.g., Langley et al., 2013; Scheff, 1997).

Another important scope condition is value, i.e., the researcher's own worldview and understanding of the phenomenon to which the construct refers. Here, philosophy of science and methodological quality criteria relevant for the chosen design and methods become important. First, which assumptions about the world, the phenomenon, and the kind of research/knowledge s/he can produce does the researcher carry with him/her into the work? How do these assumptions relate to and possibly influence the work? Suddaby suggests that "as organizational theorists, we must adopt an ongoing position of critical reflexivity about how our individual point of view, our often taken-for-granted assumptions, and our institutional biography might introduce bias and distortion into how we conceptualize and abstract reality" (2010 p. 350).

Coherence

What is the coherence of the construct of context to the overall theoretical argument we are trying to make? First, it is worth pointing out that context holds a certain place in the majority of social science theories, which Table 2.1 amply illustrates. Within health care research, context is also essential: for example, in relation to theories of institutional or organizational change, strategy, organizational behavior, organizational development, integration of care, implementation of information technology, quality-improvement efforts, policies or standards, managerial work, leadership, or patient involvement. Thus, we may assume that context has acquired layers of "surplus meaning" (Suddaby, 2010 p. 348). Because the construct of context has acquired meaning across the social sciences, broadly speaking, it may also have altered meaning depending on the field in which it is used. We see examples of this if we examine how the concept is defined and used differently in, for example, studies of language or organizational behavior (see, e.g., Fetzer & Akman, 2002; Johns, 2017).

Actions in Context

Scholars of organization and management often study phenomena that involve a great deal of action. People's actions and interactions are connected across time and space, often in complex, multifaceted ways, and the consequences of a series of inter-actions can be far-reaching and unpredictable. Thus, the fundamentally unpredictable nature of our social world places *action* as a theoretical concept, a unit of analysis, and a philosophical category at the heart of much social science research. The capability for action for doing something other than only what is expected, is what allows humans to bring innovation into the world (Arendt, 1958). Actions can be observable activities and thought processes (reflections or mental actions) and actions are embedded in interactions, and in processes including past, present, and perceived future actions. In this way, the human conditions of plurality and connectedness (i.e., that individuals are born into webs of relationships (Elias,1978; Arendt, 1958)) are important aspects of both action and context.

The open and fluid character of human interaction leaves room for uncertainty and contingency, from "external" conditions, from the course of action itself (unanticipated consequences), or as a result of re-evaluation (change of mind) (Strauss, 1993). This "openness" and continuous possibility for actors to perform or interact in unforeseen ways is a potential power to act (Arendt, 1958); the capacity of human consciousness to reflect and recontextualize is at the "very core of our perceptual and cognitive processing mechanisms" (Givón, 1989 p. 4). This is an important point in the analysis of context, and it recognizes the socially constructed dimensions and unbounded nature of the concept (Akman, 2000; Scharfstein, 1989), as it draws attention to the fundamental and challenging conditions for contextual analysis: people repeatedly contextualize and recontextualize actions (observable and mental) throughout their daily lives, in relation to past, present and expected future actions. This also applies to the concept of work, when perceived as a central form of human interaction embedded in processes that include continuous recontextualization and relation to past, present, and potential future actions. In this process, whether individuals are at work or not, contingencies need to be handled that may change the course of action or the way an action is evaluated and understood in a given situation: "consequences become conditions" (Strauss, 1993 p. 37).

At the same time, Strauss reminds us that when people perform actions (e.g., work or are actively creating a context for understanding an event), they do so through/with a body, and this aspect is particularly pertinent to remember in health care (Strauss et al., 1997). Stating that the body is an essential condition for action may seem unnecessary, but we argue that it is important to remember that health care work is carried out in settings where the main source of sensory input and bodily experiences arises from interactions with people (bodies) who are experiencing health problems. Depending on the types of illness and the needs of individual patients, health care work may well be carried out in severely stressful or emotionally charged situations, which actors experience with their minds and bodies (bodily expressions, sense of smell, hearing, sight, and feelings such as fear, anger, sorrow, joy, or compassion). The significance of acting and experiencing through the body in such situations is particularly important for the concept of context in health care, as the "bodily" contributions to continuously making sense of and re-evaluating actions and contexts in which actors perform are based on nonverbal, contextually bound experiences.

Note

1. See, for example, Nicolini (2012), for a discussion of the limited uptake of the philosophical underpinnings of practice-based theories into organization and management research.

References

Akman, V. (2000). Rethinking context as a social construct. *Journal of Pragmatics, 32*(6), 743–59.

Akman, V. & Bazzanella, C. (2003). The complexity of context: Guest editors' introduction. *Journal of Pragmatics, 35*(3), 321–9.

Arendt, H. (1958). *The human condition*. Chicago: University of Chicago Press.

Barley, S. R. & Tolbert, P. S. (1997). Institutionalization and structuration: Studying the links between action and institution. *Organization Studies, 18*, 93–117.

Blackler, F. (1995). Knowledge, knowledge work and organizations: An overview and interpretation. *Organization Studies, 16*(6), 1021–46.

Brown, J. S. & Duguid, P. (1991). Organizational learning and communities of practice: Toward a unified view of working, learning and innovation. *Organizational Science, 2*(1), 40–57.

Brown, J. S. & Duguid, P. (2001). Knowledge and organization. *Organizational Science, 12*(2), 198–213.

Cicourel, A. (1992). The interpenetration of communicative contexts: Examples from medical encounters. In A. Duranti & C. Goodwin (eds.), *Rethinking Context: Language as an interactive phenomenon*. Cambridge: Cambridge University Press, pp. 291–311.

Clarke, A. (2005). *Situational analysis: Grounded theory after the postmodern turn*. Thousand Oaks, CA: Sage.

Cole, M. & Engeström, Y. (1993). A cultural historic approach to distributed cognition. In G. Salomon (ed.), *Distributed cognitions*. Cambridge: Cambridge University Press, pp. 1–46.

Currie, G. & Lockett, A. (2011). Distributing leadership in health and social care: Concertive, conjoint or collective? *International Journal of Management Reviews, 13*(3), 286–300.

Dilley, R. (ed.). (1999). *The problem of context*. Oxford: Berghahn Books.

Dopson, S. & Fitzgerald, L. (2005). *Knowledge to action? Evidence based health care in context*. New York: Oxford University Press.

Dopson, S., Fitzgerald, L., & Ferlie, E. (2008). Understanding change and innovation in health care settings: Reconceptualizing the active role of context. *Journal of Change Management, 8*(3–4), 213–31.

Duranti, A. & Goodwin, C. (eds.). (1992). *Rethinking context: Language as an interactive phenomenen*. Cambridge: Cambridge University Press.

Edmonds, B. (2002). Editorial: Context in context. *Foundations of Science, 7*(3), 233–8.

Elias, N. (1978). *What is sociology?* (2nd ed.). New York: Columbia University Press.

Fetzer, A. (2004). *Recontextualizing context: Grammaticality meets appropriateness*. Amsterdam: John Benjamin Publishing Company.

Fetzer, A. & Akman, V. (2002). Contexts of social action: Guest editors' introduction. *Language & Communication, 22*, 391–402.

Fitzgerald, L. & McDermott, M. A. (2017). *Challenging perspectives on organizational change in health care*. New York: Routledge.

Givón, T. (1989). *Mind, code and context:Essays in pragmatics*. New Jersey: Lawrence Erlbaum Associates, Inc.

Goffman, E. (1974). *Frame analysis: An essay on the organization of experience*. Harmondsworth: Penguin.

Hallett, T. & Ventresca, M. J. (2006). Inhabited institutions: Social interactions and organizational forms in Gouldner's patterns of industrial bureaucracy. *Theory and Society, 35*, 213–36.

Härtel, C. & O'Connor, J. (2014). Contextualizing research: Putting context back into organizational behavior research. *Journal of Management and Organization, 20*(4), 417–22.

Hernes, T. (2014). *A process theory of organization*. Oxford: Oxford University Press.

Johns, G. (2001). In praise of context. *Journal of Organizational Behavior, 22*(1), 31–42.

Johns, G. (2006). The essential impact of context on organizational behavior. *Academy of Management Review, 31*(2), 386–408.

Johns, G. (2017). Incorporating context in organizational research: Reflections on the 2016 AMR decade award. *Academy of Management Review, 42*(4), 577–95.

Klein, K. J., Ziegert, J. C., Knight, A. P., & Xiao, Y. (2006). Dynamic delegation: Shared, hierarchical, and deindividualized leadership in extreme action teams. *Administrative Science Quarterly, 51*, 590–621.

Langley, A., Smallman, C., Tsoukas, H., & Van, d. V. (2013). Process studies of change in organization and management: Unveiling temporality, activity, and flow. *Academy of Management Journal, 56*(1), 1–13.

March, J. G. (1981). Footnotes to organizational change. *Administrative Science Quarterly, 26*(4), 563–77.

Meier, N. (2015). Configurations of leadership practices in hospital units. *Journal of Health Organization and Management, 29*(7), 1115–30.

Meyer, A. D., Tsui, A. S., & Hinings, C. R. (1993). Configurational approaches to organizational analysis. *Academy of Management Journal, 36*(6), 1175–95.

Nicolini, D. (2009). Zooming in and out: Studying practices by switching theoretical lenses and trailing connections. *Organization Studies, 30*(12), 1391–418.

Nicolini, D. (2011). Practice as the site of knowing: Insights from the field of telemedicine. *Organization Science, 22*(3), 602–20.

Nicolini, D. (2012). *Practice theory, work, and organization: An introduction.* Oxford: Oxford University Press.

Ofri, D. (2013). *What doctors feel: How emotions affect the practice of medicine.* Boston: Beacon Press.

Paget, M. A. (1988). *The unity of mistakes: A phenomenological interpretation of medical work* (2nd ed.). Philadelphia: Temple University Press.

Pettigrew, A. M. (1987). Context and action in the transformation of the firm. *The Journal of Management Studies, 24*(6), 649–71.

Pomerantz, A. (1998). Multiple interpretations of context: How are they useful? *Research on Language and Social Interaction, 31*(1), 123–32.

Rousseau, M. D. & Fried, Y. (2001). Location, location, location: Contextualizing organizational research. *Journal of Organizational Behavior, 22*(1), 1–13.

Sandberg, J. & Tsoukas, H. (2015). Making sense of the sensemaking perspective: Its constituents, limitations, and opportunities for further development. *Journal of Organizational Behavior, 36*(S1), S6–S32.

Scharfstein, B. A. (1989). *The dilemma of context.* New York: New York University Press.

Schatzki, T. R. (1996). *Social practices: A Wittgensteinian approach to human activity and the social* (Digitally printed version ed.). Cambridge: Cambridge University Press.

Schatzki, T. R., Cetina-Knorr, K., & Savigny, E. (eds.). (2001). *The practice turn in contemporary theory.* London: Routledge.

Scheff, T. J. (1997). *Emotions, the social bond, and human reality: Part/whole analysis.* Cambridge: Cambridge University Press.

Scott, W. R. & Meyer, J. W. (1994). *Institutional environments and organizations: Structural complexity and individualism.* Thousand Oaks, CA: Sage.

Scott, W. R., Ruef, M., Mendel, P., & Caronna, C. A. (2000). *Institutional change and healthcare organizations: From professional dominance to managed care.* Chicago: University of Chicago Press.

Shove, E., Pantzar, M., & Watson, M. (2012). *The dynamics of social practice: Everyday life and how it changes.* London: Sage.

Smircich, L. & Stubbart, C. (1985). Strategic management in an enacted world. *Academy of Management the Academy of Management Review, 10*(4), 724–36.

Strauss, A. (1993). *Continual permutations of action* (3rd ed.). New York: Transaction Publishers.

Strauss, A., Fagerhaugh, S., Suczek, B., & Weiner, C. (1997). *Social organization of medical work* (2nd ed.). New Brunswick: Transaction Publishers, Rutgers.

Suddaby, R. (2010). Editor's comments: Construct clarity in theories of management and organization. *Academy of Management Review, 35*(3), 346–57.

Timmermans, S. & Berg, M. (1997). Standardization in action: Achieving local universality through medical protocols. *Social Studies of Science, 27*(2), 273–305.

Timmermans, S. & Epstein, S. (2010). A world of standards but not a standard world: Toward a sociology of standards and standardization. *Annual Review of Sociology, 36*, 69–89.

Weick, K. E. (2001). *Making sense of the organization.* Oxford: Blackwell Publishing.

Weick, K. E. (2006). Faith, evidence, and action: Better guesses in an unknowable world. *Organization Studies, 27*(11), 1723–36.

Weick, K. E. (2012). Organized sensemaking: A commentary on processes of interpretive work. *Human Relations, 65*(1), 153.

Wenger, E. (2000). Communities of practice and social learning systems. *Organization, 7*(2), 225–46.

Wentzer, H. & Bygholm, A. (2007). Attending unintended transformations of health care infrastructure. *International Journal of Integrated Care, 7*(4), e41.

Zerubavel, E. (1991). *The fine line: Making distinctions in everyday life.* Chicago: University of Chicago Press.

Zerubavel, E. (1999). *Social mindscapes: An invitation to cognitive sociology.* Cambridge, MA: Harvard University Press.

3

Methodological Challenges in Studying Context in Action

Sue Dopson and Ninna Meier

This chapter develops the methodological aspects of the Framework for Studying Context and Action introduced in the beginning of the book. It then presents and discusses the methodological challenges of studying context raised by our contributors, and explores why the links between an understanding of context, the unit of analysis, and methods have such an impact on a given research project and its results. Generally, the ideas and arguments put forward in this book contend that context must be understood relationally, as the interaction of context, actors, and action. This has significant implications for the design and methods adopted in research endeavors and for the results we claim to have produced. We argue that the concept of context, its relationship to action, and how this may be studied, is an underdeveloped and somewhat neglected arena in organization studies.

Context and action are concepts often used in organization research in health care and other fields. This, however, does not necessarily mean that scholars reflect upon, develop, or critically engage with these concepts as they use them. Many studies, both qualitative and quantitative in design, state that they have included context in the study, while offering minimal data or explanation of their conceptual and methodological approach to context, and this is problematic for several reasons (see, e.g., Johns, 2006; Rousseau & Fried, 2001). Frequently, context is expressed simply as "there," by a brief exposition such as "in the health care system," "in the context of primary care," or "the data were collected in a large general hospital." This is problematic, because if we take the stability of context for granted, we risk overlooking or neglecting important aspects of the social worlds we study. Buttny illustrates this problem in the following example:

We need to take context as that which can be empirically investigated rather than some factor that is a priori assumed to be at work. The proposition that gender or race is always relevant as a context to a conversation is the kind of claim being cautioned against. Although these features may indeed be relevant, we need to show in what ways they are relevant through persons' orientations, that is, their talk, noticeable silence, or other nonverbal displays. In a recent study on "talking race" [...] I found, not surprisingly, that race was relevant in discursive constructions about race but did not make a difference in describing the conversational practice of reporting speech.   (1998 p. 47)

Contextualizing research can help us to analyze both similarities and differences across situations, settings, events, or whichever focus we have adopted.

If we do not offer sufficiently detailed and nuanced descriptions of the elements we have bounded as relevant context, and why, we leave the reader of the text guessing what the author's reference to context might mean. More problematically, often the text does not even specify from which perspective or vantage point reference to context is made. Is it the researcher's evaluation of what might be the most influential contextual forces in a given setting? Is it the shared perspective of a certain group or organization under study? In both cases, the way in which the researcher determines what were the most significant aspects of context is often not made explicit. However, such lack of specification and transparency is particularly apparent in case study research, which is unfortunate, because context in this type of research helps us understand the results and—importantly—the boundary conditions for their application.

Indeed:

contextualization is a way of approaching research where knowledge of the setting to be studied is brought to bear in design and implementation decisions. This can occur at all stages of the research process, from conceptualization to writing the research article. And at the minimum stage, contextualization essentially requires a thicker description of the setting(s) to help the reader and those researchers who would build upon a study understand the factors that gave rise to the researcher's observations.   (Rousseau & Fried, 2001 p. 6)

In their editorial of contextualizing organizational research, Rousseau and Fried (2001 p. 6) provide a table with elements to consider theoretically and methodologically (construct comparability, points of view, representativeness, range restriction, time, and levels). They go on to propose that researchers aiming to produce contextualized organizational research should focus on one of three ways to move forward: rich descriptions, direct observations and analysis of effects, and comparative studies.

Two vignettes are offered next as examples of how context can be operationalized and studied, which is especially relevant in relation to the complex contexts involved in health care change. Following the unfolding of the narratives, we highlight some implications for research design and methods.

Vignette 1: Genetics Knowledge Park

Advances in biomedical innovation have heralded some radical shifts in the delivery of health care, with genetics science and technology, for example, providing a shift toward forms of diagnostics and treatments that are more personalized and preventative. There have been many major investments in biomedical science and genomics, regional development initiatives aimed at fostering biotechnology clusters, incentives for biotechnology start-ups, activities for university technology transfer, collaborative projects (e.g., EU Framework funding), and life science networks (e.g., industry, academic, and clinical networks). Many such initiatives provide mechanisms to bridge academic science, industry, and clinical practice in the hope of speeding the transfer of new discoveries, often produced in academia, into commercially viable and clinically accepted products and treatments. McGivern and Dopson studied a biomedical network specifically aimed at encouraging the translation of academic knowledge of genetic science into new clinical practices by encouraging "Mode 2" forms of knowledge production among heterogeneous groups of practitioners (including academic genetics scientists, clinicians, industrialists, legal and ethical experts, social scientists, and the public). This vignette, drawn from McGivern and Dopson (2010), illuminates the complexity of the stakeholders and subcultures that often exist in health care change contexts, as well as the impact of the interdependences on action. It also demonstrates the importance of understanding the wider policy context and the formation of the network locally.

The policy interest in genetics, and in particular, the interest in securing the monies associated with the Genetics Knowledge Park (GKP) initiative that emerged in 2001, pushed more closely together the research (University of Oxford) and clinical and science (National Health Service (NHS)) practice world in the sites successful in acquiring funding. In short, the funding opportunity offered meant that the context was changed and new patterns of local action emerged. Figure 3.1 shows the new figuration of actors following funding.

The network, at this, point was dominated by an elite group of scientists with training in medicine. These clinical researchers had worked together for some time locally and, therefore, knew and trusted one another because of the shared epistemology (having all trained in both medicine and science) and because their reputations within the university were important. Their incentives for joining this new context were clear. It represented an opportunity for

GKP (Conception: 2001)

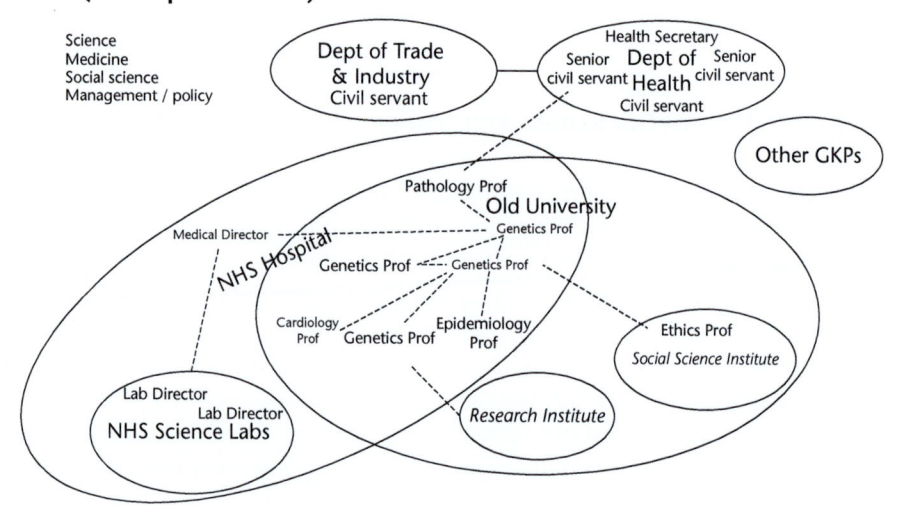

Figure 3.1 GKP (Conception: 2001)

more money to push on with their existing work and leverage other funding opportunities. This is not to say that they disregarded the importance of other possible benefits of the network: for example, as one interviewee argued, "it could provide an umbrella to bring people together." The GKP was collectively imprinted with the epistemology of the clinical researchers who founded it. Clinical researchers in this case captured the jurisdiction over the GKP from the outset.

NHS managers who were tangentially engaged with the bid were very worried about cost implications, yet failed to get such concerns on the agenda early on. As a stakeholder group, they were marginal and engaged in a rather tokenistic way. Another stakeholder group was research scientists working in a research institute within the university. These scientists' epistemology was quite similar to the clinical researchers', although they appeared somewhat less powerful because they lacked the understanding of patients and the NHS context. The NHS scientists who worked in the NHS laboratories (Labs) had a distinct epistemology from that of clinical researchers and, indeed, research scientists within the research institute. They were also enrolled in the network to perform vital genetic tests. The NHS Labs were keen to be involved in the network as they saw the GKP as being useful in terms of providing new funds and equipment and raising the Labs' local and national profile.

The call for tenders had emphasized the need to engage social science stakeholders and patients. The professor who headed an "ethics" institute within the university with an interest in the ethics of genetics was identified

Methodological Challenges in Studying Context in Action

to lead the social science aspect of the network. Patient representation took the form of a member of the Genetics Interest Group, who was invited to attend the executive meetings and to be part of a work package. In practice, this person's attendance was rare. Later, in 2005, commissioning stakeholders were involved in the network in a non-tokenistic manner.

The Changing Configurations within the Context

The GKP won funding and assembled executive and supervisory governance boards. Some of the senior clinicians who were originally and centrally involved in the GKP bid soon withdrew to roles that were more supervisory (the GKP was just one small part of the many different projects in which they were involved) or simply disappeared from the activities of the GKP, and the range of professionals became more actively involved in the project on a day-to-day basis (see Figure 3.2).

Most notably, these included: (1) the network director; (2) three consultant geneticists (two working in the Medical Genetics Department of the NHS hospital, while the other worked in both the university and the hospital, and had previous experience working in Labs, as well as current experience interfacing with policy makers regarding developing guidelines in the nascent

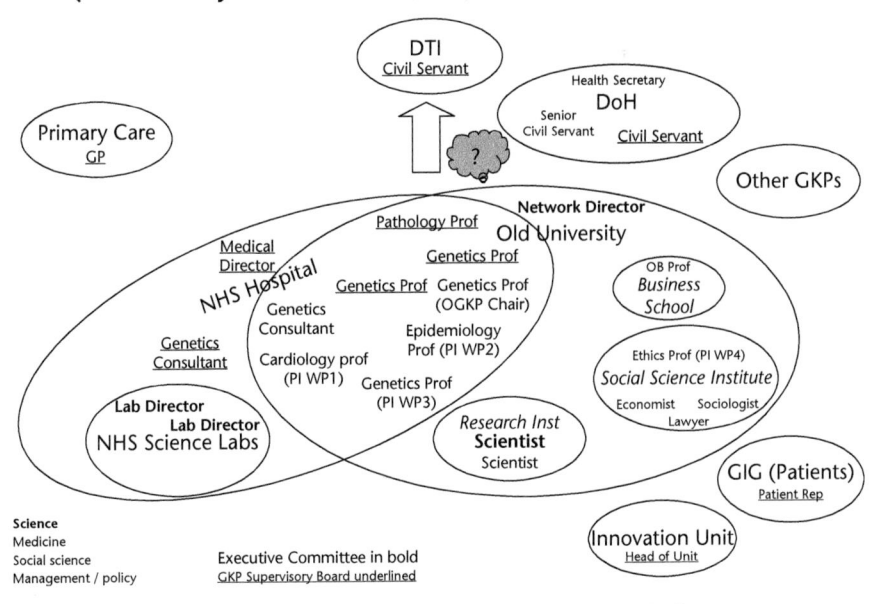

Figure 3.2 GKP (Formal early formation: 2002–3)

genetics discipline); (3) two scientists who were recruited within the research institute to do work around micro arrays for cancer and learning disabilities; (4) within the social science institute, a health economist, a sociologist, a lawyer, and an anthropologist, all at junior levels, were recruited to pursue their respective disciplinary approaches to genetics innovations within the GKP; (5) a researcher from the business school also became involved with the GKP to study the managerial aspects of the network; and (6) a professor of medicine and epidemiology, and a senior epidemiologist.

The early period of the network was characterized by hiring of new personnel, starting up research activity, introducing governance arrangements, and getting to grips with the expectations of the Department of Health (DH). By mid-2003 (see Figure 3.3), there had been several changes.

First, the network in practice revolved around an even more limited number of key individuals, particularly those in genetics medicine, the NHS Labs (although only one of the two lab leaders was included in the GKP executive board), the research institute, and the professor of ethics. Representatives from primary care, patient groups, the Trust, and the Innovation Unit had little practical involvement with the GKP other than formally sitting on the supervisory board. At this early stage, the Department of Trade and Industry, despite having jointly funded the GKPs, appeared to begin to lose interest in

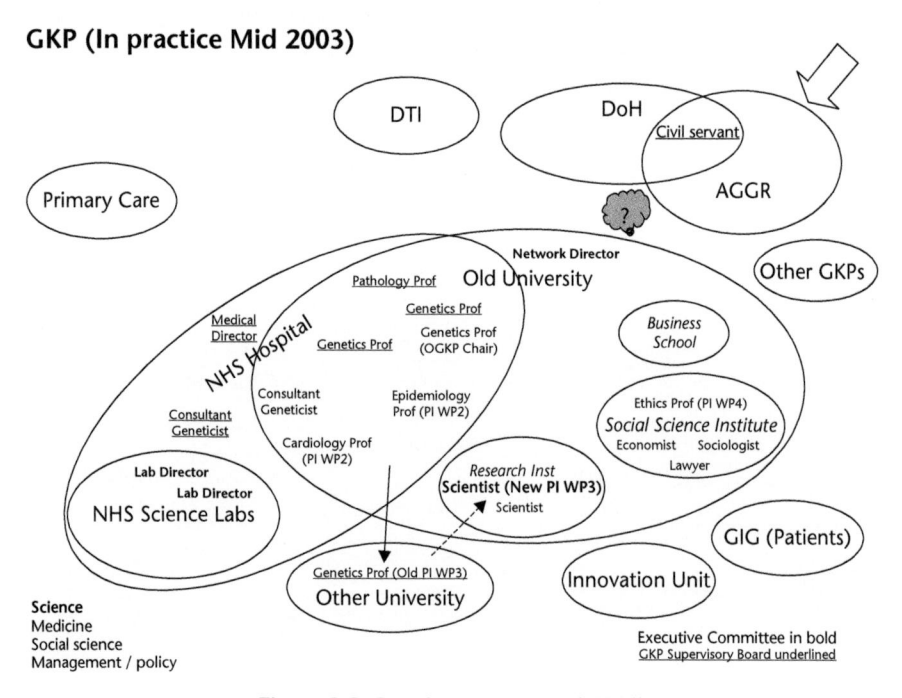

Figure 3.3 GKP (In practice mid 2003)

Methodological Challenges in Studying Context in Action

the project; perhaps because it became apparent that commercial applications were unlikely to develop within the 5-year time-frame for the project.

During this period, the DH acknowledged that it had little understanding of the ongoing activities within the GKPs, and brought in a group of "experts" as a governance mechanism (known as the Advisory Group on Genetics Research (AGGR)) to help it regulate the GKPs. The DH also imposed quarterly reporting on the GKPs. Almost immediately, this contributed to one genetics professor leaving the university for another and delegating operational responsibility for his work package, and quarterly reporting, to a junior scientist within the research institute.

By the end of 2004 (see Figure 3.4), the DH and AGGR appeared to have a better understanding of what was happening within the GKPs, and showed concerned that the GKPs were not doing what the DH would retrospectively have intended; in particular, there appeared to be little networking going on between the six GKPs they had funded, and results were slower than anticipated. Thus, the DH applied pressure to the network director, who in turn put pressure on the different work packages within the GKP, to meet the espoused goals of translation into the NHS.

The DH/AGGR could be seen as attempting to re-establish jurisdiction over the network, which, after all, it was paying for, and steer it away from doing

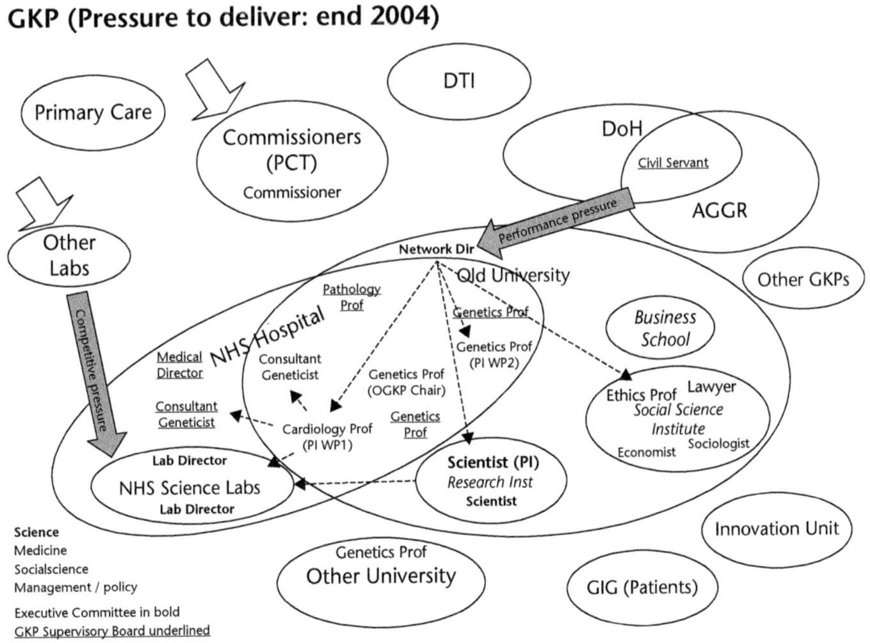

Figure 3.4 GKP (Pressure to deliver: end 2004)

GKP (end 2007)

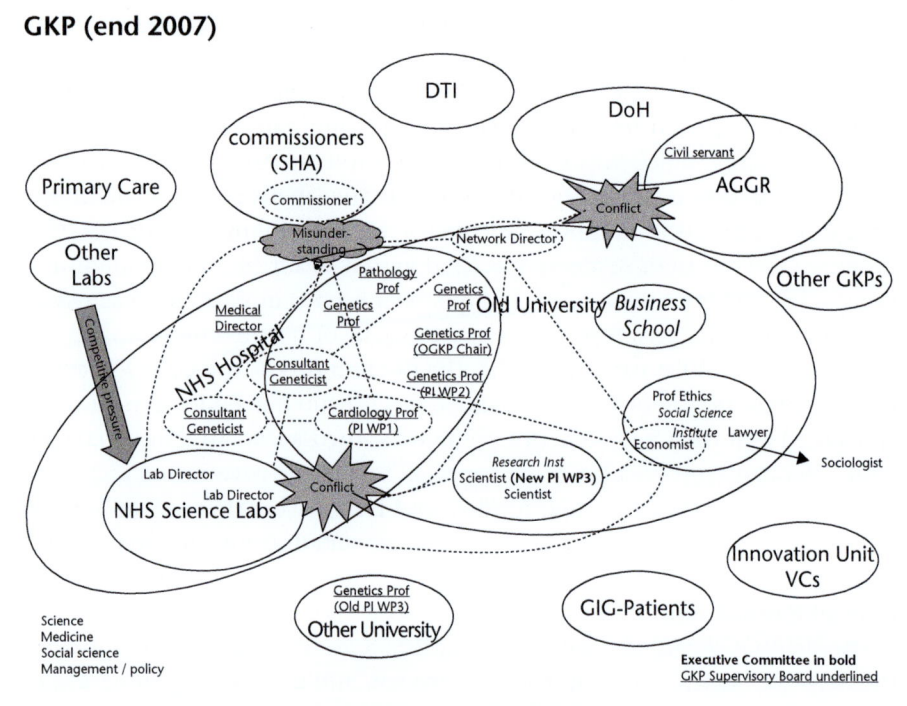

Figure 3.5 GKP (end 2007)

academic science alone and toward translation into the NHS. Concurrently within other parts of the GKP, a number of pressure points emerged (see Figure 3.5).

Cooperation was beginning to break down between the NHS scientists, the clinical researchers, and the molecular genetics lab leads, mainly related to their very different approaches to genetic testing. Labs are interested in 100 percent accuracy of results, in case they might be faced with litigation in the future, but this meant that results were slow, whereas clinical researchers and research scientists in the university and the hospital wanted results returned quickly, with reasonable but not necessarily 100 percent accuracy.

A related concern reported by the lab scientists as adding to the tension "was a fear that this new technology (microarrays) was actually going to replace what they were doing." Wider of the GKP under scrutiny, a national network of Labs was being rationalized. Competition for business between NHS Labs began to undermine the GKP Labs' willingness to disclose information about their costs to the GKP economist for fear that it might leak to other labs and undermine their competitive position. Molecular genetics labs in England have to work as a network because tests are rationalized around the country. Conflict between the NHS Labs and the rest of the network intensified as a result of the Labs' unwillingness to disclose pricing, and this distrust appeared to spread to other parts of the GKP.

A second clash point can be traced to pressure from the DH to get the genetic test developed in practice. Researchers who had developed the test looked to the network director to broker the conversation with the commissioners about how to turn the test into a funded NHS service. The commissioner appeared to make an effort to understand the benefits of the test for sudden cardiac death for the local population for whom he commissioned NHS services. The NHS members of the GKP initially felt excluded from the commissioning conversation and spoke of needing to get involved "to ensure the commissioning process went smoothly." The commissioner was perplexed that the network had only thought about genetics in isolation, ignoring the wider context. Although the GKP network leadership argued that the test was clinically and economically viable, it had implications for limited local budgets; testing people with a family history of sudden cardiac death would be expensive, and those found with the condition would need to be provided with defibrillators, which were even more expensive. Local budgets were limited, and the test's economic benefits deemed "academic."

Another conflict was in evidence in respect of the role and contribution of the sociologist to the network, who were seen as "these weird sort of sociology people" doing "wooly" research (NHS Labs scientist). When it became clear that his position would not be refunded, the sociologist focused on personal research, which enabled him to leave the network and take up a position elsewhere.

Reflections on Bounding Contexts for Change over Time

When my colleague Professor Gerry McGivern and I (Sue Dopson) began our study of this network, we started with a bounding of context that included only the actors who set up the local network. The research focus at that point was to understand how a science network operated, with particular consideration of the barriers and facilitators to translation of genetics science. At the end of our longitudinal study, we realized that the GKP story was profoundly influenced and shaped by the "set-up" stage of the network, in particular, the role of the funding body and policy makers. This set the context. Another insight was that the actors and actions in the network were influenced profoundly by social relationships that local actors had with people they did not know, and in some cases, of whose existence they were not aware. The idea that context comprises face-to-face relationships—and that people with whom individuals have personal or direct relationships with have the most impact on actions—is naive in the extreme. We can also see from

Vignette 1 how action is affected by the activities of past generations, not only in terms of material things such as buildings, but also in terms of language and education systems. Therefore, we cannot understand people's actions adequately outside of their social and historical context. Many studies of health care change do not properly locate agency within this broader social and historical context, and because of this, offer a partial understanding of management problems and actions. The complex network showcased in Vignette 1 necessarily involves power relationships, which tend to be unequal across a range of dimensions. These networks are always dynamic, that is, they are in process. They can be conceived of, in terms that are more abstract, as processes such as the division of labor, but it is important to note that these processes only exist in and through the actions of people.

We see in operation in the context very different time-frames for the different communities of practice involved: for policy makers, the results of the research took too long, but for the scientists the time-scales involved were normal. Vignette 1 highlights the importance of seeking to understand factors such as career structures, incentives, social capital, trust, ways of working, and, crucially, power differences, as potent mediators of context and action in collaborative and translational work. McGivern and Dopson (2010) argue that policy makers, when considering funding innovations and networks such as the GKP, need to attend to the incentives operating in the context and the impact on communities' desire to collaborate with one another, and how these compare with other incentives and disincentives provided by the wider systems in which they are situated. Neither universities nor health services provided adequate incentives for ongoing conversations between researchers, clinicians, social scientists, or managers. Furthermore, genetics innovation and knowledge has to cross another significant and poorly understood contextual boundary to be successful: the boundary between the health service and the patients and their families.

Vignette 2 shows how organizational actors in health care settings are not isolated individuals. Individuals live within and are a part of a network of social relationships that extend well beyond the organization to which they in name belong. The point we wish to make is that we started to study a network of people and actions, and during the process of researching this, we realized that our contextual awareness needed to be broadened, as well as deepened, by understanding context from a communities of practice perspective. Furthermore, we realized how actors have been, and continue to be, influenced by the shadow of past periods and historic decisions, which they have inherited. This important involuntary temporal aspect of the creation and development of context (that the context for one's actions and interactions with others can be influenced substantially by past events and decisions) has been under-researched, but in our view, it has been demonstrated to be critical, and, crucially, it needs to inform a more sophisticated notion of context.

Vignette 2: Comparing across Contexts in Action

Between 2013 and 2016, I (Ninna Meier) carried out a process study of multi-level organizational change processes, specifically managers' and staff members' efforts to improve coherence in and across hospital wards in emergency medicine, oncology, and internal medicine. The three areas were chosen as cases to represent different aspects of challenges to create coherence e.g., high levels of unpredictability, severity of illness, and chronic illness and multi-morbidity (Bohmer, 2009; Klein et al., 2006; Strauss & Corbin, 1988; Strauss et al., 1997). Over a period of 3 years, organizational consultants and clinical partners (hospital ward managers, clinical managers, and staff) developed organizational improvements aimed specifically at creating coherence in patient pathways.

Coherence can be understood as the result of successful coordination. It is both process and product: an on-going achievement and an outcome of how work is organized, managed, and practiced, and as such, it is an important element of patients' experiences of continuity in their own care over time (Guthrie et al., 2008; Haggerty, 2003). Based on my earlier research into hospitals, I understood coherence as resulting from formal and informal coordination practices and mechanisms at multiple organizational levels (management and operational level), and that efforts to create coherence at the different levels needed to be aligned. Starting out, I chose cases that would allow me to study my unit of analysis ("coherence") in what I initially operationalized as different clinical contexts. Based on prior work, I assumed that the level of clinical uncertainty and organizational unpredictability (Meier, 2013) would impact the coordination mechanisms and practices needed to handle contingencies and to keep the individual patient's pathway progressing, as well efforts to keep work in the given hospital unit on track. I also assumed that IT infrastructure and standardization would support some coordination practices, while other, emergent coordination practices would need to be flexible and tailor-made to the coordination challenge at hand (Meier, 2012). Such assumptions were built into the design. Next, I explain how and what these choices afforded.

I focused on how actors organized and practiced work to improve coherence in the three different areas. To study the actual work practices (Barley & Kunda, 2001; Star & Strauss, 1999), needed to create coherence continually in such a system, I designed a process study of "creating coherence" in three different cases. I assumed prolonged engagement in the field and with the participants would be central to my ability to understand what they perceived to be relevant and meaningful improvement efforts, and why (Langley et al., 2013; Langley, 1999; Pettigrew, 1990; Van de Ven & Huber, 1990; Van de Ven, 2007).

Based on several streams of organization and management research (Currie & Lockett, 2011; Fitzgerald et al., 2013; Gittell, Seidner, & Wimbush, 2010; Gittell & Weiss, 2004; Gronn, 2009; Strauss, 1988; Strauss et al., 1997), I focused on leadership and coordination practices. I chose this focus because I wanted to study how different actors worked to create coherence in the day-to-day routines at multiple organizational levels in a complex, multiorganization system, and, importantly, to capture how practices were or became connected across time and space (Shove, Pantzar, & Watson, 2012). I was interested primarily in the work, and not the individual person who was performing the work because I wanted to study how the coherency of the interdependent "fabric of health care work" (Meier, 2013) was achieved. Here, the area of specialty and/or type of diagnosis is essential to understanding the clinical work and the leadership and coordination practices needed to keep individual patients' pathways on track. In hospitals, health care work is practiced 24 hours a day, every day of the year, and by multiple people simultaneously. Moreover, health care work is organizationally fragmented and geographically distributed across the larger health care system consisting of primary and secondary care sectors. "Gaps" in care in such systems (e.g., during handovers or transfers) present vulnerabilities and represent significant risks for adverse events (Nemeth et al., 2008; Siemsen et al., 2012).

From previous research into leadership, coordination, and change in health care work (Dopson, Fitzgerald, & Ferlie, 2008; Dopson & Fitzgerald, 2005; Dopson, Earl, & Snow, 2008; Meier, 2015b), I knew that context would play an important role in the project. I knew I would have to specify carefully how I understood context, what role I assumed context would play, and how I would operationalize context into something I could study meaningfully. However, I also knew that my approach to context, the vantage point I worked from, and whose context I would claim to represent, would come to matter.

Approach to Context Made Vantage Point a Central Theme

I decided to approach context analytically as a configuration of contextual forces influencing, and influenced by, actors dynamically and over time (Dopson et al., 2008; Dopson & Fitzgerald, 2005). My approach to context was to "trace" what I had constructed as relevant contextual forces during the 3-year process. Because coherence was the focus of the research, I constructed a configuration of contextual forces derived from the characteristics of work: for example, purpose, tasks, types of work, pace, organizational features (such as structure, size, and distribution/layout of department), and governance (here I focused on health policies and national standards). I divided this analytically into the elements related to the core clinical work, at which the improvement efforts were aimed (see Table 3.1).

The research was carried out in Denmark, a country with a predominantly public health care sector with universal access to services. Thus, national health policies acted as a central contextual force because these can impact the structuring, management, and practice of clinical work (Burau & Vrangbaek, 2008; Kirkpatrick, Dent, & Jespersen, 2011; Kuhlmann & Saks, 2008; Meier, 2012). I traced national health care policies because of the high degree of political governance on multiple levels of health care organizations. I focused on policies that targeted either the organization or the practice of the core clinical work: for example, policies of standardization, documentation, and benchmarking of performance, and specific time-frames, for diagnosis and treatment (30-day "guarantees" in both somatic and psychiatric care), clinical pathways for cancer, and national standards for "arrival to treatment" (also known as "door to doctor") times in A&E Departments, for example. Health care policy as a contextual force was traced for each area of medical specialty: accident and emergency medicine (A&E), oncology, and internal medicine.

In bounding a certain context for the process study of actors' efforts to improve coherence, I was particularly mindful of the relationship between context and action: how the actors, their actions, and what I had constructed as relevant context influenced one another over time. Here, I was inspired by Barley and Tolbert's (1997) method to trace how talk and action change over time, and I divided the research into three phases, so I could explore changes in talk and action at the different times.

I designed pilot studies for each case to qualify the fieldwork (Czarniawska, 2007, 2008) to be carried out in each department. Here, I read national clinical standards for care in the three areas chosen, policy papers concerning the political governance of work in these areas, and general policy papers on, for example, involvement of patients and relatives. I soon realized that, for oncology and internal medicine, I would have to choose one or two diagnoses to focus on, because the clinical variety and complexity of treatment and care depending on diagnosis within these two types of departments made it necessary to be specific in this regard.[1] I went on informal site visits and talked to staff in different positions. During these talks, I gave them a sheet of paper and asked them to draw where their patients typically came from (Home? GP?), where they would see them (Office? Bed unit? Theatre?), what would happen

Table 3.1 Examples of Contextual Forces in Health Care Work

	Purpose of work	Types of patients	Types of work procedures/tasks	Central policies influencing work
A&E	Initial diagnosis and treatment	All acutely ill or injured patients	Triage, treatment of minor injuries, referrals for further exams/admission	Standard "arrival to treatment" measures Treatment Plans 24-hour coverage by A&E physicians Medical specialists on call Clinical standards for procedures/treatments
Oncology	Nonsurgical oncological treatment and care	Patients diagnosed with oncological illness	Outpatient treatment and care Individualized treatment plans Chemo-, radiation, and immune therapies Consultations Palliation Few admissions	Diagnose specific "cancer packages" with designated time-frames and Multidisciplinary Team Conferences Maximum waiting times for diagnosis and treatments Treatment of side effects and complications in patients' local hospital Rehabilitation in municipality
Internal Medicine	Diagnosis, treatment and care	All medical patients (composition of patients vary day to day)	Admissions for treatment and care Complex diagnosis Outpatient treatment and controls in clinics	"Right to diagnosis" (30 days) "Treatment guarantee" (30 days) National Care Paths for chronic diseases Clinical standards for procedures/treatments

Abbreviation: A&E, accident and emergency medicine.

then, and the possible paths from there (Intensive care unit? Home?). These drawings made me aware of the importance of the vantage point because they illustrated the vast net of actors in different positions involved in the work. Additionally, the drawings made me aware of the importance of place, and how where you are may influence how you experience things.

Throughout the data collection process, I became acutely aware that what to a researcher might look like the same context for a phenomenon might be experienced differently by people: these experiences might vary across actors in the *same* situation and across *different situations*. I became curious to explore why and how a lack of shared understanding of "the situation" could be problematic for achieving coherence. However, physical movement to interact face to face, as well as relational aspects of collaboration and coordination, seemed to mediate this important boundary work (Meier, 2015a). I repeated the pilot studies before the last iteration of the field studies, as the improvement efforts by the organizational development consultants and the clinical partners had resulted in organizational changes in all three departments. For me, this meant my unit of analysis had moved: efforts to create coherence were now practiced in forums or collaborations, which had not existed before. Thus, I needed to investigate where and when the coordination and leadership practices aimed at creating coherence took place, as well as who was involved.

The Three "Clinical Contexts"

A&Es are the sorting machinery, the gatekeepers so to speak, to the hospitals, the medical specialties and their resources (e.g., examinations, treatments, or beds). I chose emergency medicine as my first case study because the nature of work there is fast-paced and highly dynamic: length of stay varies greatly depending on the patient's condition, and this can develop—sometime rapidly or urgently—during the patient's time in A&E. Moreover, the number and types of patients/diagnoses is unpredictable: an A&E Department is never closed, and the composition of patients can change fast. The core task, "initial diagnosis and treatment," calls for collaboration and coordination across professions and medical specialties. In A&Es, flow is central (Arkun et al., 2010): a large portion of patients is "turned at the door," meaning that patients are not referred to a bed in one of the other departments. The "flow" of patients and an individual patient's pathway influence each other: at any given time, the capacity of a hospital is influenced by the capacity of its A&E and vice versa. Coordination and leadership practices (e.g., the allocation of staff to certain patients, decisions about the next step in a patient's process, referral to diagnostic imaging, or admission to a surgical department) made in A&E are embedded in the core, clinical work here and are connected to the coordination and leadership practices in the Radiology or Surgical Departments, which in turn influence capacity for examinations or surgical procedures. Because time and flow in A&Es matter for patients and staff in the A&E and in the rest of the hospital, flexible and recurring coordination mechanisms, such as "capacity conferences," are being implemented increasingly in the field (Resar, Nolan, Kaczynski, & Jensen, 2011). Here, coordinator nurses from A&E and the other departments meet and coordinate their patient flow in a 15–20-minute meeting several times a day.

Oncology Departments carry out oncological (typically nonsurgical) treatments: chemo-, radiation, and biological therapies. The task here is to treat and care for different types of cancer patients in the various stages of their disease, with rehabilitation and palliation being offered where needed. In many modern health care systems, cancer treatment is outpatient treatment with control scans and consultations in specialized hospital wards. Oncology was chosen for my second case study because the nature of work here is urgent, highly specialized, and emotionally charged: patients here are severely—often life threateningly—ill, and I assumed this would impact the work to create coherence. Patients in oncology wards are referred for treatment and care, here, and their treatment follows diagnose specific national clinical standards (care pathways) that are subject to strict deadlines and controls. Unpredictability in cancer care often arises from the individual patient's process because each patient deals with or responds to the diagnosis and treatment processes differently, both mentally and physically. Because oncology is primarily organized as outpatient treatment, coherence needs to be achieved across geographical, organizational, and professional boundaries—and patients and families are important parts of their own process (see Chapter 10 in this book, on patients' experiences of context).

Internal medicine departments are typically divided into medical specialties (bed units or wards), primarily treating "their" patients: for example, patients with respiratory diseases are cared for in the Pulmonary Medicine Ward. However, if a given ward or bed unit is full, a patient might be admitted to a "sister" ward or unit, where relevant consultations can be given by medical specialists. I chose to study an internal medicine ward with two clinics and two large bedded units (Endocrinology and Gastroenterology), which also cared for "generic" medical patients. This allowed me to study efforts to create coherence in a clinical context where patients are severely, and often chronically, ill. The current pressures on health care systems have generally reduced the length of stay in hospitals and reallocated several types of treatments or procedures to outpatient attendance and/or primary care services in the patient's own home. As a result, the types of patients admitted in bedded units in hospitals are often very ill: suffering from a combination of multimorbidity, chronic disease, or severe illness, all of which require complex treatment plans and tailor-made coordination across the different organizations in the health care system. In some circumstances (e.g., in case of neurodegenerative diseases or substance abuse), creating coherence in patients' pathways can be especially difficult, if the patient and/or his/her family are not capable of collaborating with the medical staff. One reason why some patients and relatives are "not capable of collaborating" might be the current generic assumptions in policies or standards of what being a patient or a relative is and patients and relatives in turn should be able to do, because such general assumptions do not take the various experiences and circumstances of individual patients into account.

Methodological Reflections on Bounding Context for Comparison

In Vignette 2, the approach to context I chose meant including the clinical microsystem, and the specificity of different clinical areas, as well as a focus on how this work was organized and practiced. This required a flexibility in the process study design to capture the elements of context that changed and interacted over time. Additionally, the pilot studies highlighted the variety of ways in which coherence challenges were experienced and handled, and how, by the different actors, even within the same "clinical context," in this case, oncology. Analytically, I attempted to handle the multiplicity of levels and complexity of context through the construction of configurations of contextual forces relevant to each area, but this did not fully encompass the various subjective experiences of different actors, which also changed over time as the process unfolded. These dynamic elements of context—and the relationship between context and action in practice over time as a multilevel process—were to some degree captured by the process study design. However, further work can be done to improve designs to capture these dynamic and multilevel elements of change processes (including the work done to produce stability in settings characterized by simultaneous, fast-paced, and complex change initiatives). As the vantage point in this study was clearly the researcher's "outsider" position, several relevant actors' experiences of context were represented only partially in the material. In line with Chapters 9 and 10 of this book, I propose that further research focuses on what patients and relatives experience as relevant contexts for their illnesses, as well as how these experiences influence their interactions with health care professionals.

Methodological Lessons from the Vignettes

Both vignettes highlight the naivety of a view of context as a stable, layered, and unidirectional set of influences, where the outer layer involves influences from government health policy, which moves inward to regional/local influences, and finally to influences specific to a single organization and individual practitioners. We support Dopson and Fitzgerald (2005) contention that there are three difficulties with such a unidirectional view of context. First, organizations, groups, and individuals are portrayed as being passive recipients subject to aspects of the health care context that shapes behavior, but with no leeway to choose which aspects of context to bring into the organization, and with no influence with which they could reshape context. Second, these contexts are in some way separated rather than being treated as an "integrated configuration." Third, such a view implies a static view of context: that is, context is seen as a particular setting at a particular point in time rather than as evolving and changing over time.

A more sophisticated notion of context must acknowledge the capacity of individuals to influence context. Actors perceive and interpret aspects of context in different ways. In practice, individuals do not view the facets of context as being separate, but rather, they experienced them as a maelstrom or at least a morass. Individuals seek to make sense of multiple contexts by drawing on a mixture of cognitive and emotional judgment to create an "integral context," and it is with this in mind that action takes place. Yet the ways in which actors construe their environment is a social act. Collectively, they make sense of their context and thereby create—or "enact" (Smircich & Stubbart, 1985; Weick, 1995; Weick, Sutcliffe, & Obstfeld, 2005)—that environment, which then, in turn, impacts the actors' ability or willingness to effect the change.

The work carried out Pettigrew and colleagues demonstrate that the existing health care literature base is weak because we lack research that is processual (an emphasis on both action and structure), comparative, pluralist (a description and analysis of the often-competing versions of reality seen by actors in change processes), contextual (operating at a variety of different levels with specification of the linkages between them), and historical, thus taking into account the historical evolution of ideas and stimuli for change, as well as the constraints within which decision makers operate (Pettigrew, 1990; Pettigrew, Woodman, & Cameron, 2001; Pettigrew, 1992). Langley's (1999) overview of process methods in organizational studies reveals the radically different approaches that can be undertaken with these methods and what might be achieved with this approach. Moreover, in their 2013 editorial of a special issue of process studies, Langley and colleagues (2013) provide an overview of the types of questions posed, which includes not only the traditional forms of narrative-based process research reviewed here, but also forms of analysis that are more quantitative. However, this latter approach appears to lose the strong internal validity and holistic portrayal of a phenomenon that might be thought to be the distinctive strength of process research.

We are not alone in recognizing the need for a more sophisticated view of context. Fitzgerald et al. (2002) seek to reconceptualize the importing of context into organizational action using health care data. Their data draw attention to the interplay of features of the outer and inner contexts, and note multiple differences of value, structures, education, and relationships between the acute and primary sectors of health care. Fitzgerald et al. (2002) conclude by arguing: "Ultimately, the behaviour of the stakeholders and the features of context are interlocked. The combination of multilayered, two-way influences, multiple stakeholders with interpretative schemes, innovation seeking behaviour by individuals and groups, and differing absorptive capacity in organizations, produces a situation in which context is an actor" (p. 1447).

Research designs for contextual research must acknowledge that local contexts are multidimensional, multifaceted configurations of forces, which change over time. Furthermore, no "context" is discrete. There are complex connections and interactions, of which individuals often are not aware. It is also important that researchers think carefully about where they have set the boundaries on context, and how that affects analysis, as several of this book's contributors have done in their chapters. The concept of context is tied to the meaning one is trying to convey, to boundary conditions of validity and claims, to construct clarity, and to the question of providing sufficiently detailed descriptions to enable readers to evaluate research studies and results. The way researchers operationalize context and, thus, draw the boundaries that include certain aspects and exclude others matters significantly for the specific analysis we can produce, and for the collective body of work we can draw on and contribute to with our work. One aspect often omitted from studies of organizational change in context is the way in which actors draw on experiences *outside* work and organizational life to impact organizational change.

In terms of vantage point, we suggest that researchers specify the perspective of the analysis: is it from a "traditional" researcher-as-outsider or synoptic position? Does the analysis adopt the perspective of a certain group (e.g., patients or managers?) or focus on the relationship between two phenomena? In the film industry in particular, and in storytelling in general, this is a matter of choosing where to position the camera, so to speak (Pullman, 2017): from whose perspective is the story told?

In terms of representation, we suggest that researchers make transparent whose context they are attempting to represent and, perhaps most importantly, reflect on the potentially privileged or underprivileged position they are attempting to represent. Anthropologists have long discussed matters of representation. For instance, can one ever claim to understand and represent something from another person's point of view? (Geertz, 1993). But discussions concerning the potential power and normativity inscribed in language and discourse can be found across different disciplines: for example, within the field of sociology of standards and classification systems (Bowker & Star, 1999; Star & Bowker, 2007; Star & Strauss, 1999). The point here is that when researchers bound context for a phenomenon in a certain way, they highlight some elements as being relevant and others as less so, and, in these choices, issues of power and normativity tend to become less visible. Duranti and Goodwin (1992) point to three important aspects of performing context analyses: (1) include the perspectives of the actor/group studied, (2) examine actions and activities performed, and (3) recognize the multiple, concurrent, and changing contexts. This is relevant advice, which, in turn, requires several occurrences of boundary drawing to establish which actors and activities are included in the study, as well as how "context" is operationalized. The point we are trying to make here is that these boundaries can be drawn by the researcher in a multitude of ways, and, depending on the research question, different designs and methods might be relevant.

We have organized the thematic contributions in Chapters 4 through 14 around the three main research questions of the book:

Question 1: *What constitutes an event, situation, or phenomenon?*
Question 2: *How do actors understand, experience, and engage with context?*
Question 3: *How do contexts change, and what is the role of actors in such processes?*

Below we briefly present the methodological lessons to be learned from these chapters.

Methodological Reflections Relating to *Context*: Question 1

The majority of the work on contexts in health care has been operationalized and has made the object for analysis using the often-proposed macro-, meso-, and microlevels of context. What have been analyzed as macrolevels of context have received the bulk of scholarly attention, often through studies of national setting, governance, system structures, and the relationship between health care professions and the state, primarily through document analyses, historic analysis, surveys, or interviews. Additionally, research into organizations and their environment has contributed to scholarly work on understanding these interactions (see Chapter 2, Table 2.1).

Methodological Challenges in Studying Context in Action

Many of the chapters argue the importance of being mindful of the ways in which the theoretical lens shapes what constitutes context of an event as well as research design and methodological choices. Fitzgerald's Chapter 4 illustrates this point well. The chapter begins with a relatively brief review of context as understood from an interactionist perspective. The empirical illustrations included form the foundation for an analysis that seeks to elaborate and develop emergent ideas of layers of contextualization and the manner in which actors' sensemaking and sensegiving leads to decisions and responsive actions, which, in their turn, influence and reshape context. The chapter traces the development and understanding of an interactionist view of context in health care that connects context, actors, and action interactively. These views are elaborated to build our understanding of the processes by which context influences and is enacted by actors. It is suggested that the outer and inner contexts do not exist in a stable relative position to each other; an argument also made in Chapters 1 and 2. Rather, the individual actor *connects* these elements, through a focus on a problem or topic, and through action. The actor blends context fluidly into form by selectively melding contextual elements. Therefore, one might argue that the crucial difference between the elements of the external context and the elements of the personal context is one of perceived distance. In daily life, the individual experiences the totality of context, and selectively attends to and interprets a fluid mix of elements of the external and the personal organizational contexts. Chapter 4 argues that the interaction of context, actors, and action have significant implications for the design and methods adopted in research. A direct implication is that it requires the analysis of multilevel data. The chapter proposes that for studies featuring health care, significant levels of analysis include the national, political, and cultural and the organizational, or interorganizational, level and the individual level. Each aspect of context raises potential methodological issues. Such complex situations will be best understood through prolonged observations of interactions in real time or through longitudinal designs.

We see in all of the chapters the acknowledgment of the influence of the researchers focusing on shaping what counts as context, and why? The attention to certain elements of context is driven dynamically by focus, and selective attention is framed by sensemaking and by an individualized judgment of what is "relevant." The significance of what is framed as relevant (and, thus, bounded as context) is embedded in the socialization of the individual, the influence of sensegiving processes, personal experiences, goals, the system of knowledge, and the will and power to act. Both sensemaking and contextualization are theoretical constructs that refer to how humans make meaning as they live their lives. This, as Weick (2006) points out, introduces "self-referential inconsistency": " . . . I sometimes act as if I have an accurate view

53

of a world in which only plausibility is possible...I claim to know how others make sense, but my efforts are nothing more or nothing less than that same sensemaking" (p. 1733).

The bounding of context is a critical and difficult issue. Initially, researchers need to identify clearly whether they are adopting a researcher perspective on context or are endeavoring to provide a view from the "eye of the beholder." In either case, we believe researchers attempt to be reflective and transparent about choices, and the consequences for their own understanding is especially important in relation to context, because the act of carrying out research, of analyzing empirical material, and of writing to convey such findings may resemble sensemaking processes (Meier, 2018; Wegener, Meier, & Maslo, 2018). As an example: at the national level, it will never be possible to collect comprehensive data on every aspect of national life. Researchers need to identify trends or policies at national level having specific effects in relation to the unit of analysis. This is by no means a straightforward task. Chapter 4 gives one example of a comparative, multicase research design in which the research team attempted to specify a set of organizations that faced "high-change" environments. Drawing on prior research, the team developed a careful, evidence-based group of criteria to underpin the notion of a high-change environment, and then the team spent a considerable period of time matching organizations to these criteria and gaining access to study them. Nevertheless, this eventually proved to be relatively worthless as a comparative explanation. Because of the dynamic nature of organizations, during the period of study some organizations altered rapidly from "high change" to "low change" and vice versa.

Chambers, in Chapter 5, makes a plea for the study of the lifecycle of a policy for a deep appreciation of policy as a component of the health care context to be understood. The chapter describes policy at multiple levels, and how this shapes the context in which health care is delivered that influences all efforts to attain specific health and health care outcomes. Chambers notes that policy can influence actions at every level, from affecting individual patient access to care, to provider delivery of interventions, and to organization, system, and national settings in which care is delivered. He also notes that teasing apart the specific measures related to policy is a complicated task. For the research process, this includes identifying a common lexicon for both policy development and policy outcomes. For the former, several groups (e.g., the Kaiser Family Foundation and the National Institutes of Health) have attempted to construct databases to support policy research. These efforts are important to improve the quality of research studies on health policies, ensuring that sufficient tools are available to maximize the learning from these policy experiments.

Chambers notes that, consistent with the notion of a learning health care system, our understanding of the policy context will improve greatly where there is an expectation that, with each policy activity, simultaneous evaluation efforts are launched to best learn from each experience. This concept has been referenced in building improvements in behavioral health care and in understanding intervention adaptation, and in learning from policy experiments relevant to obesity, but it could be expanded to consider the health policy environment across multiple countries.

The physicality of context is highlighted as an absent but important aspect of research designs by Tryggestad, Harty, and Holm Jacobsen in Chapter 6. They foreground what is usually considered as contextual background—the building—as they shed light on and call attention to the ways in which buildings matter in design and for work. These authors argue that the relationship between space and practice is a long-standing debate within sociology and organization studies, from the early studies of the Chicago School of Urban Sociology in the 1920s and 1930s, through the links between social inequalities and spatial distribution of resources to general contemporary debates over shifts to late/postmodern society (Harvey, 1989). They draw on ethnographical studies of two large public hospital building projects, part of a current Danish health care reform. The project, therefore, embodies a host of national and regional policy requirements for, and visions about, the organization and provision of health care. Based on the empirical studies, they show how these innovative design requirements are negotiated and materialize as visualizations of the physical building, and how these design visualizations in turn are active in shaping the organization and provision of health care services: that is, the building as both object and context of health care work.

The building is, therefore, not just a physical entity, an object, but a process, a project, and a matter of concern. In terms of implications for research, the authors argue that future studies should be designed to account for how multiple tensions, and that concerns emerge and play out in the interaction between people and their different devices and methods for designing a building, and its spatial organization, functions, work processes, and services. Further research is called for into the role of methods and devices in shaping stakeholders' interest and design contributions in the setting of the built environment.

Methodological Reflections Relating to *Actors*: Question 2

What is perceived and treated as context is shaped by, and shapes, the actions being performed in a given situation, and this central aspect of the dynamic relationships between context and action can be found in the practice-oriented philosophical contributions to the larger field of social science, although these were only limitedly adopted by organization and management scholars (Nicolini, 2012). It is a methodological challenge to study and analyze contexts in action, particularly in studies of social processes where the interrelated nature of context and action becomes a central, yet challenging, part of the research. The challenges of studying a phenomenon such as "context" are also a question of *how* we perceive and make meaning of our surroundings (Smircich & Stubbart, 1985). Yet this process is embodied and, to an extent, unarticulated, even sometimes outside the attention of the individual actor. At the same time, contexts can be, and often are shared, inherently social, and mediated and reproduced through interactions and relationships or communities/networks that can be distributed across time and space. The communities and networks of practice that Brown and Duguid (2001) describe in their work are examples of such shared contexts. Another important and yet challenging aspect of studying context and action is the simultaneously shared, durable structure-like and yet potentially brief, elusive, and highly personal nature of contexts for action: what matters most as context may change in an instant, and how such changes are experienced and interpreted by participants in a given situation may differ.

Korica and Nicolini argue in Chapter 7 that it matters less, and is less empirically accurate, to speak of what context *is*, than to trace the ways in which *context is made to matter*, in characteristic ways, by particularly influential individuals during their ordinary activities. In this chapter, the authors "make context visible," by tracing connections in actions as part of CEOs' daily activities. As practice and process-oriented scholars, they designed the research with an existing analytical orientation toward context, although this was not the formal focus of the study. The analytical guidance here is to ensure that investigations of context and its relevance pay attention to both situated expressions and doings within that organization (which includes "sayings" and "materialities"), but also how references are established to "wider" features, such as other organizations, legal oversight, and political norms characteristic of that time and place (Nicolini, 2012). To this end, methodological approaches that facilitate attention to both, such as Nicolini's (2009) "zooming in and out," are particularly appropriate.

Between March 2011 and May 2013, Korica and Nicolini conducted an ethnographic study of seven health care CEOs of acute and mental health NHS trusts in England. They also conducted formal semistructured interviews with CEOs and consulted approximately a thousand pages of documents, including meeting papers, articles the CEOs referenced, and external publications consulted. As is common with ethnographic studies, the richness of the data far exceeded the scholarly space available to analyze and share it. In terms of representation—Who's context is it?—the authors openly acknowledge that the particular "theory method toolkit" (Nicolini, 2012) they engaged with allowed them to trace and see context in some specific ways, but not others. As such, this analytical account is enabled and, in part, produced by their methodological choices. It was driven by clear analytical aims: the relative dearth of dynamic, processual studies of context, and a commitment to the "strong programme" to allow for theorization that is more nuanced of complex practices. Such studies are likely to contribute meaningfully by "complexifying" already complex organizational realities, rather than reducing these to fit limitations of outlets, or preferences for simple representations (Tsoukas, 2017).

Wentzer's Chapter 8 highlights the methodological and analytical capacity within methodology programs such as Sociology and Technology in Society (STS), and Activity Theory that draw attention to the entanglement of technology in human practices, and organizational and societal contexts. STS argues that human and nonhuman actors cannot be differentiated ontologically, as they are both historical and political "actants" (Latour, 2005, 1993). They co-shape and enact semimaterial reality together (Akrich, 1992; Akrich & Latour, 1992). Time and space are enfolded in technologies, and technology refolds time and space when implemented into practice. For contextual research, this means that technology and other nonhuman actors/actants should not necessarily be positioned as "background": such positioning should be a matter of the specific research question and empirical investigation. Additionally, Chapter 8 articulates possible learning situations based on a case study of operation support work in surgery, as an example of the role of technology in context. Wentzer's choice of ethnographic methods affords a detailed, nuanced close-up study of the use of technology in different surgical contexts. Based on these studies, she demonstrates how the dynamic relationship between context and action unfolds, and, specifically, how aspects of what we can call the clinical context co-produce vulnerability and safety in collaboration with technology and people. Wentzer ends her chapter by concluding, "the examples of the interruptions of flow and security in the practice of surgery draw attention to the importance of context, as something mediated and multilayered, that can be learned from when it breaks down, or rather 'breaks open.'" She goes on to remind readers that context is usually taken for granted, "but when something breaks down we especially 'see' context and how it is essential to human action."

Duranti and Goodwin (1992) argue for an interactionist view of context, which places the social person at center stage. The methodological implication of such an approach is that the researcher should consider adopting the perspective of those studied as the starting point of an understanding of the context. This has many important implications for the selection of "voices" to be heard through a research project. For this individual level of analysis, researchers need to specify who the interviewees or observed individuals were, and why they were selected. Too often, this explanation is rudimentary or based on numbers. Researchers should be encouraged to explain the logic of selecting voices in relation to the research question or focus, and they have an obligation to consider why some voices are privileged over others. Rarely heard voices may offer useful and critical perspectives. In health care research, these would include, for example, the views of the nonprofessionals, such as patients, cleaners, and health care assistants.

Locock et al. (Chapter 9 in this volume) seek to demonstrate the potential of adopting a microlevel approach, as well as the need for further explorations of patients' and families' voices, in health care contexts. Locock et al. note several methodological considerations that have arisen. First, there is scope for greater attention to studying how patients and relatives engage with the different aspects of the system, such as the physical buildings and artifacts, geographical distribution of work, health IT, staff, or other patients and relatives, and how such actions, in turn, reshape the context for other patients and relatives, as well as health care staff. This would be highly relevant in several under-researched areas: in studies of patients, not just as recipients of care, but also as care providers for others during or after their treatment, and in exploring patients, their families, and their home environment as central elements of the larger health care system. To contribute here, they suggest further detailed empirical analysis of who does what when providing care in different settings, and by which means interactions between patients, families, and staff are integrated more or less successfully across these. Particularly in the case of long-term conditions, May et al.'s (2014) reflections on the "burden of treatment" are relevant, as here patients become the providers of their own care, and their home becomes the care setting. There is work involved in shaping this care context that often remains invisible to professionals, systems, and, indeed, to researchers interested in studying context in health care.

Second, Locock et al. (Chapter 9 in this volume) argue that more could be done to enlist "patient/family ethnographer" observations as an alternative and supplementary perspective on important questions: for example, how teams function, how care decisions are made, why mistakes and miscommunication happen, and what happens to other patients. The authors acknowledge that patients can see contexts in ways that are different from staff views of them, and they may have important feedback that the health care system needs. However, they stress that enlisting patient and family ethnographers should be done with due attention to issues of power relationships, negotiations of perspective and knowledge, and ethics. This would require a more participatory stance to research and a continuous and relational engagement with the field, characteristics of qualitative methods such as shadowing (Czarniawska, 2007) or engaged scholarship (Van de Ven, 2007). Finally, they highlight a challenge to organizational research, namely to focus on the continual and changing interplay between context and how a wider range of actors "see," "are," and "shape" context, as neither can be viewed satisfactorily in isolation.

Meier's Chapter 10 here discusses the question of how patients might experience context for their illness in a multiorganizational health care system. Based on examples from cancer care, she reflects on the significance of *place*—where people are—for how they engage with and experience contexts for their actions. Assuming that actors engage with and experience contexts differently, Meier discusses potential consequences for the current fragmented and distributed organization of cancer care. She argues that the predominance of outpatient care in oncology, which means patients are primarily at home, results in a situation where the traditional close monitoring of patients by health care professionals is no longer feasible. Thus, the current organization of oncology separates the specialized knowledge located in hospitals from the patients' bodies, which are at home. Place matters, Meier concludes, because the lack of co-location of patients and professionals creates a situation in which patients are expected to act according to the specialized knowledge of one place (the hospital), regardless of where they are. Contexts for such actions, however, are always constructed locally by individual actors, depending on their own point of view. In the case of the organization of cancer care and patient involvement, these points might provide valuable insights into how to address current challenges in patient involvement.

The perspective of those for whom health care is provided has been almost entirely absent in research discussions of context, with potentially detrimental effects on how research organizational issues are understood in specific health care contexts such as cancer care, mental health, and chronic diseases, where quality of care also rests on patients' and relatives' abilities to take an active part in their own care process. The turn to patient-centeredness means that researcher-led definitions and demarcations of what is context and how it should be studied are no longer sufficient. Locock and colleagues helpfully outlined a number of methodological and theoretical challenges in Chapter 9—specifically, the question of how to study emotional and relational aspects of contexts in various illness settings.

Often, the unit of analysis for research refers to parts of peoples' subjective experiences and understandings of a situation or an event. But not all elements of such experiences can be expressed through language, however: for example, embodied or tacit aspects. Comparing such phenomena across actors or illness settings will require systematic attention to how both researcher and participants understand the phenomena, and what constitutes their context, such as this book presents.

Murray's Chapter 11 explores the role of researchers in bounding context for their study. Drawing on theories of liminality, she shows how liminality can help researchers to understand change in social systems and the role of actors within them, and how—as researchers—we are always constructing/bounding "the context," and, thus, the center and the periphery, and the liminal spaces. Through methodological and analytical reflections on how Murray constructed context in a specific study of changes to achieve integration of care in a health care system, she shares her model of context construction, reflecting how she, as a researcher, acted as boundary constructor, delineating the context for change, including the boundaries of the transitioning liminal space and the health care system. She does this through sharing, in Chapter 11, her own work of constructing context with readers, how her work with documental analysis brought out these important reflections as she was working to analyze her data material "by stitching together elements across levels and organizations to produce both actors' understandings of what is happening and based on this, our understanding of what is happening." Moreover, Murray demonstrates the importance of including temporal and spatial elements in contextual studies of change in complex systems, and—importantly for our purpose—she shows how this requires a more nuanced and dynamic understanding and engagement with context.

Methodological Reflections Relating to *Change*: Question 3

Ferlie's Chapter 12 in this book considers the processual nature of context and action and, in particular, how "context" can evolve over time. *Time* is defined over the long duration (e.g., 30 years) rather than over the life of a single government (say, around 4 to 5 years), often the time-frame taken within UK health policy analysis. Theoretically, Ferlie argues, most attention is paid to how researchers might study the evolving "outer context" (which includes but goes beyond the national political economy) and best analyze how it is changing over the longer term. The chapter highlights the insights of Pettigrew, Ferlie, and McKee (1992 p. 6), who adopted a contextualist perspective, noting that too much organizational change research was, "ahistorical, aprocessual and acontextual in character. There are remarkably few studies of change that allow the change process to reveal itself in any kind of substantially temporal or contextual manner." The heuristic device of the "Pettigrew triangle" (Pettigrew, Ferlie, & McKee, 1992 pp. 6–7) is discussed by Ferlie as an analytical framing: "theoretically sound and practically useful research on change should involve the continuous interplay between ideas about the context of change, the process of change and the content of change, together with skill in regulating the relations between the three." Ferlie noted that here was an attempt to move away from linear accounts of the implementation process and an over-reliance on rational analysis as a driver for change (while not discarding reason and data altogether).

Methodological Challenges in Studying Context in Action

Ferlie offers a number of frameworks to help specify the "context" and to analyze changes over the longer term. There are well-known frameworks that can help to assess an organization's external environment, such as a PESTELI (i.e., Political, Economic, Sociological, Technological, Legal, Environment, Industry) analysis. *Socially*, for example, the gradual aging of the population evident since the 1980s may well pose significant challenges for health care organizations and lead to attempts to change patterns of service delivery. A long-term and major *technological* development has been the rapid growth of powerful new information and communication technologies (ICTs) since the 1990s, leading to a distinct narrative of so-called digital era governance (DEG) (Dunleavy et al., 2006), where these new ICTs can help to reintegrate New Public Management (NPM)-style fragmented organizations and service processes. DEG principles could affect UK health care organizations as they can other public agencies, leading to the ICT-driven redesign of complex care pathways. It is the *political* dimension of the "outer context" that is of great interest, at least in largely publicly funded health systems (such as the NHS), where it assumes great importance. The assessment of this dimension—and of significant but perhaps only occasional changes in it—requires interpretive skill and cannot simply be read off from a conventional PESTELI trends analysis.

Other long-term changes in the "inner context" of the health care delivery system organizations, he argues, should also be considered. The notion of "inner context" in UK health care organizations, however, has become more complex since the study discussed in the chapter. The focus in Pettigrew, Ferlie, and McKee (1992) was largely on the role of the then focal District Health Authority, which had—at least in formal terms—hierarchical control over "its" hospitals (though a couple of chapters on the reprovision of mental health and learning disability services did consider the role of non-health agencies). There is now also an increased interest in the so-called wicked problems in health policy that are complex, multifaceted, and beyond the jurisdiction of any single agency (Ferlie et al., 2013). So the level of systemic capacity at the subregional level represents an increasingly important aspect of the inner context. Future contextualist work, therefore, might well look further at how these health and social care systems operate as systems (or not) in relation to such wicked problems, and where it is that stronger joint working has been built up, and why. This switch of focus from the single organization to the local system may also require new basic ideas.

In many of the thematic chapters, comparative designs were typically preferred to single-case studies in the exploration of context over time. Kessler's Chapter 13 outlines a complex and ambitious research design to explore the contextual influences on the development of the health care support worker (HSW) role. The research design adopted for the work presented in Kessler's chapter was based on a multimethod case study approach. The research was explicitly informed by an interest in the influence of context on the shape of the HSW role, and the case study has long been recognized as a research design well-suited to examining phenomena in-depth in a real-life context (Yin, 1984). Four NHS acute health care providers or trusts were deliberately selected by location, being drawn from different parts of the country (London, South, North, and Midlands—the terms used in referring to the cases in the text). They fell into pairs: two of the trusts (Midlands and London) were medium-sized, single-site district general hospitals, whereas the other two (South and North) were large multisite teaching hospitals. However, in each case, attention focused on the same two clinical areas: inpatient surgical and medical wards.

Such a research design generated questions that allowed Kessler's team to probe the influence of context at different levels over time:

- How diverse were the forms assumed by the HSW role across the four trusts? The greater the diversity, the more permissive the national context, and the greater the scope for agency at the organizational level.

- If organizational context was active in shaping the HSW role, what properties were influential at this level? In selecting trusts from different regions, the impact of local labor markets could be picked up. More significantly, the emergence of diverse HSW-role types would encourage an interest in the contextual effect of bespoke trust policies and practices.

- How permissive or restrictive was the organizational context, and what residual scope remained for the HSW role to be shaped by the workplace context? Just as diverse HSW roles at the trust level would suggest a permissive national context, so diverse HSW-role types across clinical areas and wards would point to a permissive organizational context. This would encourage the search for aspects of the workplace context shaping the HSW role.

A number of the chapters encourage the more longitudinal designs. Estabrooks and Chamberlain argue in Chapter 14 that longitudinal designs work because measurement over time is a powerful tool for change. With data gathered over 10 years, the authors can now begin to observe secular trends, monitor disparate trends (e.g., increasing complexity of resident health issues combined with static staffing levels), and examine intended and unintended consequences of policy decisions. Estabrooks and Chamberlain struggled with the absence of a valid measure of context. Consequently, they undertook to develop, pilot test, and validate a pragmatic tool to assess organizational context: the Alberta Context Tool (ACT). The completed ACT included eight domains of context: *leadership, culture, evaluation* (grouped as feedback of information), *formal interactions, informal interactions, social capital, structural resources*, and *organizational slack* (grouped as staff, time, and space). With three "slack" elements, the ACT contained ten elements. Using a "variance" approach, the authors argue that context could be separated into measurable and modifiable variables reflecting the eight domains. They required the context tool to meet three criteria: have a basis in theory, measure *modifiable* elements of context, and be parsimonious. Brevity was critical for two reasons: the instrument was embedded within a larger survey, and the long-term care (LTC) setting was unusually resource strapped, necessitating the least amount of time possible being taken from direct care.

The team has approached an empirical examination of context in two ways. First, they have developed and run traditional multilevel models to assess the contributions of each of the ten elements in the ACT. Second, they have developed and used context classifications that are more meaningful to their decision makers, and made their models more parsimonious. While they have conducted significant psychometric testing of the measure of context, elements of the measure did not always perform well in empirical modeling (e.g., leadership and culture) or perform better when they examine specific subgroups of residents (e.g., a 12-months-before-death cohort). Estabrooks and Chamberlain argue that quantitative data are not sufficient for understanding mechanisms of context influence, yet despite any lack in measurement or conceptual precision, they believe they gain in being able to identify modifiable elements of context that can be addressed by LTC facilities, and by regional health systems. With these elements, they are able to design pragmatic intervention studies that lead to change.

In the following ten thematic chapters, we hope readers will find inspiration and helpful contributions to their own work exploring the context–action relationship.

Note

1. For oncology, I chose breast cancer and esophagus, cardia, and ventricle cancers, because these two cancer types allowed me to study efforts to create coherence in very different kinds of patient pathways.

References

Akrich, M. (1992). The de-scription of technical objects. In W. E. Bijker & J. Law (eds.), *Shaping technology-building society: Studies in sociotechnical change*. Cambridge, MA: MIT Press, pp. 205–24.

Akrich, M. & Latour, B. (1992). A summary of a convenient vocabulary for the semiotics of human and nonhuman assemblies. In J. L. W.E. Bijker (ed.), *Shaping technology/ building society: Studies in sociotechnical change*. Cambridge, MA: MIT Press, pp. 259–64.

Arkun, A., Briggs, W. M., Patel, S., Datillo, P. A., Bove, J., & Birkhahn, R. H. (2010). Emergency department crowding: Factors influencing flow. *The Western Journal of Emergency Medicine, 11*(1), 10.

Barley, S. R. & Kunda, G. (2001). Bringing work back in. *Organization Science, 12*(1), 76–95.

Barley, S. R. & Tolbert, P. S. (1997). Institutionalization and structuration: Studying the links between action and institution. *Organization Studies, 18*, 93–117.

Bohmer, R. M. J. (2009). *Designing care: Aligning the nature and management of health care.* Boston, MA: Harvard Business Press.

Bowker, G. C. & Star, S. L. (1999). *Sorting things out: Classification and its consequences.* Cambridge, MA: The MIT Press.

Brown, J. S. & Duguid, P. (2001). Knowledge and organization. *Organizational Science, 12*(2), 198–213.

Burau, V. & Vrangbaek, K. (2008). Institutions and non-linear change in governance: Reforming the governance of medical performance in Europe. *Journal of Health, Organisation and Management, 22*(4), 350–67.

Buttny, R. (1998). Putting prior talk into context: Reported speech and the reporting context. *Research on Language and Social Interaction, 31*(1), 45–58.

Currie, G. & Lockett, A. (2011). Distributing leadership in health and social care: Concertive, conjoint or collective? *International Journal of Management Reviews, 13*(3), 286–300.

Czarniawska, B. (2007). *Shadowing and other techniques for doing field studies in modern societies.* Malmö: Liber AB.

Czarniawska, B. (2008). Organizing: How to study it and how to write about it. *Qualitative Research in Organizations and Management, 3*(1), 4–20.

Dopson, S., Earl, M., & Snow, P. (eds.). (2008). *Mapping the management journey: Practice, theory and context.* Oxford: Oxford University Press.

Dopson, S. & Fitzgerald, L. (2005). *Knowledge to action? Evidence based health care in context.* New York: Oxford University Press.

Dopson, S., Fitzgerald, L., & Ferlie, E. (2008). Understanding change and innovation in health care settings: Reconceptualizing the active role of context. *Journal of Change Management, 8*(3–4), 213–31.

Dunleavy, P., Margetts, H., Bastow, S., & Tinkler, J. (2006). New public management is dead—Long live digital-era governance. Journal of Public Administration Research and Theory, *16*(3), 467–94.

Duranti, A. & Goodwin, C. (eds.). (1992). *Rethinking context: Language as an interactive phenomenon.* Cambridge: Cambridge University Press.

Ferlie, E., Fitzgerald, L., McGivern, G., Dopson, S., & Bennett, C. (2013). Making wicked problems governable? The case of managed networks in health care. Oxford: Oxford University Press.

Fitzgerald, L., Ferlie, E., McGivern, G., & Buchanan, D. A. (2013). Distributed leadership patterns and service improvement: Evidence and argument from English healthcare. *The Leadership Quarterly, 24*(1), 227–39.

Fitzgerald, L., Ferlie, E. Wood, M., & Hawkins, C. (2002). Interlocking interactions: The diffusion of innovation in health care, *Human Relations*, 55(12), 1429–49.

Geertz, C. (1993). *Local knowledge: Further essays in interpretive anthropology* (2nd ed.). London: Fontana Press.

Gittell, J. H., Seidner, R., & Wimbush, J. (2010). A relational model of how high-performance work systems work. *Organization Science, 21*(2), 490–506.

Gittell, J. H. & Weiss, L. (2004). Coordination networks within and across organizations: A multi- level framework. *Journal of Management Studies, 41*(1), 127–53.

Gronn, P. (2009). Leadership configurations. *Leadership, 5*(3), 381–94.

Guthrie, B., Saultz, W. J., Freeman, K. G., & Haggerty, L. J. (2008). Continuity of care matters. *BMJ (Clinical Research Ed.), 337*(a867), 548–9.

Haggerty, L. J. (2003). Continuity of care: A multidisciplinary review. *BMJ, 327*, 1219–21.

Harvey, D. (1989). The condition of postmodernity. Oxford: Blackwell.

Johns, G. (2006). The essential impact of context on organizational behavior. *Academy of Management Review, 31*(2), 386–408.

Kirkpatrick, I., Dent, M., & Jespersen, P. K. (2011). The contested terrain of hospital management: Professional projects and healthcare reforms in Denmark. *Current Sociology, 59*(4), 489–506.

Klein, K. J., Ziegert, J. C., Knight, A. P., & Xiao, Y. (2006). Dynamic delegation: Shared, hierarchical, and deindividualized leadership in extreme action teams. *Administrative Science Quarterly, 51*, 590–621.

Kuhlmann, E. & Saks, M. (2008). Changing patterns of health professional governance. In E. Kuhlmann & M. Saks (eds.), *Rethinking professional governance*. Bristol: The Policy Press, University of Bristol, pp. 1–15.

Langley, A. (1999). Strategies for theorizing from process data. *Academy of Management Review, 24*(4), 691–710.

Langley, A., Smallman, C., Tsoukas, H., & Van, d. V. (2013). Process studies of change in organization and management: Unveiling temporality, activity, and flow. *Academy of Management Journal, 56*(1), 1–13.

Latour, B. (1993). *We have never been modern*. Trans. C. Porter. Cambridge, MA: MIT Press.

Latour, B. (2005). *Reassembling the social—An introduction to actor-network-theory*. Oxford: Oxford University Press.

May, C., et al. (2014) Rethinking the patient: Using burden of treatment theory to understand the changing dynamics of illness. *BMC Health Services Research, 14*(281), n.pag.

McGivern, G. & Dopson, S. (2010) Intre-epistemic power and transforming knowledge objects in a bio-medical network. *Organizational Studies, 31*(12), 1667–86.

Meier, N. (2012). Coordination in clinical managerial practice: Moving things around and making things happen. *Scandinavian Journal of Public Administration, 15*(4), 57.

Meier, N. (2013). *Between policy and practice: An investigation of clinical managerial work in hospital units*. (Unpublished PhD thesis). Aarhus University, Aarhus.

Meier, N. (2015a). Collaboration in healthcare through boundary work and boundary objects. *Qualitative Sociology Review, 11*(3), 60–82.

Meier, N. (2015b). Configurations of leadership practices in hospital units. *Journal of Health Organization and Management, 29*(7), 1115–30.

Meier, N. (2018). Knowing across time and place. In C. Weneger, N. Meier, & E. Maslo (eds.), *Cultivating creativity in methodology and research: In praise of detours*. New York: Palgrave Macmillan, pp. 131–41.

Nemeth, C., Wears, R., Woods, D., Hollnagel, E., & Cook, R. (2008). Minding the gaps: Creating resilience in health care. *Advances in Patient Safety: New Directions and Alternative Approaches, 3*, 1–13.

Nicolini, D. (2009). Zooming in and out: Studying practices by switching theoretical lenses and trailing connections. *Organization Studies, 30*(12), 1391–418.

Nicolini, D. (2012). *Practice theory, work, and organization: An introduction.* Oxford: Oxford University Press.

Pettigrew, A. M. (1990). Longitudinal field research on change: Theory and practice. *Organization Science, 1*(3), 267–92.

Pettigrew, A. (1992). The character and significance of strategy process research. *Strategic Management Journal, 13*(Special Issue: Fundamental Themes in Strategy Process Research), 5–16.

Pettigrew, A., Ferlie, E., & McKee, L. (1992). *Shaping strategic change.* London: Sage.

Pettigrew, A. M., Woodman, R. W., & Cameron, K. S. (2001). Studying organizational change and development: Challenges for future research. *Academy of Management Journal, 44*(4), 697–713.

Pullman, P. (2017). *Daemon voices: Essays in storytelling.* Oxford: David Fickling Books.

Resar, R., Nolan, K. M., Kaczynski, D., & Jensen, K. (2011). Using real-time demand capacity management to improve hospital-wide patient flow. *The Joint Commission Journal on Quality and Patient Safety, 37*(5), 217–27.

Rousseau, M. D. & Fried, Y. (2001). Location, location, location: Contextualizing organizational research. *Journal of Organizational Behavior, 22*(1), 1–13.

Shove, E., Pantzar, M., & Watson, M. (2012). *The dynamics of social practice: Everyday life and how it changes.* London: Sage.

Siemsen, I. M. D., Madsen, M. D., Pedersen, L. F., Michaelsen, L., Pedersen, A. V., Andersen, H. B., & Østergaard, D. (2012). Factors that impact on the safety of patient handovers: An interview study. *Scandinavian Journal of Public Health, 40*(5), 439–48.

Smircich, L. & Stubbart, C. (1985). Strategic management in an enacted world. *Academy of Management.the Academy of Management Review, 10*(4), 724–36.

Star, S. L. & Bowker, C. G. (2007). Enacting silence: Residual categories as challenges for ethics, information systems, and communications. *Ethics and Information Technology, 9*(4), 273–80.

Star, S. L. & Strauss, A. (1999). Layers of silence, arenas of voice: The ecology of visible and invisible work. *Computer Supported Cooperative Work, 8*(1–2), 9–30.

Strauss, A. (1988). The articulation of project work: An organisational process. *The Sociological Quarterly, 29*(2), 163–78.

Strauss, A. & Corbin, J. M. (1988). *Unending work and care.* San Francisco: Jossey-Bass Publishers.

Strauss, A., Fagerhaugh, S., Suczek, B., & Weiner, C. (1997). *Social organization of medical work* (2nd ed.). New Brunswick: Transaction Publishers, Rutgers.

Tsoukas, H. (2017). Don't simplify, complexify: From disjunctive to conjunctive theorizing in organization and management studies. *The Journal of Management Studies, 54*(2), 132.

Van de Ven, A. H. (2007). *Engaged scholarship: A guide for organizational and social research.* Oxford: Oxford University Press.

Van de Ven, A. H. & Huber, G. P. (1990). Longitudinal field research methods for studying processes of organizational change. *Organization Science, 1*(3), 213–19.

Wegener, C., Meier, N., & Maslo, E. (eds.). (2018). *Cultivating creativity in methodology and research: In praise of detours*. Basingstoke: Palgrave McMillan.

Weick, K. E. (1995). *Sensemaking in organizations*. Thousand Oaks, CA: Sage.

Weick, K. E. (2006). Faith, evidence, and action: Better guesses in an unknowable world. *Organization Studies, 27*(11), 1723–36.

Weick, K. E., Sutcliffe, K. M., & Obstfeld, D. (2005). Organizing and the process of sensemaking. *Organization Science, 16*(4), 409–21.

Yin, R. (1984). *Case study research: Design and methods*. London: Sage.

Part I
Context
What Constitutes the Context of a Situation/Event or Phenomenon?

4

Enacted Context

Louise Fitzgerald

Introduction

This chapter aims to explore and develop an understanding of an interactionist view of context that includes the interaction of context, actors, and action. The word *context* comes from the Latin *contextus*, meaning, "a joining together" (Duranti & Goodwin, 1992; Scharfstein, 1989). Thus, the chapter adopts a distinct viewpoint: an interactionist perspective of context. Then, it examines the methodological implications of these ideas. Thus, the chapter argues that context is not a given, nor merely a backcloth to action.

The chapter begins with a relatively brief review of context as understood from an interactionist perspective, focusing on developments in the field of organization studies. The second part of the chapter provides illustrative examples of the processes of interaction between actors and facets of their context at differing levels of analysis. These empirical illustrations form the foundation for an analysis that seeks to elaborate and develop emergent ideas of layers of contextualization and the manner in which actors' sensemaking and sensegiving leads to decisions and responsive actions that, in their turn, influence and reshape context. Based on this analysis, the final section explores the methodological implications, and it questions the analytical processes that may be used.

Differing disciplinary perspectives on the issues in understanding and studying context have been appraised. Attention has been drawn to the centrality of the concept of context in anthropology, and to the work of anthropologists in developing knowledge of aspects of cultural context (Daryl Slack, 1996; Dilley, 1999b; Duranti & Goodwin, 1992; Scharfstein, 1989). Dilley (1999a) introduces the issues by stating that interpretation is context-dependent, but context itself is problematic. The issues, Dilley argues, center on framing and delimiting context, essentially bounding context. He argues that context might be delimited by perceiving it as a set of connections relevant to someone or some problem, or aspects of context may be selected and analyzed as being useful in answering a research question. His perspective is that context is "that which environs the object of interest and helps by its relevance to explain it" (Dilley, 1999a p. 1). Importantly, these ideas draw attention to what is left out or thought not to be connected to the object of study. Current views in anthropology have shifted from being a direct focus on culture to a focus on the relationship between the individual and the object of study that produces the frame of analysis. Fabian (1999) and Tabakowska (2002) explore the question of how context is to be bounded. They promote the argument that context does not require bounding if transparency is evident and the relevance explained. (Later in this chapter, we shall return to the issue of relevance and to the methods for elucidating transparency.)

Referring to linguistics, Duranti and Goodwin (1992) take as their core theme "the capacity of human beings to dynamically reshape the context that provides organization for their actions within the interaction itself" (p. 5). They promote four basic parameters of context: (1) setting, (2) behavioral environment, (3) language, and (4) extrasituational context, background knowledge, or frames of reference. Parameter 4 is described as the "policing" effects of domains of cultural knowledge on what counts or does not count. These authors argue that it is crucially important to take the perspective of the participants being studied as the point of departure for analysis. This viewpoint highlights two issues. First, what the participant treats as relevant context is shaped by the specific activities being performed, and, second, participants are always situated in multiple contexts. Duranti and Goodwin observe that, in analyzing context, it is especially difficult to describe the socio-historical knowledge employed in acting.

Tracing the Development of the Interactionist Concept of Context in Organizational Studies, Focusing on Health Care

This section selectively reviews the literature on organizational context within the field of organization studies. Specifically, it explores the development of an interactionist view of context, which places the person in connection with the context. Unlike the anthropologists, who focus a significant volume of research on national contexts or national cultures and how these were played out in local communities, this section emphasizes organizational contexts. There has been a direct development of the anthropological approaches to research and methodology in the development of ethnographic methods in organization studies (Ybema et al., 2009; Van Maanen, 2011).

While this remains a relatively underdeveloped and specialized stream of research, more evident in European studies, it is a vibrant research field, but is not explored here (McCann et al., 2015; Watson, 2011).

Broad, early research on context emphasized the importance of external environmental variables and their influence on the organization (Burns & Stalker, 1966; Katz & Kahn, 1966; Lawrence & Lorsch, 1986); and internal organizational characteristics and the dynamics and relationships between them (Child & Smith, 1987; Pugh et al., 1963; Warmington, Lupton, & Gribbin, 1977). The extensive research program known as the Aston Studies attempted to relate the organizational context to internal aspects of organizational structure and behavior (e.g., Pugh & Payne, 1977) and to develop conceptualizations of the environment which Hage (1997) described as "brilliant."

Moreover, in processual studies of organizations, the exploration of context is a consistent theme. Within this stream of research, there has been considerable conceptual development of our understanding of organizational context and of interactionist perspectives of how actors and context interrelate. Pettigrew's 1985 book and later articles (1987, 2012) frame a number of key issues and are particularly significant for their contributions. They offer the context–content–process triangle as the lens through which to study organizational change, directly including the organizational context as key to understanding events in organizations. Pettigrew delineated the concepts of outer and inner context. The former was used to describe the influential characteristics of the context beyond the organizational boundary, including macrolevel influences, such as the economy and the competitive landscape, but also the social and political environment in which the organization operates. By contrast, the inner context detailed characteristics within the organizational boundary, such as the structure, corporate culture, and political context within the firm. These concepts of outer and inner context embraced both historical and current factors and together emphasized a multifactorial concept of context.

Subsequently, Pettigrew and Whipp (1991) and Pettigrew, Ferlie, and McKee (1992) seek to link the context, content, and process of change to outcomes. The former study identifies five central factors that differentiated high performers from low ones. The high performers (1) conducted environmental assessments, (2) led change, (3) linked strategic and operational change, (4) managed their human resources as assets and liabilities, and (5) managed coherence in the overall process of competition and change. The second study (Pettigrew, Ferlie, & McKee, 1992) focuses on health care and investigates variability in performance between health care units. The results describe "receptive" and "nonreceptive" contexts for change, and attempt to establish the dynamism between change processes and context, focusing on interconnections, patterns, and mechanisms. Using a comparative case study method with sixteen paired cases in eight Health Authorities, the researchers highlighted factors differentiating receptive from nonreceptive contexts for change, including availability of key people leading change; the intensity, scale, and orchestration of external environmental pressure; and the fit between the change agenda and the locale. These were described as a *linked set of conditions* (Pettigrew, Ferlie, & McKee, 1992 p. 275) that clearly involve external and internal contextual factors. Thus, the range of factors highlighted emphasizes the multifactorial nature of organizational contexts. Significantly, this analysis links aspects of both the local and national context to actions and events within particular organizations. Abelson's (2001) definition of *context* separated the notion into outer, societal, "predisposing" influences and inner, "precipitating," political influences. However, the data in Pettigrew, Ferlie, and McKee (1992) demonstrate the interplay of outer and inner context. McNulty and Ferlie (2002) propose that context has to be analyzed at three levels. These are the macrolevel of the public sector, the mesolevel of the organization, and the micro-individual level. This conceptual relayering began to challenge and elaborate the previous dichotomy between outer and inner context.

These data set the scene for Fitzgerald et al.'s (2006) later theoretical contribution, moving away from considering cause-and-effect relationships toward what Goldstone (2003) terms "conjunctural causation," whereby combinations rather than individual factors are significant. Conceptually, this thinking aligns with Witteloostuijn (1997), who made the point that dynamism exists in both internal and external contexts/environments. Witteloostuijn underlines the impact of internal organizational functioning on external contexts. Using the example of organizational failure, he identifies that such an event matters to both local and national societies.

An interactionist perspective on context perceives context in relation to someone or some object, or more precisely, someone focusing on a topic or issue. Examining government restructuring of UK health care via the introduction of a quasi-market, authors Ashburner and Fitzgerald (1996); Ashburner, Ferlie, and Fitzgerald (1996); and Ferlie et al. (1996) stress that actors' perceptions of policy and responses to the stated objectives led to unintended consequences. A focus on actors and their interpretations of the elements of their context helps to explain the linkages between elements of the context at all levels and the events pathway, which, in its turn, may influence the context. Change generates reactions from actors in the system. They are not passive. They respond intentionally, and frequently utilize opportunities to achieve personal, group, or organizational objectives. The intention to introduce private-sector ideas and models into health care was redirected partially by clinical professionals moving rapidly into key roles, and nuanced intraprofessional shifts in medical power.

Studies of innovation-adoption processes in health care further elaborate the conceptual understanding of the interactionist view of context. Fitzgerald et al. (2002) emphasize the nature of the adoption decision and argue for a more context-sensitive treatment of the phenomenon. Other authors offer perspectives on the contextual influences on the innovation-adoption process. Van de Ven et al. (1999) portray the fluid nature of participation by personnel at differing times throughout the process of adoption. Robertson, Swann, and Newell (1996) show the influential role of cross-organizational professional networks, importing external ideas into the organization from bone fide sources.

Further analysis (Fitzgerald et al., 2002) evidences interactions between actors in a multilayered context. Nationally, there were different patterns of diffusion of the same innovation in the acute and primary care sectors of health care, so that the subsectoral characteristics of the contexts influenced the process. Robust evidence demonstrated group-level variance within the communities of practice, with, for example, surgeons in a tightly bounded professional world having few external influences. Adoption and diffusion processes were shaped by local contexts and dependent on the interlocking interactions of actors and context. The differing interactions between elements of context and actors and groups were evident when comparing acute hospitals with General Practice in primary care. The data provide evidence of multiple differences in values, education, and the quality of interprofessional relationships, with people also working within different structures: hierarchies in acute care and partnerships in primary care. Fitzgerald et al. (2002) conclude: "Ultimately, the behaviour of the stakeholders and the features of the context are interlocked. The combination of multi-layered, two way influences, multiple stakeholders with interpretative schema, innovation seeking behaviour by individuals and groups and differing absorptive capacity in organizations, produces a situation in which context is actor."

The arguments thus far promote the view that an important element in understanding the interactionist concept of context, and the construction and bounding of context, is to recognize and acknowledge the sensemaking and sensegiving processes of individuals and groups. Sensemaking is fundamentally a "social process... [where] organization members interpret their environment in and through interactions with each other" (Maitlis, 2005 p. 21). Sensemaking is likely to be especially significant in periods of change and major job decisions, as evidenced in both private and health care sectors (Fitzgerald et al., 2002; Fitzgerald et al., 2005; Rothausen et al., 2017). Sensemaking of complex contexts involves paying selective attention to certain aspects over others. In reviewing the myriad contextual data surrounding them, individuals are influenced by personal motivation and perceived local or organizational needs (Ferlie et al., 2013). Sensemaking addresses the perception and interpretation of power, especially in top-down change. Ferlie et al. (1996) and McDermott, Fitzgerald, and Buchanan(2013) stress that the actors' differing perceptions of policy and their responses framed action. Whittle et al. (2016) illustrate that sensemaking interpretations of power relations at a local level may also lead to the withholding of information from senior managers, or "sense-censoring" as they describe it. It is the processes of focus and selection that act to bound context.

The actions that follow from interpretations of aspects of context will also be influenced by processes of sensegiving, defined as the "process of attempting to influence the sensemaking and meaning construction of others toward a preferred redefinition of organizational reality" (Gioia & Chittipeddi, 1991 p. 442). In a review of the literature on sensegiving, Maitlis and Lawrence (2007) point out that actors at all levels of an organization may engage in sensegiving. Identifying what motivates individuals to engage in sensemaking, they note, in particular, that one key motivator is when stakeholders perceive the issue as being important to themselves. They then progress to identifying the enablers of sensegiving. It is apparent from research (McGivern et al., 2015) that sensegiving can have a major influence on change processes.

These findings are reinforced by data from seven studies of innovation and innovation diffusion (Dopson and Fitzgerald, 2005). The authors sought to extend and elaborate the interactions between elements of context and actors, presenting evidence to substantiate the points made previously. They summarize a more nuanced view of active context. Context is not discrete: local contexts are multidimensional, multifaceted configurations of forces, and individuals are influenced by social relationships and history, and thus, actors perceive and interpret context in different ways. Individual elements are rarely viewed as being separate or distinct. Instead, an individual experiences the totality of context as a maelstrom, or at least as a morass. Individuals strive to make sense and create an integral context, so that context looks different from the perspectives of various stakeholders, and individuals select from and prioritize aspects of their context in differing ways.

In a reflective article, Dopson, Fitzgerald, and Ferlie (2008) underline the core elements of this analysis of context. They suggest that the cumulative effect of a conjunction of positive factors led to successful change outcomes. This line of thinking shifts attention from a view of single elements of local context as the "external" influences acting on an organization, and underlines the temporal elements of the processes. Accumulation involves the gradual build-up of pressure, and the combined impact of a conjunction of factors from different organizational sources to generate an outcome.

Using ten comparative cases of service improvement in health care, Fitzgerald et al. (2013) elaborate on the concept of accumulated and conjunctive forces building up and resulting in change, by identifying the specific combinations of factors leading to positive or negative outcomes. The authors focus on distributed leadership roles in front-line service improvement. These results illustrate the variable interactions and consequent configurations of actors in leadership roles and contextual factors through time and then connect these processes to intermediate outcomes. Particular contextual characteristics, especially poor or sound foundations of good-quality interprofessional relations connect interactively with individual, distributed and collective leadership to produce both positive and negative effects. This finding is echoed by McDermott andKeating's (2012) analysis of service improvement in Irish hospitals, in which they suggest that a supportive social context can help change agents to address challenging dimensions of their external contexts.

Illustrative Examples of the Processes of Interaction between Actors and Facets of Their Context at Differing Levels of Analysis

These illustrative examples start by displaying the influence of and reactions to a multilayered context, and they explore how actors interpret elements of context at differing levels of "distance" from their core activities and focus.

Illustration 1: The Political Economy and Willowtown Primary Care Trust

The first example draws on Dopson et al. (2013) and Ferlie et al. (2016), and it evidences the influence of distant national or cultural elements of the health care context. This macrolevel analysis highlights the influence of two facets of the national health care domain: the underlying political economy of public services reform and the strongly developed business school/management consulting knowledge nexus. The authors describe the continuing, active, politically driven process of health care reform. They characterize two recent reform "narratives": the first, New Public Management (NPM) reform under Prime Minister Margaret Thatcher, which sought to introduce businesslike, market-based reform; and the second, post-NPM or New Labour reform, which emphasized service quality, networks, and system-wide collaboration. Of these reform periods, neither pursued a uniform approach, but employed a mix of targets and incentives. The research examines whether one can find evidence of management and clinician attention being drawn to the knowledge around these themes and a consequent selection of texts. Ferlie et al. (2016) present Willowtown Primary Care Trust, facing productivity and savings targets as the staff struggle to implement an improved integrated care initiative. This latter initiative is based on systems thinking and whole systems approaches to change, emphasizing collaboration and shared learning.

These ideas come under pressure to give priority to "hard" data and knowledge on financial risk, accounting, and performance management. Ultimately, management, and to a lesser extent, clinician attention shifted toward saving money, and the whole systems initiative was summarily stopped.

This attention shift can be detected within the organization and within the discourses, and it gradually becomes apparent that the relative influence of management knowledge on accounting and performance management has become dominant, leading to behavior change. These new behaviors alter the organization, which creates an altered context for action and sensemaking.

Illustration 2: New Service-Delivery Systems in Maternity Care

The evidence-based medicine (EBM) movement has generated substantial shifts in care throughout the health system, and it has created strong pressures for clinicians to access and use the most up-to-date scientific knowledge. But frequently the evidence base for change is not clear-cut. In the wake of the document "Changing Childbirth" (Department of Health, 1993), policy changes and targets were set out to provide women with better-informed choice and a range of options when giving birth. These changes were contested, and there was (and is) controversy about the extent to which childbirth should be medicalized. The evidence to support midwife-led care for low-risk mothers was challenged. This case (Fitzgerald et al., 2005) focuses on a maternity unit in an acute hospital, with high levels of ethnically diverse demand and old buildings with outdated design (e.g., the unit had to operate over three floors).

In this case, driven by overcrowding in the antenatal clinics and the lack of hospital space to improve this, senior midwifery managers had begun a process of producing a protocol to allow low-risk mothers to be cared for in the community. Gradually, in a staged manner, a number of changes were introduced to services, such as a "booking" meeting in which mothers were categorized by risk, a new midwife-led unit, and community midwives operating in two group practices.

It is evident that the changes to organizational systems, clinical behavior, and standards of care were influenced by the national policy-level context and by EBM. Yet the effective processes of change were also significantly influenced by local conditions. These are important for an understanding of this case. These local conditions included long-standing relationships of trust and respect between the obstetricians and the midwives, general agreement that the changes would meet urgent local needs, and a senior midwifery manager with political and strategic skills who sought alliances with obstetricians who wanted change. So, here, we may perceive key actors attending to and interpreting national contexts, but framing their positive responses through the lens of local needs.

It is apparent from the two illustrations presented thus far that the broad national-level context may have influence in a multitude of ways: through policy directives, EBM, research; and targets. But this national-level context cannot be viewed as deterministic. The actors in the organizations select elements of this context as "relevant" partially according to the dictates of policy or cultural influences, but a considerable body of research exemplifies the varied and competing influences of education, prior practices, networks of relationships, and the demands of the local context (see the Glue Ear case in Fitzgerald et al., 2005 pp. 171–4, for an illuminating mixture of competing influences). So each individual makes judgments and selections before acting, creating a sometimes-circuitous and nonlinear process.

Illustration 3: Extrapreneurial Responses to Policy Implementation

The third illustration is drawn from McDermott, Fitzgerald, and Buchanan (2013), and it is based on four cases of acute hospitals in England and Ireland. These cases also underline the unintended outcomes of mandated policy changes. However, this example traces in greater detail how change recipients can interpret, react to, translate, and contribute to policy change initiatives. Significantly, these differing responses to policy demands emphasize how individual actors attend to and blend aspects of the local and national contexts, frequently giving some precedence to local context. The data demonstrate four patterns of responses and action (or inaction) across the four cases. These profiles are labeled:

- systematic and dispersed entrepreneurial change agency;
- systematic clinical entrepreneurial change agency;
- fragmented entrepreneurial change agency; and
- disinterested and limited intended change agency.

These labels convey a complex set of responses to national-level contexts in which actors interpret, select, and decide on actions they consider relevant to their positions and aims. The range of responses is particularly illuminating because it displays how the selection of contextual elements may be interpreted as constraints, challenges, or opportunities.

In addition to the profile of responses across the organizations, the article identifies a subset of individuals, called *extrapreneurs*. In the data, these extrapreneurs are predominantly powerful clinicians with the skills and strategic knowledge to enable them to shape the context. Extrapreneurs go well beyond what is demanded, to obtain improvements for their local domains.

They adopt a form of contextualized change agency to influence others both within and outside their organization to gain support for actions that in some cases radically alter and reshape their local context.

To understand the interactive concept of context, one must view the entire, multilayered, multifactorial context from the perspective of the person within it. The context influences the person, and through selective attention and interpretation, the person decides which aspects of context are relevant in their case and, in acting, reforms and reshapes the context, most evidently at the local level.

Methodological Implications

The ideas and arguments put forward in this chapter for an interactionist view of context, which includes the interaction of context, actors, and action, have significant implications for the design and methods adopted in research. Indeed, it might be argued that the concept of context, and *how* it may be studied, is an underdeveloped and somewhat neglected arena in organization studies. Many studies, both qualitative and quantitative in design, state that they have included context in the study, while offering minimal data or explanation of their conceptual and methodological approach. Frequently, context is simply expressed as "there," by a brief exposition such as "in the health care system" or the "the data were collected in a large general hospital." This lack of specification and transparency is particularly apparent in case study research. It may readily be argued that a critical and essential component of a case study is multifaceted data on the context of the case (Fitzgerald and Dopson, 2009; Yin, 2014). So the first methodological implication to be drawn is that researchers need to be transparent in their methods, to identify clearly the unit of analysis, and to explain their concept of context and an explanatory logic of any data.

Another direct implication of an interactionist view of context is that it requires the analysis of multilevel data. This chapter has proposed that, for studies featuring health care, significant levels of analysis include the national, political, and cultural; the organizational or interorganizational level; and the individual level. Each aspect of context raises potential methodological issues. Such complex situations will be best understood through prolonged observations of interactions in real-time, or longitudinal designs. As previously discussed, the bounding of context is a critical and difficult issue. Initially, researchers need to identify, clearly, whether they are adopting a researcher perspective on context or are endeavoring to provide a view from "the eye of the beholder." Second, at the national level, it will never be possible to collect comprehensive data on every aspect of national life. So transparency is again necessary. Researchers need to identify trends or policies at the national level, having specific effects in relation to the unit of analysis. This is by no means a straightforward task. Based on our own experiences, one example is of a comparative, multicase research design in which the research team attempted to specify a set of organizations that faced "high-change" environments. Drawing on prior research, the team developed a careful, evidence-based group of criteria to underpin the notion of a high-change environment. Then the team spent a considerable period of time matching organizations to these criteria and gaining access to study them. Nevertheless, this proved relatively worthless as a comparative explanation. Because of the dynamic nature of organizations, during the period of study, some organizations altered rapidly from "high change" to "low change" and vice versa.

Duranti and Goodwin (1992) argue for an interactionist view of context that places the social person center stage. The implication of this is that the researcher should consider adopting the perspective of those studied as the starting point of an understanding of the context. This has many important implications for the selection of "voices" to be heard through a research project. For this individual level of analysis, researchers must specify who and why interviewees/observed individuals were selected. Too often, this explanation is rudimentary or based on numbers. Researchers must seek to explain the logic of selecting voices in relation to the research question or focus. Researchers have an obligation to consider why some voices are privileged over others. Rarely heard voices may offer useful and critical perspectives. In health care research, these would include the views of nonprofessionals, such as patients, cleaners, and health care assistants.

Further developments will be needed for social science researchers to progress from post hoc analysis of events (which is useful) toward the capacity and ability to assess/predict between alternative scenarios. To enable such assessment, researchers must weigh the influence, affect, and effect of differing configurations of context on events. Such development will require better methods for understanding complex interactions, and while progress once achieved may not enable precise prediction, it will ensure improved assessment of trends. Current developments in methods, such as the adoption of network analysis (Lin, 1999; Wellman, 1983), illustrate hopeful progress in the analysis of complex sets of relationships. The method of Qualitative Comparative Analysis, both crisp and fuzzy, is a further development that facilitates multilevel analysis (Andrews, Benyon, and McDermott, 2015; Ragin, 2013).

Louise Fitzgerald

Emerging Developments and Elaboration of the Interactionist Concept of Context in Health Care

This chapter has traced the development and explored the understanding of an interactionist view of context in health care, which connects context, actors, and action interactively. Here, these views have been elaborated to build our understanding of the processes by which context influences and is enacted by actors. The chapter has projected the concept of context as multilayered and multifactorial, sensed, experienced, and constructed. Exploring the issue of a layered context, here I argue that the delineation and separation of an outer and inner context, or the suggestion that context should be analyzed at the macro-, meso-, and micro levels of analysis, represents a view that is too inflexible and limited. Instead, it is suggested that the outer and inner contexts do not exist in a stable, relative position to each other. Rather, the individual actor connects these elements through a focus on a problem or topic. The actor *fluidly blends context into form* by selectively melding contextual elements. The external ("outer"), broader context may be experienced less directly by the individual and be perceived as distant, and understanding or knowledge of it may be shared via a network of relationships. Certain elements of this external context may be inherited beliefs and cultural norms, barely acknowledged overtly by the individual. The personal ("inner") context is experienced and interpreted directly, exercising a strong influence on decision-making and action. Therefore, one might argue that the crucial difference between the elements of the external context and the elements of the personal context is one of *distance*. In daily life, the individual experiences the totality of context, and selectively attends to and interprets a fluid mix of elements of the external and the personal organizational contexts.

The attention to certain elements of context is dynamically driven by focus, and selective attention is framed by sensemaking and driven by an individualized judgment of what is "relevant." The significance of what is framed as *relevant* (and thus bounded as context) is embedded in the socialization of the individual, the influence of sensegiving processes, personal experiences, goals, the system of knowledge, and the individual's will and power to act. This explanation perceives the *bounding of context* as an act of individual sensemaking, embodied cognition, and judgment.

References

Abelson, J. (2001). Understanding the role of contextual influences on local health care decision making: The case study results from Ontario, Canada. *Social Science and Medicine, 53,* 777–93.

Andrews, R., Beynon, M. J., & McDermott, A. M. (2015). Organizational capability in the public sector: A configurational approach. *Journal of Public Administration Research and Theory, 26*(2), 239–58.

Ashburner, L., Ferlie, E., & Fitzgerald, L. (1996). Organisational transformation and top down change: The case of the NHS. *British Journal of Management, 7*(1), 1–16.

Ashburner, L., & Fitzgerald, L. (1996). Beleaguered professionals? Doctors and institutional change in the NHS. In H. Scarbrough (ed.), *The management of expertise.* New York: St. Martin's Press, pp. 190–216.

Burns, T. & Stalker, G. M. (1966). *Management of innovation* (2nd ed.). London: Tavistock.

Child, J. & Smith, C. (1987). The context and process of organizational transformation: Cadbury Ltd in its sector. *Journal of Management Studies, 12*, 12–27.

Daryl Slack, J. (1996). The theory and method of articulation in cultural studies. In D. Morley & K.-H. Chen (eds.), *Stuart Hall, critical dialogues in Cultural Studies.* London: Routledge, pp. 112–27.

Department of Health. (1993). *Changing childbirth, part 1: Report of the Expert Maternity Group.* London: HMSO.

Dilley, R. (1999a). Introduction: The problem of context. In R. Dilley (ed.), *The problem of context.* New York and Oxford: Breghahn Books, pp. 1–47.

Dilley, R. (ed.) (1999b). *The problem of context.* New York and Oxford: Breghahn Books.

Dopson, S., et al. (2013). *Health care managers' access and use of management research,* Final Report to the NIHR HS&DR—08/1808/242, Department of Health, May. www.nets.nihr.ac.uk/projects/hsdr/081808242. (Accessed 11 November 2017).

Dopson, S. & FitzGerald, L. (eds.). (2005). *Knowledge to action? Evidence based health care in context.* Oxford: Oxford University Press.

Dopson, S., Fitzgerald, L., & Ferlie, E. (2008). Understanding change and innovation in health care settings: Re-conceptualising the active role of context. *Journal of Change Management, 8*(3/4), 213–41.

Duranti, A. & Goodwin, C. (1992). *Rethinking context: Language as an interactive phenomenon.* Cambridge and New York: Cambridge University Press.

Fabian, J. (1999). Ethnographic misunderstanding and the perils of context. In R. Dilley, (ed.), *The problem of context.* New York and Oxford: Breghahn Books, pp. 85–105.

Ferlie, E., Ashburner, L., Fitzgerald, L., & Pettigrew, A. M. (1996). *The new public management in action.* Oxford: Oxford University Press.

Ferlie, E., Fitzgerald, L., McGivern, G., Dopson, S., & Bennett, C. (2013). *Making wicked problems governable? The case of managed networks in health care.* Oxford, Oxford University Press.

Ferlie, E., et al. (2016). From evidence based management to the political economy of knowledge—the case of English health care organizations. *Public Administration, 94*(1), 185–203.

Fitzgerald, L. & Dopson, S. (2009). Comparative case study designs: Their utility and development in organizational research. In D. Buchanan & A. Bryman, (eds.), *The Sage handbook of organizational research methods.* London: Sage, pp. 465–83.

Fitzgerald, L., Dopson, S., Ferlie, E., & Locock, L. (2005). Knowledge in action. In S. Dopson & L. Fitzgerald (eds.), *Knowledge to action? Evidence based health care in context.* Oxford: Oxford University Press, pp. 169–71.

Fitzgerald, L., Ferlie, E., McGivern, G., & Buchanan, D. (2013). Distributed leadership patterns and service improvement: Evidence and argument from English healthcare. *The Leadership Quarterly, 24*(1), 227–39.

Fitzgerald, L., Ferlie, E., Wood, M., & Hawkins, C. (2002). Interlocking interactions: The diffusion of innovations in health care. *Human Relations, 55*(12), 1429–49.

Fitzgerald, L., et al. (2006). *Managing change and role enactment in the professionalized organization*. London: National Coordinating Centre for NHS Service Delivery and Organisation R&D (NCCSDO).http://www.nets.nihr.ac.uk/projects/hsdr/081201021 (Accessed 10 October 2016).

Gioia, D. A. & Chittipeddi, K. (1991). Sensemaking and sensegiving in strategic change initiation. *Strategic Management Journal, 12*, 433–48.

Goldstone, J. A. (2003). Comparative historical analysis and knowledge accumulation in the study of revolutions. In J. Mahoney & D. Rueschemeyer (eds.), *Comparative historical analysis in the social sciences*. Cambridge: Cambridge University Press, pp. 41–90.

Hage, J. (1997). Aston Group. In A. Sorge & M. Warner (eds.), *The IEBM handbook of organization behaviour*. London: International Thomson Business Press, pp. 57–63.

Katz, D. & Kahn, R. (1966). *The social psychology of organizations*. London: Wiley.

Lawrence, P. & Lorsch, J. (1986). *Organization and environment* (Revised ed.). Boston, MA: Harvard University Press.

Lin, N. (1999). Building a network theory of social capital. *Connections, 22*, 28–51.

Maitlis, S. (2005). The social processes of organizational sensemaking. *Academy of Management Journal, 48*, 21–49.

Maitlis, S. & Lawrence, T. (2007). Triggers and enablers of sensegiving in organizations. *Academy of Management Journal, 50*(1), 57–84.

McCann, L., Granter, E., Hassard, J., & Hyde, P. (2015). Where next for the paramedic profession? An ethnography of work culture and occupational identity. *Emergency Medicine Journal, 32*(5), e6–e7.

McDermott, A. M., Fitzgerald, L., & Buchanan, D. (2013). Beyond acceptance and resistance: Entrepreneurial change agency responses in policy implementation. *British Journal of Management, 24*, S93–S115.

McDermott, A. M. & Keating, M. A. (2012). Making service improvement happen: The importance of social context. *Journal of Applied Behavioral Science, 48*(1), 62–92.

McGivern, G., Currie, G., Ferlie, E., Fitzgerald, L., & Waring, J. (2015). Hybrid manager-professionals' identity work: The maintenance and hybridisation of professionalism in managerial contexts. *Public Administration, SI, 93*(2), 412–32.

McNulty, T. & Ferlie, E. (2002). *Reengineering health care: The complexities of organizational transformation*. Oxford, Oxford University Press.

Pettigrew, A. M. (1985). *The awakening giant: Continuity and change in imperial chemical industries*. Oxford: Basil Blackwell.

Pettigrew, A. M. (1987). Context and action in the transformation of the firm. *Journal of Management Studies, 24*, 649–70.

Pettigrew, A. M. (2012). Context and action in the transformation of the firm, a reprise. *Journal of Management Studies, 49*(7), 1304–28.

Pettigrew, A. M., Ferlie, E., & McKee, L. (1992). *Shaping strategic change*. London: Sage.

Pettigrew, A. M. & Whipp, R. (1991). *Managing change for competitive success*. Oxford: Basil Blackwell.

Pugh, D. S., Hickson, D. J., Hinings, C. R., Macdonald, K., Turner, T., & Lupton, T. (1963). A conceptual scheme for organizational analysis. *Administrative Science Quarterly, 8*, 289–315.

Pugh, D. S. & Payne, R. L. (1977). *Organizational behaviour in its context: The Aston Programme III*. London: Saxon House.

Ragin, C. C. (2013). *The comparative method: moving beyond qualitative and quantitative strategies*. Berkeley/Los Angeles and London: University of California Press.

Robertson, M., Swan, J., & Newell, S. (1996). The role of networks in the diffusion of technological innovation. *Journal of Management Studies, 33*(3), 333–60.

Rothausen, T. J., Henderson, K. E., Arnold, A. K., & Malshe, A. (2017). Should I stay or should I go? Identity and well-being in sensemaking about retention and turnover. *Journal of Management, 43*(7): 2357–85.

Scharfstein, B.-A. (1989). *The dilemma of context*. New York and London: New York University Press.

Tabakowska, E. (2002). The regime of the other, "us" and "them" in translation. In A. Duszak (ed.). *Us and others: Social identities across languages, discourses and culture*. Amsterdam, PA: John Benjamins, pp. 449–62.

Van de Ven, A. D., Polley, D. E., Garud, R., & Venkataraman, S. (1999). *The innovation journey*. Oxford: Oxford University Press.

Van Maanen, J. (2011). Ethnography as work: Some rules of engagement. *Journal of Management Studies, 48*(1), 218–34.

Warmington, A., Lupton, T., & Gribbin, C. (1977). *Organizational behaviour and performance: An open systems approach to change*. London: Macmillan.

Watson, T. (2011). Ethnography, reality and truth: The vital need for students of "how things work" in organisation and management. *Journal of Management Studies, 48*(1), 202–17.

Wellman, B. (1983). Network analysis: Some basic principles. *Sociological Theory, 1*, 155–200.

Whittle, A. Mueller, F., Gilchrist, A., & Lenney, P. (2016). Sensemaking, sense-censoring and strategic inaction: The discursive enactment of power and politics in a multinational corporation, *Organization Studies, 37*(9), 1323–51.

Witteloostuijn, A. v. (1997). Internal contexts and external environments. In A. Sorge & M. Warner (eds.), *The IEBM handbook of organization behaviour*. London: International Thomson Business Press, pp. 163–72.

Ybema, S., Yanow, D., Wels, H., & Kamsteeg, F. H. (eds.). (2009). *Organizational ethnography: Studying the complexity of everyday life*. London: Sage.

Yin, R. K. (2014). *Case study research: Design and methods*. Thousand Oaks, CA: Sage.

5

Context of Health Policies and the Impact on Implementation of Health Care and Health Interventions

David A. Chambers

Introduction

This chapter will discuss the interface between the context, health and health care policy, and health care delivery, using examples primarily from the experience of cancer control and mental health care within the US health care systems, though drawing on more general trends in the influence of policy on health care. The chapter will briefly describe policy as existing in two major dimensions: (1) the set of legislative and regulatory actions that governments and organizations use to influence the provision and receipt of health care, which form the context upon which health care is delivered, and (2) a set of strategies that may support or impede the implementation of health and health care interventions. Moreover, the chapter offers a discussion of how research can be advanced in this space. In doing so, the chapter principally addresses two of the main research questions of the book, Question 1 (i.e., What constitutes an event, situation, or phenomenon?), with an examination of Question 3 (i.e., How do contexts change, and what is the role of actors in such processes?) and how dynamism affects the implementation of health interventions.

Since the 1980s, researchers focusing on the dissemination and implementation of effective health interventions have developed a plethora of conceptual models (Tabak et al., 2012), helping to map the influences on clinical practice change. In most of these models, policy represents an external influence on the provision and receipt of health care at the macrolevel of the socio-ecological framework. In reality, influence is bidirectional, and policy is multilevel. Policy provides both a central aspect of context for health care delivery and an advantage point to affect that care over time. Through this lens, we see that the context is not just a component of the background against which health care delivery is set: it also enables a set of actions that can directly shape health care delivery itself. This chapter will be constructed with the following components.

First, the chapter discusses the ways in which policy at multiple levels shapes the context in which health care is delivered, which influences all efforts to attain specific health and health care outcomes. The chapter notes that policy can influence actions at every level, from affecting individual patient access to care, to provider delivery of interventions, and to organization, system, and national settings in which care is delivered. Second, the chapter discusses how health policy can be employed as a driver for change in the delivery of health care and the support of health, influencing the implementation of a range of interventions that can improve health and health care practice. The chapter concludes with a discussion of opportunities for further advances in policy-relevant research and practice.

The Context of Health and Health Care Policy

Policy serves as a context for the delivery of health care and the support of health. Traditionally, researchers have focused primarily on policy with a "big P" to represent national or state/provincial legislative and regulatory activity, but we recognize that policy is enacted at local levels, by public systems and health care organizations, and can influence the provision of health care, payment for it, and the built environment, either promoting the attainment of health or inhibiting it. For example, schools may be impacted by national, state, or district policy that affects their ability to provide healthy lunches, supply opportunities for physical activity, and enable access to health care services on-site, as well as to create policy that further specifies each of these. Similarly, a workplace may be subject to varying smoke-free air laws, which in turn affect the health and health care of its employees and others who enter the workspace. Given the wide range of influences on health and health care, commentators have recognized the opportunity to incorporate health into decision-making across multiple sectors, and create what many have referred to as "health in all policies" (Public Health Institute, n.d.).

Multiple Levels of Policy

There are a number of health care frameworks that recognize the multilevel nature of the context in which provision and receipt of health care occurs.

David A. Chambers

One framework, arising from a US National Cancer Institute meeting on multilevel initiatives, recognizes each level of health care as being akin to a layer of an onion (Taplin & Rodgers, 2010). At the center of the model is the individual patient, with family and social support surrounding. The next layer is the provider or team, followed by the organization and/or practice setting. The outer layers include the local community environment, the state health policy environment, and finally, the national health policy environment (Taplin & Rodgers, 2010). We notice that while the word *policy* is only included in the outer two levels, there are policies that can also affect the inner layers, as we shall describe later in the chapter. Figure 5.1 represents a similar depiction of the multiple layers of context.

Another framework frequently referred to by health care researchers is the socio-ecological model, which organizes health activity into four distinct levels: individual, settings, sectors, social and cultural norms and values (Social-Ecological Model, 2015). Typically, policy is relegated to the outermost level of the model, but, again, we recognize that policy can influence health and the health care actions of the individual, the settings in which they receive care, and the communities, cities and towns, states, provinces, and countries in which they live. One can also observe that health and health care decision-making (and indeed the policies that affect them) will also be influenced by the cultural norms and values of individuals, communities, and broader populations.

Broad Categories of Policy

At a basic level, health-related policy can be broken down into public and private categories. Public policy making relates to the creating of policies that

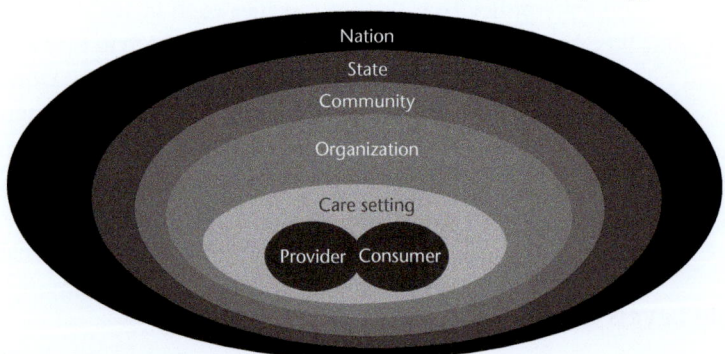

The multilevel nature of health care (and health policy)

- Nation
- State
- Community
- Organization
- Care setting
- Provider Consumer

Figure 5.1 Policies Can Affect Health and Health Care at Multiple Levels, and Can Be Targeted at One or More of Those Levels

Context of Health Policies and the Impact on Implementation

are intended to affect the broad citizenry, whether in a local jurisdiction or at the more macrolevels, including all the way up to national policy. Private policy relates to the enacting of rules and procedures by organizations in the private sector that govern those who deliver and receive services under the domain of that organization (American College of Health Executives, n.d.). For example, a corporation may offer specific benefits to employees that affect their ability to access and afford health and health care services, or may influence health in the workplace (e.g., policies related to exposure to toxic chemicals). Across both private and public sectors, we can further distinguish between policies that influence the broad area of health and those related more specifically to the provision, organization, and payment of health care services, which is described as "health care policy" (American College of Health Executives, n.d.).

A full description of the many types of policies related to health and health care is beyond the scope of this chapter, but, briefly, we shall consider those policies related to health care financing (e.g., insurance regulations, direct coverage of services, and eligibility requirements for the public payment of health care), access to services (e.g., medication formularies and health care infrastructure support), the conduct of medical research (e.g., public and private funding of research and human-subject protections), support of the health care workforce (e.g., licensing of professionals and regulation of health care professional education), and public health (e.g., smoke-free public places, immunization requirements, and clean water) (Wikipedia, n.d.). One might note that each of these policy categories can manifest at multiple levels. For example, in the USA, each state may have different public health policies, different requirements for health insurance, different licensure for professionals, and different reimbursement levels for health services. Policies may also be enacted that impact health and health care at the city level (e.g., city policies related to smoke-free restaurants and bars, and the size of sugar-sweetened beverages), and, of course, policies can exist at the national level. In short, policy affects almost every aspect of health and health care, and at every level of the system.

The Multiple Stages of Policy Making

To understand policy as a component of the health care context, it is useful to consider the life cycle of a policy. Various frameworks have laid out the policy cycle, such as including iterative phases of agenda setting, formulation, adoption, implementation, evaluation, and support or maintenance of the policy over time (Nakamura, 1987). Below, we consider two aspects of policies as a recognition of the need for researchers to attend to context over time: formulation and implementation. In many countries, federal policy often has an initial formulation to set out the overall characteristics of a policy and some guidance on how it should be implemented, and a more extensive implementation process where rules and regulations governing implementation are crafted and then mechanisms to support implementation are established. Below are two brief illustrative examples of these aspects.

Example 1: Mental Health Parity and Addiction Equity Act of 2008

In 2008, the US Congress passed the Paul Wellstone and Pete Domenici Mental Health Parity and Addiction Equity Act (MHPAEA) of 2008 that would prevent group health plans and health insurance issuers in the USA from benefit imposing limitations that are less favorable on mental health and substance-abuse services than on medical/surgical benefits (Frank et al., 2014). MHPAEA, which derived from similar requirements within the Federal Employees Health Benefits program, was intended to enable mental health and addiction services to be given coverage that is more adequate compared with historical practice, where these services were either not covered at all or were covered so minimally as to prevent individuals with these disorders from receiving evidence-based care (Health Affairs, n.d.).

While MHPAEA set out broad requirements in the text of the bill, the legislation did not specify what would be considered adequate coverage (i.e., medical/surgical benefits vary by type of health problem, meaning that one needed to identify equivalent areas to compare with mental health and substance abuse), how enforcement of the law would be carried out, and how performance would be measured. Each of these and other issues with policy implementation needed to be crafted within the US Department of Health and Human Services to enable the legislative intent of the policy to be fulfilled, and it needed to engage key stakeholders to ensure that health benefits would be gained by the population.

Example 2: The NHS Internal Market

In the UK, a set of National Health Service reforms in the 1980s and 1990s created the dynamics of a marketplace within the UK, where hospitals (formed into Trusts) were expected to compete with one another to provide optimal health care to the population (Propper & Söderlund, 1998). The argument was that an internal market would drive higher quality and improved efficiency as "customers" would favor the health care providers who brought a better product to the marketplace. Similarly, the designing of the policy required a whole set of regulations that would define how the marketplace would function, how the NHS would incentivize high quality delivery, and what consequences might emerge should Trusts fall behind on quality indicators.

The market, while established to reap benefits from natural competition, could not exist solely on the basis of the guidance set out initially, but rather on the set of regulatory steps that supported policy implementation across the districts of the NHS and into each local Trust.

In both of these examples, we see that there were initial steps taken to author policy directives to govern the health care marketplace, but that the full extent of policy making requires an extra set of regulatory actions to create and implement a set of rules needed to ensure the policies are embedded within the health care sector. The policy activity is thus a process rather than a single action of governmental decree, with a myriad of steps and layers that impact multiple levels of the socio-ecologic model.

Features of the Policy Context

Dynamism

The maxim "The only thing that is constant is change" is attributed to the Greek philosopher Heraclitus. One of the biggest challenges in understanding the health and health care policy context is its dynamism. With each legislative session at city/town, state/province, or national level, the potential for the policy environment to change expands. Changes to the legislative body in each new election cycle may bring new priorities, and changing societal norms may influence the policy agenda. A good example of the dynamism in policy can be seen in the shifts in smoke-free laws. For decades, entertainment establishments (e.g., bars and restaurants) had few or no regulations about smoking. Gradually, though, cities and towns began to see these establishments create separate sections for smokers and non-smokers. Over time, many of these cities passed broad laws prohibiting smoking completely in restaurants and bars, despite concerns that these businesses would suffer unrecoverable losses of income. At present, smoking in such establishments has become the exception rather than the rule in most cities in the USA. Other industries (e.g., airlines and gaming) have seen similar shifts in policies across the decades, as social norms have changed in terms of expectations of smoke-free environments (Chapman & Freeman, 2018).

Uncertainty

Alongside this dynamism, policy carries with it a great deal of uncertainty. The potential for and presence of ongoing change creates an environment where activities may need to be adjusted continually to account for new laws and regulations, and, increasingly, in anticipation of them. We return to the smoke-free environment as a salient example. In the USA, efforts to expand smoke-free housing have been ongoing for many years (King et al., 2010). Not just a response to health, smoke-free housing has been desirable for the potential to reduce fires and minimize costs of rehabilitation of housing units as they pass from one occupant to another, but limited efforts have been made historically to create policy to require smoke-free housing environments at the national level (King et al., 2010). Since around 2010, however, multiple local public housing authorities (over 500 of them) have moved to create smoke-free housing in their local jurisdictions, with variation in terms of how these policies are enacted and enforced. As the Department of Housing and Urban Development began to enact national smoke-free policies with their federally owned units (Housing and Urban Development, n.d.), the early adopters became uncertain as to whether their own efforts could remain as locally constructed or would needed to adjust to new regulations. As the presidential election grew closer, a new level of uncertainty was reached, as there was no guarantee that a new administration would maintain similar policy priorities within the department. The local housing authorities then faced the challenge of determining whether to move according to existing policy activities or to wait until it was clearer what the new administration's stance would be on this issue. In the policy realm, uncertainty, like dynamism, is the rule rather than the exception.

Short-Term versus Long-Term Focus

Another challenge for enacting, understanding, and studying the policy context is that of the general focus on the short term. Because the legislative lifecycle exists within the political realm, where terms of office may be no more than a couple of years in length, policy decisions may be influenced greatly by their likely impact on the next election cycle, as well as past policy actions that the current actors are seeking to move away from, and the current priorities of policy makers. In the USA, the Affordable Care Act represented an enormous shift in how health insurance would be accessed by millions of people when it was passed in 2009. While it was offered as a long-term policy solution to health care by the authors of the legislation, in practice, it was (and continues to be) impacted by a series of short-term activities, each brought on within the legislative sessions at federal and state levels. As follow-up legislation proposed to change or repeal the law, each state needed to determine its course of action on expanding the numbers of people eligible for Medicaid (government health insurance for lower socioeconomic status groups within each state), each of which might only be relevant through the current legislative session and may need updating as population demographics continue to shift.

Similarly, policy within health care organizations is often crafted with a short-term financial picture in mind. A publically traded company may be primarily concerned with the impact of policy activities on revenues or costs within the next quarter or fiscal year, and whether their shareholders benefit. In an area of massive consolidation within the health care delivery industry, survivability may preclude longer-term planning. As health care expenditures are focused primarily on the acute illness or emergency service rather than preventive care that might not reap benefits for decades, so too is the policy environment.

External Impacts (Sectoral versus Universal)

Policy affecting the delivery of health care is not limited to the health care sector, nor is the influence of health care policy restricted in its impact on society. It is thus crucial for understanding the context of policy that we are aware of the sectoral and universal impacts of different policy activities, some originating within the health care sphere and others elsewhere, but having a clear impact on the context of both health and health care. For example, the correctional system within a country (i.e., prison and similar facilities) will determine its own policies regarding the degree to which incarceration includes opportunities for education, behavioral health, work training, and other developmental services. In the USA, a large percentage of inmates have diagnosable mental disorders, low educational status, and a limited work history, and the degree to which these services can be offered are likely to have an effect on health care and other federal spending on these individuals when they return to society, and, in turn, may affect recidivism. The converse is also true: health care policy can have a direct impact on other sectors, including social work, education, and the labor market, among others. Availability of medication for chronic diseases, for example, can affect an individual's ability to work and, therefore, impact economic production. Ultimately, understanding the impact of health policy on other sectors, and other policies on the health care sector, is essential if we are to utilize policy to maximize health, productivity, and overall well-being. This is particularly important when we consider the study of policy activities; if we choose to look only at the impact of health policy on health, we risk misattributing change that may be a result of policy activity in other sectors rather than health. Similarly, we may miss the potential impact of health policy on activities in other sectors. This may require researchers to collect data that extend beyond the health sector, and draw on sufficient expertise to understand the influences of multiple domains of policy on health and health care.

Policy Framing

The interface between policy and its sensemaking by various stakeholders is a sometimes- overlooked but important area to understand, particularly as

Table 5.1 Summary of Selected Features of Health Policy and Their Influence on the Health Care Context

Features of health-related policies	Examples
Dynamism	Use of marijuana (health-related and recreational) has varied across jurisdiction and over time. States have gradually moved toward legalization in opposition to US federal law, and federal prioritization of prosecution of offenders has varied over time.
Uncertainty	The reorganization of the UK's National Health Service under Conservative government leadership in the 1980s and 1990s grew uncertain as power in the government seemed to shift to the Labour party; uncertainty re-entered the policy consciousness with the return of the Conservative Party leadership in 2010.
Temporal focus	Prioritization of comparative effectiveness research led to the creation of a Patient Centered Outcomes Research Institute in the USA in 2010, to support head-to-head research on different health interventions; the Institute was created with a 10-year funding window, requiring reauthorization or dissolution by 2019.
External impacts	Changes in the tax rates of corporations may have a direct effect on the hiring of health care staff, as well as health care coverage determinations by insurance companies.
Policy framing	Policies that support the provision of the human papillomavirus vaccine have been framed either as preventing cervical and other cancers or as encouraging adolescents to engage in sexual behavior.

potential policy actions are often determined by their support by constituents. For example, vaccinations have long been offered to children as an effective approach to reducing morbidity and mortality from serious illnesses, including polio, mumps, rubella, measles, and other viruses. Since 2000, the anti-vaccine movement has grown (Gangarosa et al., 2006), with supporters expressing concerns about the potential link between vaccine administration and autism (Plotkin, Gerber, & Offit, 2009). Where vaccines were framed as causing autism, states and cities modified policies enabling individuals to opt out. This arguably led to an increased incidence in a number of diseases thought to have been eradicated from the population. Framing a vaccine instead as preventing fatal illnesses might help societal understanding and support for vaccines, and impact policy formulation and implementation. Additional examples of these features of the policy context are found in Table 5.1.

The Context for Implementation of Health Policies and Interventions

Since 2001, implementation science has quickly developed as a vibrant research discipline, replete with conceptual models, field capacity, and empirical studies, all contributing to a knowledge base supporting the integration of a range of health interventions into health care and community settings (Glasgow et al., 2012; Neta et al., 2015). Recent reviews (Tabak et al., 2012; Nilsen, 2015; Mitchell et al., 2010) have identified dozens of models that conceptualize facilitators of and barriers to dissemination and implementation, stages of dissemination and implementation processes, and key constructs that must be targeted for interventions to be integrated successfully into local settings. Across most of these models, both the local context and the broader environment are centrally linked to the success of implementation, although we note that many of these models may require additional testing to determine the specific impact of both the local and "outer" context. For example, Everett Rogers' Diffusion of Innovations model (1995) posits that successful adoption and implementation of health interventions results from an understanding of the characteristics of an intervention that make it preferable to standard practice, and both the organizational characteristics of the health care setting that is trying to implement it and the broader environment (e.g., financing, policy, and cultural norms) that either support or impeded its integration. Damschroder et al.'s (2009) Consolidated Framework for Implementation Research (CFIR) uses the terms *inner* and *outer context* to relate to the importance to implementation of the local health care delivery setting, and the systemic and political influences that surround it. The CFIR identifies over sixty key constructs crucial to successful implementation, which scientists have worked to operationalize (see, e.g., www.cfirguide.org) and to assess the availability of instruments for data collection (Rabin et al., 2016).

Greg Aarons and colleagues' Exploration, Planning, Implementation, Sustainment (EPIS) model expands the many dimensions of outer and inner context, arguing that, at different stages of the implementation process, including the ultimate sustainment of an intervention, contextual factors may vary over time. The policy climate, for example, has a central role, both in the organizational setting and the external environment, throughout the process; however, policies that affect adoption or implementation may differ from those that impact long-term sustainment of an intervention (Aarons et al., 2011). These and other models have laid the foundation for the development and testing of implementation strategies (Powell et al., 2012; Powell et al., 2015).

Notably, the CFIR and EPIS models comprehensively describe context as multilevel, and they argue that strategies to support implementation will vary over time (dynamism) and will succeed through optimizing the "fit" with a health intervention as context. They, like many models, are not as well-developed to consider the ongoing change and uncertainty of policy within these levels of context, emphasizing the current policy environment within a discussion of context, rather than the dynamism and uncertainty described in the previous section. There is an opportunity for the research community to address this in the future, which would enhance the utility of these models in capturing the essence of the policy context.

Policy as Implementation Strategy

As we consider the impact of the policy context on health and health care, we recognize the powerful influence that specific policy activities may have on the delivery of evidence-based interventions. In this sense, policy is not only a component of the context that surrounds health care but also a substantial opportunity to drive deliberate change through its use as an implementation strategy.

Recent efforts to describe and classify implementation strategies (Powell et al., 2012; Powell et al., 2015) have been helpful in identifying the scope to which practice change can be impacted and, relevant to the discussion in this chapter, how policies at different levels can support or hinder the implementation of new health interventions. For example, policies within a hospital can promote or inhibit the delivery of evidence-based health interventions; reimbursement policy can similarly influence whether health interventions can be accessed by patients; and policies governing the health care workforce can determine the availability of health care workers to deliver care. Powell et al. (2012) identified sixty-eight discrete implementation strategies (expanded to seventy-three in Powell et al., (2015)), categorized into six different groups (Powell et al., 2012). One of those groups is a set of strategies that are applied in the policy context, referring primarily to strategies that impact provider credentialing and legal exposure, but among the other five categories (plan, educate, finance, restructure, and manage quality), there are a host of ways in which these strategies can be enacted through policy change.

One prime example is that of changing financing policy to support the uptake of evidence-based interventions. The Depression Improvement across Minnesota—Offering a New Direction (DIAMOND) project was an effort in the state of Minnesota to improve the provision of evidence-based depression care management in primary care (Solberg et al., 2013). Care management for depression has been tested in over 40 trials (Gilbody et al., 2006) but lagged in implementation because elements of the chronic disease management model (care management phone calls, and team meetings) were not reimbursable through typically fee-for-service payments. In 2006, the major health plans in the state came together to change the way in which reimbursement would occur, shifting from fee-for-service to a monthly case rate that would be designed to cover previously sunk costs for delivering depression care. As a result of this improved reimbursement, in conjunction with academic detailing processes at participating practices, DIAMOND saw increased use of evidence-based depression care (Solberg et al., 2013). This "policy activity as implementation strategy" was later expanded to cover other chronic diseases through a demonstration project supported by the Center for Medicare and Medicaid Services (Rossom et al., 2017).

In the State of Oregon, during the 2000s, the state developed and implemented policy that required 75 percent of all addiction and mental health services to meet the "evidence-based practice" definition: "programs or practices that effectively integrate the best research evidence with clinical expertise, cultural competence and the values of the persons receiving the services" (State of Oregon, 2007). While these policies targeted overall provision of care rather than a specific evidence-based practice, they were in the service of increasing the implementation of a set of mental health and substance-abuse interventions supported by scientific evidence. Again, we see the policy activity in the role of driving health care change proactively compared to a more traditional view as a backdrop to health and health care.

Policies related to the health care workforce can also influence efforts to implement high-quality care. For example, changes to requirements in provider training, credentialing, and who is eligible to deliver different health care services can all influence uptake and sustainment of evidence-based practices. Policies governing the use of medications and other interventions (i.e., coverage determinations by the US Food and Drug Administration, state Medicaid, and private insurance medication formularies) will similarly influence the accessibility of interventions. For example, because of a shortage of psychiatrists in certain areas, some states in the USA allowed psychologists without a medical degree to prescribe psychotropic medications (McGrath & Moore, 2010), while other states licensed people with mental illness or substance-use disorders to be reimbursed for providing support services as a Certified Peer Specialist (West, 2011).

Globally, health-related commerce (e.g., rules governing the sale of tobacco, alcohol, and other substances) also plays a major role in determining the level of use within the population and, indeed, the likely impact on the population's health. A recent National Cancer Institute monograph on the Economics of Tobacco, for example, stressed the many policy drivers in the tobacco space that affect the retail environment, eligibility to purchase, and connectedness to addiction services within the point of sale. All of these will serve as strategies toward promoting (or potentially inhibiting) the uptake of various interventions, and for policy makers to consider how these tools may promote population health and health care (National Cancer Institute, 2016).

Operationalizing Policy in the Context of Research

Teasing apart the specific measures related to policy is a complicated task. For the research process, this includes identifying a common lexicon for both policy development and policy outcomes. For the former, several groups have attempted to construct databases to support policy research. The Family Foundation, for example, tracks health policy across a number of domains, along with data on the impact of those policies on access, cost, quality, and disparities in care (Kaiser Family Foundation, n.d.). The National Institutes of Health, in turn, supported the construction of a State Health Practice Database for Research (SHPDR), which permits comparison at the state level of over a hundred indicators related to state-level policies and practice (Chambers & Rupp, 2015; State Health Practice Database for Research, n.d.). Organizational Research Services was commissioned by the Annie E. Casey Foundation to create A Guide to Measuring Advocacy and Policy, to describe outcomes related to policy and advocacy work. Six key categories related to outcomes were identified, including shifts in social norms, strengthened organizational capacity, strengthened alliances, strengthened base of support, improved policies, and changes in impact (Annie E. Casey Foundation, n.d.). These efforts are important to improve the quality of research studies on health policies, ensuring that sufficient tools are available to maximize the learning from these policy experiments. However, these valuable efforts may ignore some of the important features of the policy context that were described earlier in this chapter. The degree to which these and other guides recognize the ongoing change to policies in different jurisdictions, and the need to consistently monitor and reflect that change, will directly affect the validity of the research that is conducted.

Beyond specific resources, there is a range of considerations in terms of the research design and methods to be used. For studying context, particularly in the light of ongoing change and uncertainty, some researchers have turned to ethnographic methods to ensure a depth of understanding of the characteristics of the environment as it shifts over time. Several investigators have pioneered the use of rapid ethnographic methods (Green et al., 2015; Balasubramanian et al., 2015) to assess primary care and other environments, which could be applicable to policy research. Still others have argued for a blend of qualitative and quantitative approaches, typically referred to as mixed methods, which allow both breadth and depth of information related to context (Palinkas et al., 2011).

For those studies that intend to generate information on policies as they are implemented, there is a range of approaches that permit comparisons in situations where randomization to policy condition (e.g., the Oregon Health Insurance Experiment) may be possible, or where quasi-experimental or other designs may be more feasible. These multiple options each have strengths and weaknesses, helpfully laid out in a recent paper by Hendricks Brown and colleagues (2017), and all represent opportunities to consider the temporal nature of policy, its variability across sites, and its impact on the pursuit of health and the provision of health care.

Opportunities for Future Research and Practice

With the tremendous complexities laid out in the policy context surrounding the delivery and receipt of health and health care services lie significant opportunities for researchers, practitioners, and policy makers alike to advance upon what is already known and use that knowledge to drive better policy decision-making. As several articles have pointed out, population health may benefit greatly where evidence-based policy is a reality (Black, 2001; Baicker & Chandra, 2017). Toward that end, there are a few key recommendations to enhance research and practice in this space.

Expansion of Common Measures of Context for Implementation

One significant limitation in both understanding the policy context and shaping it toward optimal health outcomes is the variation within which policy activities are measured. Several recent efforts (Rabin et al., 2016) have attempted to pull together available measures and assess their quality for use in research and practice. As progress is being made, coordination, operationalization, and utilization of common measures to assess policy activities across systems will be important. The SHPDR mentioned above is a start for states, but is quite modest in its scope, as well as limited in its ability to capture local culture, climate, and structures. These will be vital for us to unpack the impact of policies on health outcomes across time and space. Given the recognition of the complex and dynamic policy environment, measuring these key variables over time and in multiple settings will greatly enhance our ability to address the correlations between policy activities, health and health care actions, and the resulting individual and population health outcomes. If we do not use shared measures (and use them consistently over time), our ability to capture the dynamism and multiple levels of policy will be severely limited.

Promoting Ongoing Learning from Policy Efforts

Consistent with the notion of a learning health care system (National Academies, 2012.), our understanding of the policy context will improve greatly where there is an expectation that, with each policy activity, simultaneous evaluation efforts are launched to best learn from each experience. This concept has been referenced in building improvements in behavioral health care (Stein, Adams, & Chambers, 2016), in understanding intervention adaptation (Chambers & Norton, 2016), and in learning from policy experiments relevant to obesity (Ackermann et al., 2015), but it could be expanded to consider the health policy environment across multiple countries. Using the example of smoke-free laws differing across jurisdictions, we currently lack the ability to detect the relative benefit of policy efforts over time to impact smoking rates. Where evaluation is included to discover the impact of these natural experiments, we gain a nuanced understanding of the impact of policy on health, and fuel future experiments that build on lessons learned about context.

Developing, Expanding, and Testing Conceptual Models to Support Evidence-Based Health Policy

As mentioned earlier in this chapter, implementation scientists have developed a large number of conceptual models intended to explain concepts affecting the uptake, implementation, and sustainability of evidence-based practice. In a 2012 review of sixty-one of these models (Tabak et al., 2012), only eight of the models were found to be focused on the policy context, and within this subset, the prevailing view is of policy as a set of current conditions through which health and health care activities operate. There may be some benefit in developing new models that focus on policy dynamism, the expansion of existing models to include the fluid, multilevel policy environment, and testing of existing models to determine how well they represent policy activities over time and their role in supporting health and health care. In addition, it may be helpful to look back to the more fundamental models of strategic change, such as that by Pettigrew, Ferlie, and McKee (1992), as they recognize the complex interplay between the content of change (e.g., the specific policy being enacted), the context in which that change is set, and the complex, multistage process through which change occurs.

Coda: Toward Integration

The goal of this chapter has been to travel briskly through the health policy context, both in its influence on health care overall and in the specific use of policy to drive improvements in the implementation of evidence-based interventions. While the exercise has posited the ability to separate policy activities from other elements of context, the reality is that these elements are not so easily severable. Indeed, the specific characteristics laid out in the preceding pages apply as much to other aspects of context as they do to policy. The ultimate hope from this chapter is that readers see the need to include policy where they may not have done before—not as a separate entity but in concert with other aspects of context. So much of access, cost, quality, and outcomes of care can be influenced by policies at multiple levels and in multiple categories, but more can be gained when policy is understood as a component of a larger picture, in which policy creation and implementation transpires in dynamic, multilevel processes. Ultimately, health and health care are impacted by many policies that affect a range of societal functions, and the extent to which health can be considered in all policies, population benefits should follow.

References

Aarons, G. A., Hurlburt, M., & Horwitz, S. M. (2011). Advancing a conceptual model of evidence-based practice implementation in public service sectors. *Administration and Policy in Mental Health, 38*(1), 4–23.

Ackermann, R. T., et al (2015). Evaluating diabetes health policies using natural experiments: The natural experiments for translation in diabetes study. *American Journal of Preventive Medicine, 48*(6), 747–54.

American College of Health Executives. (n.d.). *Introduction to health policy.* https://www.ache.org/learning-center/publications/books/2374 (Accessed 18 January 2018).

Annie E. Casey Foundation. (n.d.). *A guide to measuring advocacy and policy.* http://www.aecf.org/resources/a-guide-to-measuring-advocacy-and-policy/ (Accessed 18 January 2018).

Baicker, K. & Chandra, A. (2017). Evidence-based health policy. *New England Journal of Medicine, 377*(25), 2413–15.

Balasubramanian, B. A., et al. (2015). Learning evaluation: Blending quality improvement and implementation research methods to study healthcare innovations. *Implementation Science, 10,* 31.

Black, N. (2001). Evidence based policy: Proceed with care. *BMJ, 323,* 275–8.

Chambers, D. A. & Norton, W. E. (2016). The adaptome: Advancing the science of intervention adaptation. *American Journal of Preventive Medicine, 30*(16), 181–7.

Chambers, D. A. & Rupp, A. (2015). Sharing state mental health data for research: Building toward ongoing learning in mental health care systems. *Administration and Policy in Mental Health & Mental Health Services Research, 42*(5), 586–7.

Chapman, S. & Freeman. B. (2018). Markers of the denormalisation of smoking and the tobacco industry. *Tobacco Control, 17,* 25–31.

Damschroder, L., et al (2009). Fostering implementation of health services research findings into practice: A consolidated framework for advancing implementation science. *Implementation Science, 4,* 50.

Frank, R. G., Beronio, K., & Glied, S. A. (2014). Behavioral health parity and the affordable care act. *Journal of Social Work in Disability & Rehabilitation, 13*(1–2), 31–43.

Gangarosa, E. J., et al. (2006). Impact of anti-vaccine movements on pertussis control: The untold story. *The Lancet, 351*(9099), 356–61.

Gilbody, S., P. et al (2006). Collaborative care for depression: A cumulative meta-analysis and review of longer-term outcomes. *Archives of Internal Medicine, 166*(21), 2314–21.

Glasgow, R. E., Vinson, C., Chambers, D., Khoury, M. J., Kaplan, R. M., & Hunter, C. (2012). National Institutes of Health approaches to dissemination and implementation science: Current and future directions. *American Journal of Public Health, 102*(7), 1274–81.

Green, C. A., et al. (2015). Approaches to mixed methods dissemination and implementation research: methods, strengths, caveats, and opportunities. *Administration and Policy in Mental Health, 42*(5), 508–23.

Health Affairs. (n.d.). *Health policy brief: Mental health parity.* https://www.healthaffairs.org/do/10.1377/hblog20151113.051773/full/ (Accessed 18 January 2018).

Hendricks Brown, C., et al. (2017). An overview of research and evaluation designs for dissemination and implementation. *Annual Review of Public Health, 38*(1), 1–22.

Housing and Urban Development. (n.d.). Implementing HUD's Smoke-Free Policy in Public Housing Guidebook. https://www.hud.gov/sites/documents/smokefree_guidebk.pdf (Accessed 18 January 2018).

King, B. A., et al. (2010). Prevalence and predictors of smoke-free policy implementation and support among owners and managers of multiunit housing. *Nicotine & Tobacco Research, 12*(2), 159–63.

McGrath, R. E. & Moore, B. A. (eds.). (2010). *Pharmacotherapy for psychologists: Prescribing and collaborative roles.* Washington, DC: American Psychological Association.

Mitchell, S. A., Fisher, C. A., Hastings, C. E., Silverman, L. B., & Wallen, G. R. (2010). A thematic analysis of theoretical models for translational science in nursing: Mapping the field. *Nursing Outlook, 58*(6), 287–300.

Nakamura, R. T. (1987). The textbook policy process and implementation research. *Review of Policy Research, 7*(1), 142–54.

National Academies. (2012). Best care at lower cost: The path to continuously learning health care in America. Committee on the Learning Health Care System in America, Institute of Medicine. http://www.nationalacademies.org/hmd/Reports/2012/Best-Care-at-Lower-Cost-The-Path-to-Continuously-Learning-Health-Care-in-America.aspx (Accessed 18 January 2018).

National Cancer Institute. (2016). *Monograph 21: The economics of tobacco control.* https://cancercontrol.cancer.gov/brp/tcrb/monographs/21/index.html (Accessed 18 January 2018).

Neta, G., et al. (2015). Implementation science in cancer prevention and control: A decade of grant funding by the National Cancer Institute and Future Directions. *Implementation Science, 10*, 4.

Nilsen, P. (2015). Making sense of implementation theories, models and frameworks. *Implementation Science, 10*, 53.

Palinkas, L. A., et al. (2011). Mixed method designs in implementation research. *Administration and Policy in Mental Health, 38*(1), 44–53.

Pettigrew, A. M., Ferlie, E., & McKee, L. (1992). *Shaping strategic change.* London: Sage

Plotkin, S., Gerber, J. S., and Offit P. A. (2009). Vaccines and autism: A tale of shifting hypotheses. *Clinical Infectious Diseases, 48*(4), 456–61.

Powell, B. J., et al. (2012). A compilation of strategies for implementing clinical innovations in health and mental health. *Medical Care Research and Review, 69*(2), 123–57.

Powell, B. J., et al. (2015). A refined compilation of implementation strategies: Results from the Expert Recommendations for Implementing Change (ERIC) project. *Implementation Science, 10*(1), 21.

Propper, C., & Söderlund, N. (1998). Competition in the NHS internal market: An overview of its effects on hospital prices and costs. *Health Economics, 7*(3), 187–97.

Public Health Institute. (n.d.). *Health in all policies: A guide for state and local governments.* http://www.phi.org/uploads/files/Health_in_All_Policies-A_Guide_for_State_and_Local_Governments.pdf (Accessed 18 January 2018).

Rabin, B. A., et al. (2016). Measurement resources for dissemination and implementation research in health. *Implementation Science, 11,* 42.

Rogers, E. M. (1995). *Diffusion of innovations.* (4th ed.). New York: The Free Press; 1995.

Rossom, R. C., et al. (2017). Impact of a national collaborative care initiative for patients with depression and diabetes or cardiovascular disease. *General Hospital Psychiatry,* (16)30, 165–744, 77–85.

Social-Ecological Model. (2015). https://health.gov/dietaryguidelines/2015/guidelines/chapter-3/social-ecological-model/ (Accessed 18 January 2018).

Solberg, L. I., et al. (2013). The DIAMOND Initiative: Implementing collaborative care for depression in 75 primary care clinics. *Implementation Science, 8,* 155.

State Health Practice Database for Research. (n.d.). http://www.shpdr.org (Accessed 18 January 2018).

State of Oregon. (2007). Oregon State Authority Addiction and Mental Health Services. http://www.oregon.gov/OHA/HSD/AMH/Pages/EBP.aspx (Accessed on 18 January 2018).

Stein, B. D., Adams, A. S., & Chambers, D. A. (2016). A learning behavioral health care system: Opportunities to enhance research. *Psychiatric Services, 67*(9), 1019–22.

Tabak, R. G., et al. (2012). Bridging research and practice: Models for dissemination and implementation research. *American Journal of Preventive Medicine, 43*(3), 337–50.

Taplin, S. H. & Rodgers. A. B. (2010). Toward improving the quality of cancer care: Addressing the interfaces of primary and oncology-related subspecialty care. *Journal of the National Cancer Institute Mongraphs, 40,* 3–10.

West, C. (2011). Powerful choices: Peer support and individualized medication self-determination. *Schizophrenia Bulletin, 37*(3), 445–50.

Wikipedia. (n.d.) *Health policy.* https://en.wikipedia.org/wiki/Health_policy (Accessed 18 January 2018).

6

Bringing the Hospital Back In

Implications for Studying Organizations

Kjell Tryggestad, Chris Harty, and Peter Holm Jacobsen

Introduction

According to Latour (2008), as a matter of concern, the building is a project that is always prone to redesign. To take this approach, however, is difficult because it challenges modernist linear approaches to innovation as a final rather than an ongoing accomplishment and concern: "What is needed instead [of modernism] are tools that capture what have always been the hidden practices of modernist innovations: objects have always been projects; matters of facts have always been matters of concern" (Latour, 2008 p. 9).

In actor-network theory (ANT), the building that as object or otherwise, makes a difference to the ways in which people interact and organize their work is considered an actor or *actant*. It is a novel conceptualization of who—or what—the actor and the performer of an action are because it considers the actor that performs an act to be a composite entity consisting of both humans and non-humans such as the building. The notion of an actant has its origin in semiotics, and it is used in ANT to reconceptualize context as relational, dynamic, and heterogeneous (because it consists of both human and non-human interaction). According to ANT, context is not independent of actors' interactions, as often portrayed in structuralist and deterministic approaches, but rather it is integral to the process of association that develops, sustains, and transforms actor-networks (Akrich et al., 2002). An important dynamic aspect of an ANT analysis of context is to follow the use and circulation of textual–visual devices (inscriptions), such as a design drawing of a building (Latour, 1986). This allows the researcher to follow the actors and the chain of associations that eventually translate into a building and a new context of work for the users inscribed into its design.

In the early design phases, the hospital building is uncertain, fluid, and unresolved. It has yet to gain the stable, object-like matter-of-fact qualities of an accomplished building made of concrete, steel, glass, and wood. However, as a project, the building is always present in the form of many kinds of visualizations projecting its future. These visualizations act as the context within which design work on the new hospital building *and* the health care organization are negotiated and developed, where actors are employed, and where new design visualizations are produced and circulated. In brief, then, ANT is a semiotics extended to things, as well as a method of tracing the movement from signs/inscriptions to things and back again (but see also Latour, 1996, 2008). ANT is a socio-technical approach that we propose can provide a more profound understanding of how different spaces are visualized, and how they eventually connect or co-exist separately, and with what implications for its inscribed future users and prospective real users in flesh. This chapter makes two related contributions, the first theoretical, and the second more practical: (1) an approach studying the hospital building as both context and object that makes it possible to consider in a substantive way how buildings matter for organizational performance and the provision of health care. We summarize this (largely) theoretical contribution as "bringing the hospital back in" to organization and management studies in general, and health care studies in particular; (2) the practical contribution flows from bringing the hospital back in. Recognizing the significance of built spaces for clinical hospital practice requires the ability of present and prospective users to step back from experiences and everyday routines at the existing hospital, and instead, imagine a future scenario in different, not yet built, hospital spaces.

Such imagination and projections of future workspaces are integral to the project (Kreiner, 2014) and management. As we shall show below, it is also tied up in very practical devices such as physical scale models of a future patient room, and digital and immersive projections of how such a patient room is linked to adjacent rooms and spaces in the future hospital. Then there is "paper work" (Whyte et al., 2017), such as architectural drawings and design sketches, but also numbers on spreadsheets, such as budget estimations and cost projections of the built hospital. The devices inscribe human bodies into hospital spaces such as the patient room with its patients, clinical professionals, equipment, and furniture. Together, these many different projection devices and methods help in the practical work of "bringing the hospital back in." Yet, as we shall also show, these devices and methods do not only co-exist independently of each other to represent different aspects of a given context, but can also be active in shaping that context as they are tensioned against each other, perhaps most notably when negotiating the design and the economy (budget) of the future hospital. Fundamental to these negotiations—what is at stake—is not only the aesthetic design qualities of the future hospital, but its very function, organization, and the performance of clinical work. Thus at the core of these negotiations are the relations between the building project and construction management organization, and the client and health care organization that will use and operate the new hospital building. Relations are tensioned against each other, tested, and negotiated, while nobody knows for sure what the outcome will be for the building as project, object, and context for clinical work. But, then again, our claim is that it does matter a great deal for clinical work practices if the outcome of that process and trial is a building and physical context that can support rather than obstruct this important work.

We draw on ethnographical studies of two large public hospital-building projects that are part of a current Danish health care reform and construction program, with the aim of providing better and more efficient public health care. The hospital design and building project, therefore, embodies a host of national and regional policy requirements for, and visions relating to, the organization and provision of health care. Based on the empirical studies, we show how these innovative design requirements are negotiated, and materialize as visualizations of the physical building. Also, how these design visualizations, in turn, are active in shaping the organization and provision of health care services—that is, the building as both object and context of health care work.

The remaining parts of the chapter are organized as follows. First, we review some early and current research, mainly from management and organization studies pertaining to the physical organization of work. Next, we address two empirical vignettes that focus on the methods and devices used to design the physical workspaces for Danish hospitals. Finally, we return to our main argument about "bringing the hospital back in" and conclude by considering some further theoretical and practical-methodological implications for the design of both hospital buildings and the clinical organization of health care.

"Bringing the Hospital Back In"

Scholars of management and organization have recognized for some time that the physical organization of work is important in shaping its practices and performance (see Bresnen & Harty, 2010 for a review). The factory floor has been an important point of reference in much work in the sociology of organizations. There is a whole body of labor-process theory that has revealed the finer details of how human and machine can, in different design configurations, work together on the factory floor, and with what implications for productivity, quality, motivation, skills, rewards, power, autonomy, and self-determination. Yet very few studies have also considered the interconnectedness of workspaces. It is as if what matters most is the interface between humans and particular tools or manufacturing machines, while the physical spaces that encapsulate them are secondary or taken for granted. The "big machine" that houses them, powers them, and keeps them all warm and close to each other—or cold and separate, if that is the case—is left out of "the picture." This is why we started this chapter by placing a particular emphasis on this notion of "bringing the hospital back in" as a way of studying context. We most certainly believe that it does matter a great deal to the quality of the work environment and the quality of health and care how the hospital's physical spaces are designed, organized, and dimensioned. We also believe that these matters are sufficiently important to be described in more detail. The case vignettes appearing below are included for this purpose.

The relationship between space and practice is the subject of a long-standing debate within sociology and organization studies, from the early studies of the Chicago School of Urban Sociology in the 1920s and 1930s, through the links between social inequalities and spatial distribution of resources to general contemporary debates over shifts to late/postmodern society (e.g., Harvey, 1989). In organization studies, some have recognized physical spatial structures such as offices and buildings as organizational symbols (Hatch, 1990) and expressions of power structures (Pfeffer, 1981), as potential resources (Berg & Kreiner, 1990) and as structures with materially mediated meaning (Tryggestad & Georg, 2011). Marrewijk and Yanow (2010) note a spatial turn in organization studies. Kornberger and Clegg (2004) argue that a closer look at classics of organization and management theory, such as the Hawthorne experiments, Weber and Taylor demonstrate space as an important but implicit concern: "within scientific management what did Taylor do other than reorganize the spatial arrangement of the entire organization by dividing space into individual cells, so that every single activity had to take place within its own space (cell), separated from the others?" (p. 1096).

Research that focuses on the production of physical space in relation to hospitals shows that space matters, and can both facilitate and disrupt collaboration across organizational and professional boundaries (Davies & Harty 2013; Harty & Tryggestad 2015; Harty et al., 2015a, 2015b). Design processes are not only implicated in the production of buildings and physical spaces, but are also processes that can afford possibilities for new organizational spaces, places, practices, and performances (Kreiner, 2010). Organizational processes are at the same time spatial ones, and vice versa (O'Toole & Were, 2008). An extensive literature review of the impact of the built space within hospitals found evidence that the design of rooms and buildings is important in providing a physical environment for the "healing hospital" (Frandsen et al., 2009). Yet, the link between the processes of designing and visualizing physical spaces and organizational change processes are undertheorized (Ewenstein & Whyte, 2009; Meyer et al., 2013) and not well understood (Stang Våland & Georg, 2014). Matters of concerns and problematization of objects can also produce the context (Tryggestad & Georg, 2011 p. 185). With an ANT approach, we shall bring materiality and the building into the study of context in studies of organizations. Below we shall discuss the implications of bringing the hospital back in for research into context—in this case, the context of hospital health care.

Building Hospitals in the Danish Health Care Program: Two Case Vignettes

The two case vignettes show the interplay and emerging tensions between different inscriptions in use, such as design visualizations and budgets, with respect to particular health care spaces and functions. Vignette 1 focuses specifically on patient room size, and Vignette 2 focuses on hospital kitchen and hospital overall size and design solutions.

In researching these vignettes we used several methods, including digital immersive environments; following design and construction management practices in situ—in project management offices and meetings, in architectural competitions, and in industry conferences and design mock-up experiments (both physical and immersive); document studies, including some thousand pages of project documentation (both in digital and paper format); and short movies. We illustrate how to "bring the hospital back in" by showing how the visualizations of different yet connected spaces, and the development of the functions and conditions for future clinical practice is related to a number of emerging concerns in the design and construction of the new hospitals, such as size of rooms, as well as the hospitals themselves and their clinical functions, organizational performance, and economy.

The Danish state has established a program ("Kvalitetsfonden") with approximately 42 billion Danish Krone (DKK) dedicated to funding hospital construction projects within the public health care sector and regions. It is one of the largest-ever societal infrastructure investments in Denmark. Currently, there are some sixteen hospitals on the drawing board or under construction within the program. The projects are of different types, ranging from mega projects such as the large "greenfield" investments in new "super hospitals" in the major cities and regions in Denmark, with the largest projects having a budget of around of 6.5 billion DKK, to the upgrading of existing hospitals. Each hospital project within the program must pass the state's screening body, the "Expert Panel." It is an iterative process through which the region's original project proposals are evaluated and eventually refined before dedicated funds are allocated to a hospital construction project.

Vignette 1: Patient Room Size

In their report, the Expert Panel (2008) considered the design of the single-bed patient room in terms of how large it should be.[1] The room should not be too large because that would incur unnecessary costs to the individual hospital construction budget, as well as to the future hospital facility and operating budget. The Expert Panel's future budget concerns are further translated into an estimation of the appropriate size for the single-bed room: 33 to 35 square meters is considered appropriate for all hospitals and construction projects in the program. The economic calculations of the costs for building larger and smaller patient rooms and the two cost budgets (for the construction project and the hospital in operation, respectively) help the Expert Panel to explicate a cost-efficient hospital design and to conclude with a standard for its appropriate size. The question and concern about the appropriate design and size is thus resolved through the two budgets and the economic calculations. However, as we shall explain below, this design standard, which implies a set of related concerns, such as the size of the single-bed patient room and its construction and operating costs, are only resolved temporary by the Expert Panel's calculations, design standard, and concluding report.

In the wake of the Expert Panel's design standard, new questions, issues, and concerns emerged among key stakeholders and project owners in the Danish regions. To attain a better grasp of the clinical and economic implications related to the design standard, the project team in the Capital Region decided to establish their own inquiry. They used a comparative case method that included empirical inquiries about its own hospitals, as well as empirical material from existing hospital designs in Denmark and abroad, including making visits to Norwegian hospitals under construction. In this way, the project team could benchmark the new and smaller design standard proposed by the Expert Panel with a broad range of examples and experiences from hospital designs in use or under construction. The inquiry showed that, for the majority of the hospitals and projects considered, room sizes were larger than those suggested by the Expert Panel, and closer to 40 square meters. In addition, the inquiry included a prognosis concerning the size of future patients' bodies. The average size of patients' bodies was expected to increase quite significantly, with further possible design implications concerning the size of the patient's room. In the resulting report (Danske Regioner, 2009), new concerns were raised that challenged the design standard set out by the

Expert Panel. The team and region argued against the standard size and assumptions, on the basis that each hospital construction project is unique and located in a unique setting in terms of population size and demographic characteristics, such as age, gender, and regional socioeconomic conditions. In addition, each hospital construction project can also develop unique design solutions for all other rooms and functions, either from scratch—as in a new-build greenfield hospital construction project, or in conjunction with already existing hospital buildings if the project also includes the renovation of these. Such demographic, geographic, and location-specific contextual variables are important to consider for each hospital and construction project before deciding on a specific room size. Last but not least, the project team also argued that the Expert Panel's design standard could imply an increased risk for patients' health and safety. The team concluded their inquiry by deciding in favor of a larger room size than the standard set out by the Expert Panel. The Capital Region is also willing to accept higher costs for their hospital construction projects and operations in order to secure the design for future patients.

When project management at Region South learned about the Expert Panel's 33-to-35- square-meter design standard, new uncertainties emerged. The design standard would perhaps be economically sustainable, as the Expert Panel had argued. But, would it also be clinically sustainable, to provide quality health care? To deal with the question about clinical sustainability, project management at Region South decided to contract the task and inquiry to a nearby design laboratory, the Center for User Driven Innovation. The laboratory consisted of clinical professionals from health care with training in ethnographical methods and action research. The laboratory approached the task by first building a full-scale physical mock-up of a patient room according to the design standard and size set out by the Expert Panel. The room was further equipped with a standard hospital bed and furniture, medical equipment, and a living body in the form of a person playing the role of patient. A number of other people played the roles of nurses and doctors. Before the simulation, all the people in the room were given a script that included the simulation of a heart attack, along with immediate treatment on site. The simulation was filmed and further documented with photographs and feedback from those involved. A report concluded the simulation (Center for Brugerfokuseret Innovation, 2010).

The simulation revealed the interactions between bodies and among bodies, equipment, and furniture when in motion during the "heart attack" and its treatment. The main conclusion from the report concerned the context of treatment: if the bodies of the patient or other people in the room are larger than average, then the Expert Panel's design standard might hamper swift and adequate treatment. This is especially so in acute situations such as heart attacks, in which medical equipment must be mobilized together with a number of medical professionals. Extra time will be required for the logistics because of the limited space.

The extra time required for the logistics could, in turn, hamper a swift and efficient treatment and pose an additional risk to the patient's health and safety. Limits of space thus translate into a concern about time, notably the swift and adequate timing of treatment. Questions of space and room size raise new concerns about time, and the health and safety of patients, but also about the economy of the room size. The report points out that it might be possible to accommodate concerns for the patient's health and safety within the limited space implied by the Expert Panel's design standard. But it would require additional capital investment in new technological solutions, such as logistical robots and the "intelligent bed." While the Expert Panel based its design standard on the assumption that smaller rooms are cheaper to construct and operate, the inquiries conducted by the Danish regions question that assumption for being too simple. It appears that space and patient room size is more than simple Euclidian space, because it can be connected to so many different concerns, situations, and spaces. In an acute treatment situation, for example, room size is connected to time, logistics, and interaction between things and bodies of different sizes, technological solutions, and equipment in the patient room and in other rooms and hospital spaces, from which additional clinical staff and equipment are flowing. Paradoxically, a design standard with a smaller room size, while presumably being cheaper to construct, can also become more costly to operate in terms of health and safety and/or mitigating investments in advanced technology. What appears to be economically sustainable in a short-term perspective—a perspective and simplified context defined and sustained by the "quality program" construction budget inscription—is tensioned against a series of inscriptions, reports, and mock-up trials, which together, consider the new future hospitals' clinical sustainability in the long term. The visual devices in circulation are integral to the ongoing negotiations over what the hospital building can and cannot do economically and clinically. The context of the future hospital building is negotiated and defined through these circulating devices, and it does matter whether the building is contextualized and simplified as an individual budget item in a large 42 billion DKK building program and/or further recontextualized as part of a mock-up simulation of acute treatment in a single-patient room. The latter context can potentially challenge the economic sustainability of the 42 billion DKK budget sum for the national building program because in each hospital's many single-bed patient rooms, clinical matters of concern are always considered important, not least if there is not enough space to provide patients with quality health care in acute situations.

Kjell Tryggestad, Chris Harty, and Peter Holm Jacobsen

Vignette 2: Kitchen and Hospital Overall Size and Design Solution

Vignette 2 is about the development of the physical design of New North Zealand Hospital (NHN).[2] NHN is a greenfield hospital with a catchment area of 310,000 people, twenty-four medical specialties, 4,000 employees, and 500,000 outpatients per year. Constructing this new hospital involves the transfer of staff from three existing hospitals to a new physical work context. The three existing hospitals are due for closure when the new hospital comes into operation (in 2020–2021). This, in turn, implies a spatial-geographical centralization of regional health care to a single facility. We illustrate how visual representations of space in terms of physical infrastructure (functions, size, and so on), professionals' organizational workspaces (for clinical work), and budget are connected and negotiated, and how the physical design of health care has changed over time across the project. We illustrate how "bringing the hospital back in" is accomplished through the mobilization and use of different forms of visualization that connect the design of physical workspaces and clinical functions in ways that affect future health care practices. These different forms of visualization, in turn, are not only representing the future hospital, but are also connected to the recent past and the present as they generate a number of emerging concerns vis-à-vis key stakeholders such as the client organization about the design and construction of the new hospital.

In 2014, Capital Region, the client organization at NHN and the project organization ran an architectural competition to develop a design proposal for the new hospital. Before that, they had been working for 4 years, together with patients, relatives, and clinical staff at the existing hospitals, to develop visions for the new hospital. The title of the competition was "This Is It – Your Blank Canvas," indicating that the design teams had to think in innovative ways when developing their design proposals (Region Hovedstaden, 2013a). The resulting ambition of the brief was high, and the title of the evaluation report was "Setting New Standards" in Sustainable Design and Delivery of Public Health Care (Region Hovedstaden, 2013b). However, as we shall show below, there are as many ways to develop the future hospital as there are methods used to visualize how it will look, how large it will be, what it will cost, and what functions it will have.

The selected design for the hospital is novel when considered in relation to known hospital designs. It is "a pavilion in the woods," with a large roof garden. The jury board appreciates this architectural integration of nature into a sustainable healing hospital concept. Flexibility of future work practices is also integrated into the design. The hospital building's envelope has a flexible "snake structure" that is a physical materialization of the one of the design principles "user right – not ownership" formulated in the competition brief. The hospital's design and functions, and staff offices, research activities, and administration, are designed as "shared space," to facilitate flexibility for future, yet unknown uses. In addition, the selected design solution also promises to deliver on a general design requirement pertaining to all new hospital constructions within the Danish hospital construction program: that is, a hospital that is not only sustainable in providing a healing architecture but also economically sustainable by being 8 percent more cost effective than a baseline hospital currently in operation. The hospital's patient rooms are also organized with a similar flexible structure, and the different clinical specialties share patient rooms according to how many patients they have at any particular time. The design implies, or has embedded within it, new organizational workspaces for clinical staff.

After the architectural competition ended, we observed how the design team and the project organization worked on developing methods to communicate and visualize the new spatial-organizational principles that would change the clinical staff's work conditions. They were aware that staff might react negatively because the professionally "owned" territories and traditional ways of working would change so drastically. Because of this, the design team and the members of the project organization decided to leave architectural drawings and visualizations out of the first phase of the user-involvement process. Instead, they decided to start this phase of user involvement by discussing aspects closer to their clinical practice, such as how the clinical staff move around in the rooms, and the ways in which they have to work within that physical space. Later in the design process, in 2017, visualizations were being used more actively to prepare the clinical staff for the new work conditions by using virtual reality technologies.[3] In this way, visualizations were being used to demonstrate what it will be like to work in the new hospital.

Before the architectural competition, and in the 3 years that followed it, the project underwent a number of contradictory challenges and negotiations related to its spatial design principles. In this project, the overall size of the hospital started out at 161,000 square meters (in 2012), but was downsized to 136,000 square meters when the design competition was initiated (2014), and then a further downsizing took place soon after that, to secure the robustness of the budget frame, resulting in a new overall size of 122,000 square meters. The process of downsizing continued in the years that followed, and by February 2017, the overall size had shrunk to 112,500 square meters. The overall budget cost (3.8 billion DKK) was maintained throughout this period. The external appearance does not change much either, but the inside configuration does: it shrinks; the kitchen goes out, then comes back again, and then out—will the kitchen perhaps come in again? It depends on many things, and money seems to be the most important thing. It is not because there is no money. It is because the money is "set in stone," in the form of a budget that appears to be impossible to change. It even forbids any extra funding by the state or the regions, although the latter consider this a viable option, and they were both willing and able to implement the project if the state would approve it. The state did not approve that extra funding by the regions, however.

A budget for one hospital-building project within the larger budget for the national hospital-building program is not to be interfered with. The Ministry of Finance (MoF) was very concerned to maintain the budget sum for each individual hospital project because otherwise the total budget sum for the whole program and reform would not add up. This explains why the hospital spaces shrink, and the kitchen keeps being pushed to the outside of the hospital envelope. Project management and the client organization know that living in a house without a kitchen is less practical than living in a house with one. In addition, for this building project, food is considered a vital part of the concept of a "healing hospital"; three times this argument has pushed the kitchen back into the hospital envelope. What matters most—the MoF's budget discipline or the quality and service implied by the concept of a "healing hospital"? Amid these prolonged negotiations, nobody really knows the answer.

To sum up the two case vignettes, built spaces also seem to suggest a tension between shorter and longer time horizons. In the short term, the building needs time for its design and construction, and in the longer term—when it is in use—the spaces can facilitate or hamper vital workflows, logistics, and service provisions such as the acute treatment of a heart attack and the regular and timely preparation and delivery of healthy food. These are temporal-spatial events because they involve the more or less timely movement of people, their bodies, and equipment, within and across rooms and built spaces. The multiple time requirements and implications of built spaces are also a source of ongoing controversy and negotiation, often conflicting with short- and long-term budget concerns. But then again, the project budget for the building construction and the operating budget for the hospital in use are just two inscriptions and textual–visual devices that "bring the hospital back in" as both object and project, both as matters of fact and of concern. In addition, there are the mock-up simulations and design drawings that help in visualizing the building as a physical object and a context for health care work. It is through this cascade of visual displays that the building is negotiated and progressively translated into the final design. By following these visual traces and trials, we can see and understand how the building matters to health care. Once it is built and stabilized as a well-functioning object, it will be taken for granted by users as a result of other more pressing concerns in the here and now, such as treatment of the acute patient. The acute situation and the patient will be in the foreground, and the building will return to the background to silently supply the workspaces and physical infrastructure that is needed for quality health care. If the treatment turns out well, the patient will recover, assisted by the delicious smells from the kitchen, the skills of the clinical professionals, and a well-planned meal.

But this is a perfect future situation we know nothing about just now. In the present, the only thing we know is that the building to be is filled with conflicting matters of concern and tensions and negotiations with outcomes and implications that are unknown. The building as a matter of concern is a highly uncertain project. It is certainly not a simple object and a stabilized frame within which interactions and work practices can unfold to deliver quality health care. However, as a matter of concern, it also opens up new possibilities and spaces for intervention and action in the here and now. For such a redesign to happen, there will need to be materiality or projection devices that are able to connect present matters of concern to the imagined future generations of users and their still unknown concerns and needs.

Implications and Conclusion

This leaves us thinking about what the implications are of "bringing the hospital back in." This final section is about what we learned from using the ANT lens, and what it allows us to see when we foreground materiality and the building as context. We shall highlight two theoretical implications and one methodological one that we discovered from studying how changes in spatial designs matter for the building as context and matters of concern, how buildings matter in the health care landscape, and the implications of studying the hospital as context in action.

The Building as Context and Matters of Concern

Vignette 1, about the patient room size, suggests an important role for building design in providing a context for health care work, and for budgets in negotiating changes to its spatial designs. Supplied with the program and budget, the Expert Panel was prompted to articulate a concern about an economic size for a single-bed patient room. An economic (cost) boundary was drawn for what constitutes a feasible design and room size. In a more subtle way, the economic calculation and design standard also inscribe a particular "economic and normal" patient body size. This new and more confined patient identity (confined in a smaller clinical and economic space), in turn, produces a whole array of additional visualizations, representations, and clinical concerns among the regions and prospective hospital owners about timely and swift treatment. In the physical mock-up and simulation, these clinical concerns are delimited to focus on the interactions and treatment taking place inside the economically feasible patient room. The room's eventual links to the building envelope, as well as the overall hospital design and performance, becomes relatively more difficult to explore because of this array of interlinked representations and concerns. The tensions between different ways of representing and contextualizing the building generate further attempts to address and contain the matters of concern through these visualizations.

Vignette 2, about the kitchen and the overall hospital size, is another example of how building for health care work generates matters of concern regarding spatial size and functions that are tensioned against budget concern related to the funding of the building construction project. In both cases, the concern is about timely and cost-efficient operation, which is backgrounded as a result of more immediate and short-term concerns about the construction budget for the individual project and the overall building program. The kitchen example further shows how the Capital Region has continued to negotiate the short-term budget boundary to get the kitchen back into the building envelope. Their concern is mobilized around the integrity of their concept of a "healing hospital," and, more generally, is about the quality and service of public health care. Yet it is also about the cost efficiency of operations in the long term because to outsource the kitchen to private providers could also add to the costs of public health care, suggesting further links to other spaces and places for cooking patients' meals. In contrast with the Vignette1, which remained within the room and confined space of the individual patient, this concern spills far beyond that enclosed space.

How Buildings Matter in the Health Care Landscape

Both case vignettes illustrate how matters of concern related to the individual room and hospital are further linked to the broader health care landscape at national, regional, and municipality levels. In both cases, the spatial size "has to pay" to keep within the budget for the individual building project, as well as within that of the national Danish hospital-building program. As the older existing hospital buildings are closed and the new hospital spaces are downsized and, spatially and geographically, centralized to fewer buildings and locations, new concerns emerge about the division of labor within and across regions and municipalities. For example, municipalities across Denmark are starting to open local health care branches that deliver treatment and prevention services for general health problems (Waldorff & Greenwood, 2011;

Waldorff, 2013) to offer health care services that are closer to citizens' locations, in some cases even related to acute treatment, which is a core service and function of the regional hospital. As a context, the 42-billion DKK building program could not remain isolated from the broader health care delivery system. Rather than providing the solution for future quality health care, the hospital-building program generated new matters of concern that have spilled over to the broader health care landscape.

Context in Action: Implications for Research and Practice

What do we see when we study the building as context and matter of concern? The building is not just an object but a process and project. When studying the building, we also learn how it can shape and negotiate the context. When following the design of physical spaces for the hospital building and for health care, there is a whole array of inscription devices and methods at play, including architect drawings, physical mock-ups, 3D immersive environments, time schedules, and regional/national building programs and budgets. It is an open empirical question how such devices are used and with what effects for the design and organization of workspaces, processes, and the delivery of services. This is so because the inscription devices represent different matters of concern, and they are tensioned against each other in a process of negotiation over what the building is and what it should do in the context of health care. So we learn that the context of health care is not independent of the inscription devices but integral to the use circulation. In terms of implications for research, future studies should be designed to account for how multiple tensions and concerns emerge and play out in interactions between people and their different devices and methods for designing the building and its spatial organization, functions, work processes, and services. As building designs grow in scale, cost, technological sophistication, and complexity, such as the Danish "super hospitals," for example, there is also a related challenge regarding the involvement of clients and end users having a say in designing their own physical organization and work environment. The challenge is both a question of democratic involvement of key stakeholders who do not see themselves as experts in building design and a practical question of the methods of stakeholder involvement and co-design to make the building project and work organization a long-term success. While we believe that key stakeholders such as end users can make important and valuable contributions to the design task and challenge, our research also suggests that design methods and devices can be more or less useful in that respect. Further research into the role of methods and devices in shaping stakeholders' interest and design contributions in the setting of the built environment is called for, as further studies that trace the spatial links and changes within and across hospitals and health care facilities.

This chapter aimed to "bring the hospital back in" when thinking about hospital organization. From our research, it is surprising to us that it has been possible to "keep it out" for so long.

Notes

1. This section is an edited version of previously published work by Harty and Tryggestad (2015).
2. This section reports from ongoing research that has also been published as conference proceedings (Harty et al., 2015a, 2015b).
3. A video produced by the client organization at NHN illustrates how virtual reality technology is being used in the user-involvement process: https://www.youtube.com/watch?v=H3qxm4WfHHU (Accessed 30 October 2017).

References

Akrich, M., Callon, M., & Latour, B. Translated by Monaghan, A. (2002). The key to success in innovation, part I: The art of interessement. *International Journal of Innovation Management, 6*(2), 187–206.

Berg, P. O. & Kreiner, K. (1990). Corporate architecture: Turning physical settings into symbolic resources. In P. Gagliardi (ed.), *Symbols and artifacts: Views of the corporate landscape.* New York: Aldine de Gruyter, pp. 41–67.

Bresnen, M. & Harty, C. (2010). Objects, Knowledge sharing and knowledge transformation in projects. *Construction Management and Economics, 6*, 549–55.

Center for Brugerfokuseret Innovation. (2010). Report: "*Test af fremtidens patientstue, nyt OUH.*" Odense: Unpublished.

Danske Regioner. (2009). Report: "*Danske Regioners bemærkninger til de anvendte forudsætninger I ekspertpanelets screeningsrapport.*" https://www.regioner.dk/media/7265/danske-regioners-bemaerkninger-til-de-anvendte-forudsaetninger-i-ekspertpanelets-screeningsrapport.pdf (Accessed January 23 2019).

Davies, R. & Harty, C. (2013). Implementing "site BIM": A case study of ICT innovation on a large hospital project. *Automation in Construction, 30*, 15–24.

Ewenstein, B. & Whyte, J. (2009). Knowledge practices in design: The role of visual representations as epistemic objects. *Organization Studies, 30*(1), 7–30.

Expert Panel. (2008). Report: "*Regionernes investerings- og sygehusplaner: Screening og vurdering.*" https://sum.dk/Aktuelt/Publikationer/~/media/Filer%20-%20Publikationer_i_pdf/2008/screening_vurdering_nov_2008.ashx (Accessed January 23 2019).

Frandsen, A. K., et al. (2009). *Helende arkitektur*. Aalborg: Institut for Arkitektur og Medieteknologi.

Harty, C., Jacobsen, P. H., & Tryggestad, K. (2015a). Constructing healthcare spaces: The complex role of visualisations in negotiating hospital designs and practices. *Procedia Economics and Finance, 21,* 578–85.

Harty, C. & Tryggestad, K. (2015). The hospital building as project and matter of concern: The role of representations in negotiating patient room designs and bodies. *Engineering Project Organization Journal, 5*(2–3), 95–105.

Harty, C., Tryggestad, K., & Holm Jacobsen, P. (2015b). Visualisations and calculations of spaces: Negotiating hospital design during on-boarding. In A. Raiden & E. Aboagye-Nimo, (eds.), Proceedings from the 31st Annual ARCOM Conference. Lincoln: ARCOM, Association of Researchers in Construction Management, pp. 875–84.

Harvey, D. (1989). *The condition of postmodernity*. Oxford: Blackwell.

Hatch, M. (1990). The symbolics of office design. In P. Gagliardi (ed.), *Symbols and artifacts: Views of the corporate landscape*. New York: Aldine de Gruyter, pp. 129–46.

Kornberger, M. & Clegg, S. R. (2004). Bringing space back in: Organizing the generative building. *Organization Studies, 25*(7), 1095–114.

Kreiner, K. (2010). Organizational spaces: From "matters of fact" to "matters of concern." In A. Van Marrewijk & D. Yanow (eds.), *Organisational spaces: Rematerializing the workaday world*. Northampton, MA: Edward Elgar, pp. 200–11.

Kreiner, K. (2014). Restoring project success as phenomenon. In R. A. Lundin & M. Hällgren (eds.), *Advancing research on projects and temporary organizations*. Koege: Copenhagen Business School Press and Liber, pp. 19–38.

Latour, B. (1986). Visualization and cognition: Thinking with eyes and hands. *Knowledge and Society: Studies in the Sociology of Culture Past and Present, 6,* 1–40.

Latour, B. (1996). On actor-network theory: A few clarifications. *Soziale Welt, 47,* 369–81.

Latour, B. (2008). *A cautious Prometheus? A few steps towards a philosophy of design* (with special attention to Peter Sloterdijk). Paper presented at the Networks of Design meeting of the Design History Society, Falmouth, Cornwall, UK, 3 September. https://hal-sciencespo.archives-ouvertes.fr/hal-00972919/file/112-design-cornwall.pdf. (Accessed 30 October 2017).

Marrewijk, A. v. & Yanow, D. (2010). Introduction: The spatial turns in organization studies. In A. van Marrewijk & D. Yanow (eds.), *Organizational spaces: Rematerializing the workaday world*. Northampton, MA: Edward Elgar, pp. 1–16.

Meyer, R. E., Höllerer, M. A., Jancsary, D., & Van Leeuwen, T. (2013). The visual dimension in organizing, organization, and organization research: Core ideas, current developments, and promising avenues. *The Academy of Management Annals, 7*(1), 489–555.

O'Toole, P., & Were, P. (2008). Observing places: Using space and material culture in qualitative research. *Qualitative Research, 18*(5), 616–34.

Pfeffer, J. 1981. *Power in organizations*. Marshfields, MA: Pitman.

Region Hovedstaden. (2013a). Competition brief: *This is it—your blank canvas*. https://www.regionh.dk/nythospitalnordsjaelland/Projektet/raadgivere-og-entreprenoerer/Projektkonkurrence/Sider/Konkurrenceprogram-for-Nyt-Hospital-Nordsjaelland.aspx. (Accessed 30 October 2017).

Region Hovedstaden. (2013b). Evaluation report: *Setting New Standards*. https://www.regionh.dk/nythospitalnordsjaelland/Projektet/raadgivere-og-entreprenoerer/Projektkonkurrence/Documents/Dommerbetaenkning.pdf. (Accessed 10 October 2017).

Stang Våland, M. & Georg, S. (2014). The socio-materiality of designing organizational change. *Journal of Organizational Change Management, 27*(3), 391–406.

Tryggestad, K. & Georg, S. (2011). How objects shape logics in construction. *Culture and Organization, 17*(3), 181–97.

Waldorff, S. B. (2013). Accounting for organizational innovations: Mobilizing institutional logics in translation. *Scandinavian Journal of Management, 29*(3), 219–34.

Waldorff, S. B. & Greenwood, R. (2011). The dynamics of community translation: Danish health-care centres. In C. Marquis, M. Lounsbury, & R, Greenwood (eds.), *Communities and organizations*. Bingley, UK: Emerald Publishing, pp. 113–42.

Whyte, J., Tryggestad, K., & Comi, A. (2017). Visualizing practices in project-based design: Tracing connections through cascades of visual representations. *Engineering Project Organization Journal, 6*(2–4), 115–28.

Part II
Actors

How Do Actors Understand, Experience, and Engage with Context?

7

Tracing Context as Relational, Discursive Accomplishment

Analytical Lessons from a Shadowing-Based Study of Health Care Chief Executives

Maja Korica and Davide Nicolini

Introduction

Context is used to refer to the things "we need to know ... to properly understand an event, action or discourse" (van Dijk, 1997 p. 11). When we use the term, we implicitly operate a logical distinction between a focal "it" and its background. The idea of context is mobilized when there is an assumption or a belief that the focal phenomenon cannot be understood or represented unless one reaches beyond the phenomenon itself, and takes into consideration its circumstances. While the idea that social and human matters have "circumstances" is widely (albeit not universally) accepted in the social and human sciences, how one should conceive of the relationship between the phenomenon and context, and, therefore, what counts as context itself is much more contentious.

A major distinction exists between those who see context as causally influencing a phenomenon, and those who take a more interactive view. The first perspective is common, and probably predominant in health care management. Here, context is often operationalized in terms of a set of variables that "affect" or "impact" the phenomenon. For example, supporters of the behavioral model of health care utilization (e.g., Andersen, 1968) call environmental and provider-related factors that influence utilization "contextual variables," because "they measure the context or milieu in which utilization occurs" (Phillips et al., 1998 p. 573). Such environmental factors include the delivery system, external environment, and community. This also illustrates how, in this approach, context is often engaged as a residual category. It is used to capture the "noise" in the model, the "etcetera" that future research will have to untangle. This view is echoed in management studies more generally. For example, Mintzberg (2009) distinguishes between external context (culture, sector, and industry), organizational context (form of organization, age, stage, and size), job context, situational context, and personal context. These come together to contribute to a particular "posture" taken by certain chief executives. This leads him to suggest that "the effective manager may more usually be the one whose natural style fits the context, rather than one who changes style to fit context, or context to fit style" (Mintzberg, 2009 p. 132).

Since the 1990s, an increasing number of scholars have rejected this static and externalist view of context. They have instead promoted an alternative that is internalist, interactive, and dynamic. Rejecting the idea that context is simply the passive "out there" container of action (the "soup and bowl" idea of context), these authors consider action and context as being mutually interrelated. Action is seen as being both context dependent and context creating (Duranti & Goodwin, 1992). Because what counts as contextual is "situated," and can thus only be determined locally on a case-by-case basis, these scholars often add a very restrictive clause to the understanding of "context" as an efficient cause (see, e.g., Schegloff, 1997). Context can thus be assumed to have an influence only "insofar as a researcher can display that the participants themselves in their talk show that they have attended to or are being influenced by that feature of context" (Tracy, 1998 p. 8). Relatively little attention is given here to context outside the talk or scene of action—the "exogenous" or "broad" context of action. As Latour (2005 p. 168) notes, this exposes a researcher to an insoluble paradox: "when she sticks to interactions, [the inquirer] is requested to go away and to 'put things in their wider context.' But when she finally reaches that structuring context, she is asked to leave the abstract level for 'real life,' 'human size,' 'lived-in' sites."

In this chapter, we suggest that one of the reasons scholars are caught up in this difficult conundrum is that both of these approaches take context to be a representational issue, rather than a pragmatic phenomenon. In other words, they see *context* as a noun rather than a verb. They assume that dealing with context is an issue that concerns those who engage in explanatory and representational practices: scholars, inquirers, and other investigators. In this chapter, we instead build on a practice-based approach to understanding organizational phenomena, and our previous explorations of CEO practices of staying "in the know" (Nicolini et al., 2015; Korica & Nicolini, 2016). We also join forces with colleagues working to insert further rigor into the study of context (Fitzgerald et al., 2002; Dopson, et al., 2008). We do so to outline the contours of an alternative analytical understanding. Unlike conceptions of context as a stable, "out there" phenomenon with unmitigated power and effects, we suggest that context is understood analytically as *members' concern continually made present through particular kinds of attention and action*. This presents a direct answer to the second question driving this book: namely, how do actors understand, experience, and engage with context in a given situation or phenomenon? Specifically, contextualizing action is a continuously present concern for actors, in general, and health care executives studied here, in particular. It follows that context can be better understood (analytically) and traced (methodologically) by exploring how organizational individuals, such as chief executives (CEOs), engage it in everyday work.

For us, "engaging" here implies a *joining*: relating different events and concerns in ways that make them meaningful in specific ways, via distinct relations and discursive practices. We thus conceive context as a web of connections in action, resulting from observable, continually connecting actions. Such an approach echoes the etymological roots of the word itself, in which context, from Latin *contextus* or "a joining together," was originally formed from a past principle of *cum* ("together") and *textere* ("to weave, to make"), or "to weave together" (Burke, 2002). In other words, we argue that it matters less, and is less empirically accurate, to speak of what context *is*, than to trace the ways in which *context is made to matter*, in characteristic ways, by particularly influential individuals during their ordinary activities. This, in turn, requires taking as a point of departure the work and perspectives of managers whose behavior is under consideration, and considering how they organize and action their attention vis-à-vis events and situations they need to navigate. Put more directly, CEOs have a unique capacity to shape and set out a context for others to act within and in relation to (Ghoshal & Bartlett, 1994; Grint, 2005). They are at the center of that web of connections, and legitimized by their role to join these. In addition, their understandings of context also affect their work. As such, tracing these processes, with CEO work as our departure point, holds unique analytical promise for conceptually understanding context in ways that are more complex.

In the rest of the chapter, we develop our argument by building on a longitudinal study of seven chief executives in the UK's National Health Service (NHS). We combined extensive shadowing with informal and formal interviewing, as well as documentary and diary analysis. This empirical approach allowed us to respond to long-standing scholarly calls to "make work visible" (Barley & Kunda, 2001), by paying particular attention to complex lived experiences of individuals to better understand the work itself (Akin, 2000). We shall argue that a similar approach helped us to "make context visible" by tracing connections in action as part of the CEOs' daily activities and, thus, enabled the proposed analytical contributions to the literature on context, managerial work, and beyond.

Accounting for Context in Managerial Work: Previous Explorations, Promising Openings

As argued by scholars such as Stewart (1976), context is particularly relevant when it comes to an enriched understanding of managerial work. Specifically, if we recognize that all work is necessarily situated, the empirical question that arises is How does this come to matter to managerial work in particular? As noted previously, Mintzberg (2009) suggested managerial action is influenced by external, organizational, job, situational, and personal contextual factors. Stewart's (1976) investigation, which was part of a much wider program of work (e.g., Stewart et al., 1980), in turn, teased-out task-based categorical differences between jobs that were focused on variations in demands, constraints, and choices. Other, more recent, explorations include Tengblad's (2006) study of four Swedish CEOs, Dargie's (2000) investigations of public sector chief executives in the UK, and Matthaei's (2010) calendar and interview-based study of German CEOs (for a detailed overview, see Tengblad & Vie, 2012; Korica et al., 2017).

However, to the extent that context was acknowledged as being relevant in authors' accounts, it remained largely a descriptor of the sample studied, or a baseline for direct comparison between individuals in light of some other analytical concern. In one such exploration, Dargie (2000), for example, highlighted the relative paucity of studies comparing the differences in observed managerial work of chief executives in private and voluntary sectors versus the public sector, particularly following the introduction of New Public Management (Hood, 1991). Her study thus featured eight UK chief executives (four in public sector organizations, two in the voluntary sector, and two in the private sector) who were each studied via calendar analysis of 1 year, observations of work over a week, and interviews. The (admittedly rather short) paper engaged Mintzberg's (1973) ten behavioral roles to identify some ways in which the studied CEOs' performed roles differed. These included meeting particular local demands; institutional tensions (e.g., limited resources meant that CEOs in the NHS had to be involved in resource allocations, but could not, for instance, easily dismiss staff); environmental limitations (e.g., media coverage of adverse events in hospitals influenced a CEO's immediate priorities); and organizational actors (e.g., the presence of medical staff in NHS organizations presented unique challenges in managing professional autonomy). However, in its brevity, the paper emphasized the existence and nature of such differences, over the key underlying question of how they mattered in practice.

Specifically, the question of how such CEOs not only oriented their work and understood it under different emerging situated challenges but also came to define their own contexts by giving attention in discrete ways to some aspects rather than others has remained largely unexplored. This is regrettable, as chief executives could arguably be said to be especially concerned with the "broader" context, given that a key aspect of their work entails acting as the linking pin between the organizational environment and its internal differential experiences and understandings (and vice versa) (see Mintzberg, 1983). As Sausman argues in relation to the NHS:

> chief executives have probably a unique range of contacts and a unique perspective on information regarding policy and operations and so they form a natural information source or "conduit" within and outside the organisation, often being required to translate abstract ideas and broad policy objectives into what they mean for the organisation. (2001 p. ii17)

Despite this, the dynamics and analytical relevance of such a position have rarely been explicitly problematized vis-à-vis scholarly understanding of context. This is especially regarding how those executives come to grapple with continually shifting understandings of their setting(s) over time—a process in which they were not just passive participants, but also active ones.

As one notable exception, Stewart and colleagues (1980 p. 9) outline how NHS district administrators (today's chief executives) operated in a work setting where "both demands and constraints may vary over time and thus affect the opportunities for choice. The individual job-holder also creates his own personal demands and constraints, which will limit his [sic] choices, it least in the short term." They gave the example of agreeing to serve on a certain committee, which then brought with it subsequent demands, such as attending other meetings, as well as constraints, such as others' expectations that might result from this new role. However, to the extent that this account introduced managers as active crafters (at least to some extent), the analytical attention remained rather limited: focused on how this matters for, and restrains, that manager's work alone. If we accept, however, that a chief executive's position comes with a much broader remit of potential influence, this opens up room to recognize the relevance of such crafting beyond his or her own work choices, such as committee participation. In other words, Stewart and colleagues (1980 p. 19) acknowledge the key relevance of the "focus of attention," either inward or outward, in such administrators' daily work. *How* this focus is operationalized by a particular executive in terms of being given certain meaning, in distinct ways also of relevance to others, remains insufficiently explored.

Studying Context in Action: An Account of Our Approach

Our empirical study of NHS executives offers fertile ground to address this relative absence. Specifically, as practice- and process-oriented scholars, we designed the research with an already existing analytical orientation toward context, though this was not the formal focus of our study. The analytical guidance here is to ensure that investigations of context and its relevance pay attention to both situated expressions and activities within that organization (which includes sayings and materialities), as well as how references are established vis-à-vis "wider" features, such as other organizations, legal oversight, and political norms, characteristic of that time and place (Nicolini, 2013). To this end, methodological approaches that facilitate attention to both, such as Nicolini's (2009) "zooming in and out," are particularly appropriate. In our case, we engaged shadowing (McDonald, 2005; Czarniawska, 2007; Quinlan, 2008). This is a highly mobile method, particularly suitable for appreciating the "social embeddedness of managerial behavior" (Noordegraf & Stewart, 2002 p. 440), and for tracing relations; specifically how individuals make sense of their surroundings and themselves in relation to others (Vasquez et al., 2012).

Between March 2011 and May 2013, we conducted an ethnographic study of seven health care CEOs of acute and mental health NHS trusts in England (for further detail regarding our methodology, see Nicolini et al., 2014). The CEOs managed organizations that included multiple hospitals (e.g., three large hospitals) and a variety of clinics, annual budgets exceeding £500 million (US$800 million), and between 2,000 and 10,000 staff. Each was shadowed for 5 or more weeks (apart from one, where observations lasted only for 3.5 weeks). We were able to document most aspects of their work, or collect post hoc accounts for work we were unable to observe. We took field notes and direct quotes "in vivo," using tablet computers, or shortly after when appropriate, paying particular attention to key analytical elements of practice, including objects engaged, people referred to, and interactions undertaken (Nicolini et al., 2003; Miettinen et al., 2009; Feldman & Orlikowski, 2012). We also conducted formal semi-structured interviews with CEOs and consulted around a thousand pages of documents, including meeting papers, articles the CEOs referenced, and external publications consulted.

Joining Together in Action: Tracing the Relational, Discursive Accomplishments of Context

As common with ethnographic studies, the richness of our data far exceeds the scholarly space available to share it. As such, we have chosen to engage with two aspects to tease out the emerging analytical features of context in action that we observed.

Constructing the "Out There" in Practice and through Practices

One of the things we noted in our study is that understanding what was "out there" and staying on top of what was happening within and around their organizations were among the CEOs' main preoccupations. As we recounted in greater detail in Korica and Nicolini (2016), CEOs were perpetually scanning and monitoring their environment to become aware of new things worthy of attention because they could be linked in some way to their present work. This was something woven deeply, via observable practices, into the texture of their everyday activities. The "context" was thus actively enacted (Weick, 1979), through very specific activities that gave relevance to certain aspects and actively backgrounded others, *at certain times*, given the CEOs' tasks at that moment.

To provide one brief example, all the CEOs engaged in deliberate monitoring, such as keeping up with the specialized press and running oversight meetings. They also actively constructed the "out there," by participating mindfully in activities that ostensibly had other objectives. As one of our informants, an experienced executive newly in the job of running a large teaching hospital, put it during our fieldwork:

> what I do is I attend meetings that I've been booked into...and I use that as another data source...But the really valuable bit for me is being in a room with peers and just chatting about what your current issue is, and then you get a real sense of where we sit, as kind of benchmarking data.   [CEO 2]

CEOs thus consciously and purposely used meetings as an opportunity to understand what others considered worthy of consideration. In addition, even the most ordinary social conversation (e.g., meeting someone while walking to the cafeteria) echoed a similar posture: "Good to see you! How are you? *And what's new*?" In summary, the "context" was not something the CEOs found by chance, but rather something that they actively and routinely enacted with and through others. This context was neither an external set of objective conditions, nor a simple projection of their "internal" subjective mind. Rather, it manifested itself in practice as an evolving set of concerns and understandings regarding circumstances that needed to be taken into consideration as potentially relevant.

What Should We Care about? Accomplishing Context via Joining Together

The relational, discursive, and bodily construction of context extended beyond simply bringing to bear an "out there" understanding with pragmatic relevance for the organization. It also implied making connections between established relevancies and organizational action. Consider the following short vignette.

> *Vignette 1:* We are in the open plan office at the trust HQ. CEO6 is sitting at his desk. The CEO [who has been in the post over 4 years, following a private-sector career, and heads a successful mental health trust] attended a meeting to prepare for the [organization's Equality and Diversity] conference, and heard about sector Commissioning Board meetings being streamed live via video. He checks it out online, then immediately "emails the link to the video to his Chair." He explains to me once more, before emailing, about their discussions regarding public board meetings, which they have been having as an organization for some months now. So this is helpful in his view (that is, he is linking this to existing discussions with the team re: how the Board of the organization can demonstrate public accountability in light of FT [NHS foundation trust] requirements for public boards, and what he sees as the Chair's resistance to that, given the Chair is from the private sector and is not used to such oversight). After a few minutes, "the deputy comes in. The CEO tells her that he is just about the send an email with the video link around further. In it, the Commissioning Board explains just how they are approaching these meetings, which is quite helpful.... He then opens a PDF outlining arrangements for FT public board meeting." He then makes a call, "checks if the Chair received his email re: this. Asks him to please take a look at the link shared, noting the Commission Chair's introduction is very helpful." (Extract from research diary)

This extract importantly illustrates the CEO's practices of orienting attention, not just in terms of what he attends to, but also with regard to doing that orienting work for notable others, that is, the Chair. We can also detect the important discursive work of making connections, through which context is made present. Institutional requirements regarding public boards may exist at this time, such as those for FTs referred to in the vignette. Here we see, however, how they are made sense of within the broader scope of organizational activities, priorities, actors, and understandings, at a certain time. The process is *active*, not passive. We witness the CEO not just accessing the Commissioning Board website to keep himself informed, but also explicitly making that connection for his organization's Chair of the Board as well. This joining is importantly imbued with a distinct sense of understanding or relevance—the link is highlighted as part of a broader discussion about how public meetings might need to take place, the CEO's understanding of the Chair's existing resistance, and his efforts to position the trust as being notable for "public accountability." In other words, the linking is purposeful and strategically directive. It is infused with particular meaning, toward a particular end. This is evidenced in the CEO's follow-up call to the Chair, ensuring that particular notice would be paid to the email he had sent. As such, not only is the process of such linking continually actively accomplished, but so is context itself, as inherently variously interpreted and understood.

This is further evident if we consider another short vignette.

Vignette 2: At an 8 a.m. executive team meeting, the gathered executives "discuss the problems within the trust concerning people not showing up, using being busy as an excuse and cancelling meetings." [CEO4, a new executive brought in to turn around a highly challenging hospital] notes he is really worried about the accounting firm coming in and observing several key meetings. "They need to be a 7 [on the regulator's scale used to assess quality of their corporate governance], otherwise the regulator will lose faith in them." A few days later, "the Chair comes in to update the CEO on his chat with the regulator. The Chair gives him the surprising details of the conversation: it seems the local commissioners [who commission health care services locally for hospitals like his] have been giving information to regulator that is not accurate. He checks the shared information is indeed not correct. They agree the CEO will call the head of the regulator on Monday morning to reassure him of their exact plans."

(Extract from research diary)

This extract in turn illustrates the relational work of joining across customarily perceived "levels" of context. Here, internal challenges are given particular consideration and meaning by being linked explicitly to broader, supra-organizational concerns regarding regulator assessments. This effectively reorients what can be seen as a mundane operational issue (that is, people not attending meetings) into a much wider, and therefore consequential, matter of strategic concern (that is, people not attending meetings as a signal of a strained organizational setting or culture, one of the broader considerations the regulator takes into account in making assessments, which are important to get right because the organization is already seen as struggling). This suggests that while it may be helpful both analytically and presentationally for scholars to see them as "levels," such experiences of context are in everyday practice instantaneous, relational, ontologically "flat" phenomena (Emirbayer, 1997; Bradbury & Lichtenstein, 2000). In other words, they are experienced, found, expressed, and crafted with certain meaning in individual moments of relational joining. In addition, the example depicts other individuals bringing topics to the CEO's attention, which the CEO then uses as input into his further processes of joining, to enable further action. In other words, it highlights that while the active role of a CEO vis-à-vis context may not always feature him or her personally bringing certain aspects to initial attention, the CEO nevertheless remains an active participant in the overall, necessarily relational process. Furthermore, the example highlights that such processes happen over time, and therefore feature a number of different elements linked into particular understandings of context as continually shifting. Finally, the concluding sentence of the vignette reiterates once more the CEO's active role. Specifically, distinct understandings of the "external" context are not only made sense of by linking them to "internal" conversations and dynamics, but also conversely by CEOs making connections to inform "external" actors, such as regulator's shifting understandings, thereby also inevitably influencing to some degree the latter's work and nature.

Discussion and Concluding Thoughts

The above exploration of NHS chief executives' work highlights context as accomplished continually. The CEOs made context present and meaningful by actively constructing it via a multi-step recursive process. This involved both attending to context in certain ways (by linking it to existing understandings, with a view toward identifying certain meaning) and making that context work (by joining it with current or future activities, as well as existing understandings, to imbue further meaning and enable action beyond this point in time). Importantly, the latter reflects a unique role played by CEOs, as joiners and shapers of not only of their meaningful and, thus, actionable contexts, but also those of others, including actors beyond their own organizations. The process also suggests that features of what we customarily see as "external" or "internal" context are never simply "out there" or "in here." Instead, they become present—temporarily, in that moment—by being accorded meaning via discursive and relational dynamics of crafted joining. This implies *both* recognition and action: features are joined together toward something, even if that something, in terms of work and action, is yet to be performed.

This holds a number of wider analytical and methodological lessons for future investigations. With regard to our contribution to the literature on managerial work, one apparently similar theorization is Stewart and colleagues' (1980 p. 76) *linkman* and *shaper* roles by NHS district administrators. However, while for them the key aim of such roles appears to be functional, in our observations regarding context, the work was more interpretive. The CEOs continually outlined and, therefore, in some ways, crafted a particular understanding of the world in which such work might then be attempted. This has clear implications for better appreciating not only their managerial work, but also analytical understanding of context. With regard to the latter, it suggests that it is in those relational moments of accomplished interpretation that customary "levels" of context as an analytical category (that is, "macro, meso, and micro"; see McNulty & Ferlie, 2002) are linked *and* given meaning through such joining. In other words, to the extent that such features of so-called external (including "macro") context exist outside of these relations, this existence is of scant practical relevance to the practices of those individuals—at least at that moment in time. Interpretation of context as a *joining together of emergent sense* thus implies continued work, inherently limited or specific in both the components it chooses to bring together, and the ways in which such bringing together is accomplished. This also necessarily means that, conceptually, any such context is a temporary phenomenon. To the extent that it is ever fixed, or exists, it is only momentarily so in relation to distinct words and actions. These are then quickly dissolved or made fluid again as further relational and material actions occur.

The analytical and methodological implications for scholarship are clear. Analytically, rather than outside-in tracing of externally reportable features, such as regulator presence or scheduled meeting times, far more relevant for understanding managerial work is the internal tracing of lived realities. Relational spaces and times, in which such sense is made, may well differ considerably. The important questions, therefore, not just for a better appreciation of managerial work, but also for connected matters of accountability and regulation, are *how* and *why* such traces of accomplished sense differ, and *with what subsequent effects*. This crucially recognizes power (see Mintzberg, 1983; Grint, 2005), both in its ability to initiate such interpretations, and to have them count in certain ways beyond the CEO's work alone. It reminds us that if context can be created, including in the ways we depict above, then explicit consideration of *whose* context this may be as a result, and with what consequences, is necessary. This has clear relevance for the academic understanding of managerial work. It also relates to power, conflict, and resistance in situations of relational and constantly multidirectional, rather than solely individual and retrospective sensemaking (discussed in more detail earlier in this book). For example, Vignette 1 could have been explored further, space permitting, to situate it in the wider power struggles at this time between CEO6 and his Chair. Specifically, the latter had a particular, private-sector-driven understanding of the role of a Board, whose remit the CEO, in turn, actively tried to manage and circumscribe in certain ways. This then serves as further evidence of why CEOs in particular represent such a valuable analytical case for understanding context. It is precisely because their role features such a density of connections to join, and because it demands that they account for the nature and consequences of contexts they create, that studying their accomplishments of context in practice offers rich lessons for scholarly understanding.

Methodologically, this implies that empirical investigations of how particular "joining together" comes to advance certain understandings of context ought to ideally be supplemented by some consideration of the latter's fate. This is not just regarding the work of that individual, but for others to whom these are offered as direction, and to the (eventual) fate of the organization as a whole. Such focus echoes Nicolini's (2013) "strong program" of studying practices, in which registering them is not sufficient. Instead, turning to dynamics of difference over time to explain them is essential. To that aim, future studies that investigate how situated constructions of context by managers and individuals in different positions inform and relate to each other's work would make a valuable further contribution to the literature on context and managerial work.

Of course, the question of *whose* context must also be asked by us as researchers. In particular, we must openly acknowledge that the particular "theory method toolkit" (Nicolini, 2013) we engaged allowed us to trace and see context in certain ways, but not others. As such, this analytical account is enabled and, in part, produced by our methodological choices—we traced the phenomena that we could. However, we did so, driven by clear analytical aims: the relative dearth of dynamic, processual studies of context, and a commitment to the "strong program" to allow for nuanced theorizations of complex practices. Such work though, as well as the future opportunities we have advocated, is necessarily complex and difficult. They are made more so by our scholarly limitations regarding conducting longitudinal observational studies, which this would demand (see also Sminia (2017) on Pettigrew's (2012) approach to studying context). However, such studies are likely to contribute meaningfully by further "complexifying" already intricate organizational realities, rather than reducing these to fit the limitations of outlets, or preferences for simple representations (Tsoukas, 2017). As Walsh and colleagues (2006 p. 667) warned, "more often than not, our theories are culture bound, biased toward stability, and contextually restricted. As a result, our work is relevant to a dwindling fraction of the world's organizations and organizational contexts." Our attempt here, therefore, should also be seen as another contribution toward redressing this balance, by introducing further analytical fluidity to the key concept of context itself.

Acknowledgment: This project was funded by the National Institute for Health Research Health Services and Delivery Research Programme (project number 09/1002/36). [The chapter draws in part on the empirical material contained in its final report published in 2014.]

Disclaimer: The views and opinions expressed therein are those of the authors and do not necessarily reflect those of the HS&DR Programme, NIHR, NHS, or the Department of Health.

References

Akin, G. (2000). Learning about work from Joe Cool. *Journal of Management Inquiry*, 9(1), 57–61.

Andersen, R. M. (1968). *Behavioral model of families' use of health services*, Research Series Vol. 25. Chicago: Center for Health Administration Studies, University of Chicago.

Barley, S. & Kunda, G. (2001). Bringing work back in. *Organization Science*, 12(1), 76–95.

Bradbury, H. and Lichtenstein, B. M. B. (2000). Relationality in organisational research: Exploring the space between. *Organization Science*, 11(5), 551–64.

Burke, P. (2002). Context in context. *Common Knowledge*, 8(1), 152–77.

Czarniawska, B. (2007). *Shadowing and other techniques for doing fieldwork in modern societies*. Malmo: Liber.

Dargie, C. (2000). Observing chief executives: Analysing behaviour to explore cross-sectoral differences. *Public Management and Money*, 20(3), 39–44.

Dijk, T. A. van (1997). Discourse as interaction in society. In T. A. van Dijk (ed.), *Discourse as social interaction*. London: Sage, pp. 1–37.

Dopson, S., Fitzgerald, L., & Ferlie, E. (2008). Understanding change and innovation in healthcare settings: Reconceptualising the active role of context. *Journal of Change Management*, 8(3–4) 213–31.

Duranti, A. & Goodwin, C. (1992). *Rethinking context: Language as an interactive phenomenon*. Cambridge: Cambridge University Press.

Emirbayer, M. (1997). Manifesto for a relational sociology. *American Journal of Sociology*, 103(2), 281–317.

Feldman, M. S. & Orlikowski, W. J. (2012). Theorising practice and practicing theory. *Organization Science*, 22(5), 1240–53.

Fitzgerald, L., Ferlie, E., Wood, M., & Hawkins, C. (2002). Interlocking interactions: The diffusion of innovations in health care. *Human Relations*, 55(12), 1429–49.

Ghoshal, S. & Bartlett, C. A. (1994). Linking organisational context and managerial action: The dimensions of quality of management. *Strategic Management Journal*, 15, 91–112.

Grint, K. (2005). Problems, problems, problems: The social construction of "leadership." *Human Relations*, 58(11), 1467–94.

Hood, C. (1991). A public management for all seasons. *Public Administration*, 6(3), 3–19.

Korica, M. & Nicolini, D. (2016). Objects and monitoring practices: Understanding CEOs' information work as mundane accomplishment. In J. Swan, S. Newell, & D. Nicolini (eds.), *Mobilizing knowledge in health care: Challenges for management and organization*. Oxford: Oxford University Press, pp. 41–60.

Korica, M., Nicolini, D., & Johnson, B. (2017). In search of "managerial work": Past, present and future of an analytical category. *International Journal of Management Reviews*, 19(2), 151–74.

Latour, B. (2005). *Reassembling the social: An introduction to actor-network-theory*. Oxford: Oxford University Press.

Matthaei, E. (2010). *The nature of executive work: A case study*. Berlin: Gabler.

McDonald, S. (2005). Studying actions in context: A qualitative shadowing method for organizational research. *Qualitative Research, 5*(4): 455–73.

McNulty, T. & Ferlie, E. (2002). *Reengineering healthcare: The complexities of organizational transformation*. Oxford: Oxford University Press.

Miettinen, R., Samra-Fredericks, D., & Yanow, D. (2009). Re-turn to practice: An introductory essay. *Organization Studies, 30*(12), 1309–27.

Mintzberg, H. (1973). *The nature of managerial work*. New York: Harper & Row.

Mintzberg, H. (1983). *Power in and around organizations*. Englewood Cliffs, NJ: Prentice-Hall.

Mintzberg, H. (2009). *Managing*. San Francisco: Berrett-Koehler Publishers.

Nicolini, D. (2009). Zooming in and out: Studying practices by switching theoretical lenses and trailing connections. *Organization Studies, 30*(12), 1391–418.

Nicolini, D. (2013). *Practice theory, work and organization: An introduction*. Oxford: Oxford University Press.

Nicolini, D., Gherardi, S., & Yanow, D. (eds.). (2003). *Knowing in organizations: A practice-based approach*. New York: M. E. Sharpe.

Nicolini, D., Korica, M., & Ruddle, K. (2015). Staying in the know: Overhauling your personal knowledge infrastructure, *MIT Sloan Management Review, 56*(4): 57–65.

Nicolini, D., Powell, J., & Korica, M. (2014). Keeping knowledgeable: How NHS chief executive officers mobilise knowledge and information in their daily work. *Health Service and Delivery Research, 2*, 26.

Pettigrew, A. (2012). Context and action in the transformation of the firm: A reprise. *Journal of Management Studies, 49*(7), 1304–28.

Phillips, K. A., Morrison, K. R., Andersen, R., & Aday, L. A. (1998). Understanding the context of healthcare utilization. *Health Services Research, 33*(3), 571–96.

Quinlan, E. (2008). Conspicuous invisibility: Shadowing as a data collection strategy. *Qualitative Inquiry, 14*(8), 1480–99.

Sausman, C. (2001). New roles and responsibilities of NHS chief executives in relation to quality and clinical governance. *Quality and Safety in Health Care, 10*, ii13–ii20.

Schegloff, E. A. (1997). Whose text? Whose context? *Discourse & Society, 8*(2), 165–87.

Sminia, H. (2017). Andrew M. Pettigrew: A groundbreaking process scholar. In D. B. Szabla, W. A. Pasmore, M. A. Barnes, & A. N. Gipson (eds.), *The Palgrave handbook of organizational change thinkers*. New York: Springer, pp. 1–17.

Stewart, R. (1976). *Contrasts in management: A study of different types of managers' jobs, their demands and choices*. Maidenhead: McGraw-Hill.

Stewart, R., Smith, P., Blake, J., & Wingate, P. (1980). *The district administrator in the National Health Service*. London: King Edward's Hospital Fund for London.

Tengblad, S. (2006). Is there a "new managerial work"? A comparison with Henry Mintzberg's classic study 30 years later. *Journal of Management Studies, 43*, 1437–61.

Tengblad, S. & Vie, O. E. (2012). Management in practice: Overview of classic studies on managerial work. In S. Tengblad (ed.), *The work of managers: Towards a practice theory of management*. Oxford: Oxford University Press, pp. 18–44.

Tracy, K. (1998). Analyzing context: Framing the discussion. *Research on Language and Social interaction, 31*(1), 1–28.

Tsoukas, H. (2017). Don't simplify, complexify: From disjunctive to conjunctive theorizing in organization and management studies. *Journal of Management Studies, 54*(2), 132–53.

Vasquez, C., Brummans, B. H. J. M., & Groleau, C. (2012). Notes from the field on organizational shadowing as framing. *Qualitative Research in Organizations and Management: An International Journal, 7*(2), 144–65.

Walsh, J. P., Meyer, A. D., & Schoonhoven, C. B. (2006). Perspective: A future for organization theory: living in and living with changing organizations. *Organization Science, 17*(5), 657–71.

Weick, K. E. (1979). The social psychology of organizing. Reading, MA: Addison-Wesley.

8

Technology in Context

Exploring Vulnerability in Surgery

Helle Sofie Wentzer

Introduction

Understanding context by putting it to the forefront of attention (Schuback, 2006) is a transcending experience. Theory can be a scaffold, though, for grasping the enfolded nature of context to human action, and the role of technology therein.

Grasping Context from Theory

Methodology programs such as Sociology and Technology in Society (STS) and activity theory draw attention to the entanglement of technology in human practices, organizational and societal, as well as natural developments in general. STS argues that humans and nonhumans, including technologies, cannot be differentiated ontologically, as they are both historical and political "actants" (Latour, 1993, 1994, 2005). They co-shape and enact semio-material reality together (Akrich & Latour, 1992). Time and space are enfolded in technologies, and technology refolds time and space when implemented into practice. The cultural-historical theory in activity theory explains how techniques are learned and developed as part of interacting and participating in activities that are goal-oriented, productive, social, and value- and rule-based, and sometimes become distorted because of various kinds of internal contradictions that promote radical learning and innovation (Engeström, 1986, 1987; Cole and Engeström, 1993). Both "schools" place an emphasis on *action* as the spatial and temporal unit of analysis. In what "program of action" or "activity system" are the techniques and users participating?

What is/are the goal(s), the "detours" (Latour, 1994), or "contradictions" (Cole & Engeström, 1993) of the actions, and how are the "actants" configured and refigured in the interaction? These are central questions for research in technologies in human practice, and to answer them, researchers need to pay attention to the relationship between context and action, specifically how actors may experience and engage with context in multiple ways.

Vulnerability in Health Care ICT Solutions

Health care is fundamentally concerned with human vulnerability, and a multitude of low- and high-tech technologies constitutes an important part of health care solutions. Context-sensitive studies of the implementation of ICT in health care point to various kinds of unintended consequences. Ash et al. (2004) and Campbell et al. (2006) operate with nine categories of unintended adverse consequences, listed in order of frequency: "more new work for clinicians," "unfavorable workflow issues," "never-ending system demands," "problems related to paper," "changes in communication patterns and practices," "negative emotions," "generation of new kinds of errors," "unexpected changes in power structure," and "over-dependency on the technology." These categories are related to different levels of ICT-mediated interaction, collaboration, and infrastructure that become visible through disruptions and breakdowns in the users' practice (Wentzer & Bygholm, 2007). In other words, contexts, and in these the enfolded order of time and space—of interaction, collaboration, and socio-technical infrastructure—become visible from studying ICT implementation. This chapter elaborates on these insights and the attention to contexts and implementation as important sources for the identification of unexpected consequences. Additionally, it articulates possible learning situations based on a case study of support work in surgery as an example of the role of technology in context. Thus it demonstrates how context-sensitive analyses of action can add to research into how to improve safety, health care resilience, and continuity of patient-care paths (Engeström, 1987, Young et al., 1998; Nielsen et al., 2003; Larsen & Bardam, 2007; Nemeth et al., 2008; Gittell, 2009).

Case: Patient Safety in Operation Rooms

Surgical work is well-researched, but surgical *support* work is less well-known (Lingard et al., 2002; Finn, 2008; Havens et al., 2010; Wentzer & Meier, 2014). This research describes surgical support work from an ethnographic study with document analysis, 90 hours of observation, and twenty-six interviews (Star & Ruhleder, 1999; Mol, 2002). The study was conducted in three different hospitals located in the Capital Region of Denmark, two of which are university hospitals, with research as part of their practices. All of the hospitals have 24-hour emergency surgery and elective day surgery from 7:30 a.m. to 3:00 p.m. The study was undertaken at four surgery centers, covering the specialties of obstetrics and gynecology, and gynecological oncology at the first hospital; orthopedic surgery, urology, and abdominal surgery at the second hospital; and pediatric surgery, pediatric oncology, and vascular surgery at the third hospital. The elective day programs in nine operation rooms (ORs) were observed, with a special focus on programs of action (Latour, 1994) in operational support work. The support work of nurses, social health care workers, and technical assistance was observed in the ORs, documented through photographs and detailed notes on type of operation, action sequences, relations to humans and nonhumans, and modes of communication. Field notes and interviews were analyzed according to the theoretical frameworks of human–computer interaction and expansive learning in activity theory (Engeström, 1987; Kuutti, 1996; Bardram, 2005). The theoretical assumptions are that sign tools, such as language and techniques, mediate all learning and interaction. On the one hand, the mediation depends on the subject's "operating skills," such speaking a language or knowing how to read, write, ride a bicycle, thread a needle, and so on. On the other hand, the subject's "action with the tool" depends on "the goal," such as reading because you want to know what the book is about, riding your bicycle because you have a destination to go to, and threading a needle because you have something to mend. The concrete goal of an action is also part of a larger cultural "activity system," where the subject's motivation to participate is related to social norms, rules, and values, such as reading the book to become educated or mending your clothes to look presentable. These analytical levels of mediating action with tools, signs, and materials of various kinds depend on the goal of the activity and the norm system that the activity is part of and motivated by.

The findings of two overall programs of actions in surgery support work are presented below, and further explicated in relation to the activity model to point out central artifacts and relations to the outcome. Then the interdependency of the two programs of actions is discussed. Three examples of tensions or breakdowns are identified and explicated as sites of learning, to ensure safety in technology-mediated teamwork.

Two Programs of Action in the Operation Room

The many sequences of action, interactions, and communication in the ethnographic study can be summed up as two programs of action that explain

Technology in Context: Exploring Vulnerability in Surgery

the meaning and motives of operation support work: first, and foremost, ensuring safety and second, efficiency. These motives are mutually dependent, and they create a tension, with the risk of breakdown in the teamwork when technologies are out of order, especially in the case of advanced information technologies when the surgical support workers are not trained or have not been given sufficient user rights to solve a problem.

First Program of Action: Ensuring Safety

The first program of action is concerned with ensuring safety in the care pathway for individual patients entering and leaving the OR. Ensuring safety is paramount to surgical support work, as it is not only concerned with the patient, but also with the surgeon's need to feel safe to concentrate on the operation itself and the general safety in the team as a group, with its interdependencies and shared responsibilities. Aseptic guidelines and practices support can maintain this goal, but the support workers have a special responsibility to secure a sterile, aseptic environment around the patient and the operation table (see the inner zone in Figure 8.1). It is the responsibility of the surgical support workers to make sure team members follow the aseptic procedures, and they are expected to detect and correct risk-promoting behavior; for example, nonsterile persons crossing the boundary of the sterile zone.

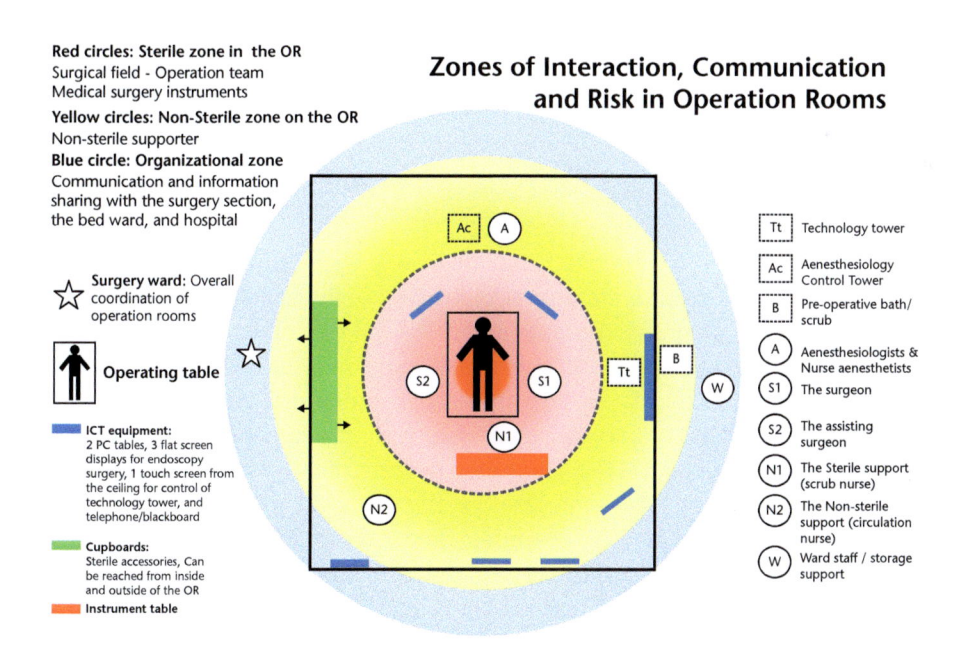

Figure 8.1 Zones of Interaction, Communication, and Risk in Operation Rooms

This sterile zone in the OR is constantly encroached by various kinds of disturbances that challenge safety in different ways: for example, by increasing the risk of the patient's wound being infected or breaking the surgeon's concentration. A chief surgeon sums up:

> *There is always a risk. We are in a sterile environment. Everything takes place in a sterile environment. This means that I can't just go to a cupboard and get what I need. Everything has to be in place from the beginning. We can plan 90 per cent, but something will always happen that wasn't planned for. For everything to be at hand, we would have to operate in the storage room, and that's not possible. That's why running adjustments will always be norm. We try to learn every time. Are there things we can do better, improve? The problem is that the more instruments you bring in from the start, the longer time it takes to prepare for the operation. It's a balance between not unpacking and packing everything again, which increases the operation time enormously, and having precisely the instruments you need. It's a balance that means that you have to send people (non-sterile) in and out of the OR/room to fetch the things you need. Or you find out that it's really another type of operation the patient needs, and you have to re-saddle. Doing emergency surgery also amplifies this. These are the terms.*

Operation support work is thus concerned with ensuring maximum safety, knowing that absolute predictability is impossible to attain. There will always be a small amount of risk to learn from, chance to be aware of, and adjustments to make (Dunne, 1993). The following section first gives an account of how the "90 percent" predictability of an operation is achieved by the team in a process with three phases: the preoperative, intraoperative, and postoperative phases. Then, examples of different orders of adjustments in relation to the critical 10 percent are provided.

First Phase: The Preoperative Coordination of Safety Roles and Security Tasks

In the preoperative phase, everything practical is planned and prepared, from the choosing of instruments and equipment for the specific operation, to receiving and positioning the patient on the surgery table. The anesthesia and various sedatives are administered. The surgeon and the surgery support workers plan and collect the instruments. A standard sterile container for surgical instruments contains no fewer than forty instruments, and for endoscopic surgery, the quantity of equipment—especially technological and the more advanced machinery—increases greatly. Every item has to be carefully unpacked with coordinated movements, and nonsterile hands and surfaces must never touch sterile surfaces. Two surgical support workers, assigned the roles of sterile support and nonsterile support, respectively, together perform this task of unpacking the items in an infection-safe manner. The sterile support continues to build up the sterile zone, the surgery bed, tables, and tools. The nonsterile group continuously facilitates all information, material, and technologies coming into or going out of the OR—from phones, PCs, screens, sutures, and technologies and machinery towers that run video, lighting, gas, electricity, and so on. The nonsterile support person and the nurse anesthetists receive the patient and help him or her onto the operating table. Following anesthesia, performed by the anesthesiologist and the anesthesia nurse, the patient's body is carefully arranged by the support assistant into a safe position that is also suitable for the specific operation. They continue to prepare the patient's body for the operation by using an aseptic wash and sterile drapes. In total, the operating team has six members, excluding the patient. These are the surgeon, the sterile and nonsterile supporters (also called the scrub nurse and assistant), the nurse anesthetists, the anesthesiologist, and the surgeon's assistant. Of this team, only the supporters and nurse stay in the room with the patient the whole time. The anesthesiologist is present in the pre- and postoperative phases, whereas the surgeon's assistant and the surgeon are mainly present in the intraoperative phase.

Second Phase: Rituals and Rhythms of Distributed Attention and Interaction in the Intraoperational Phase

The intraoperational phase begins with the ritual of "the Surgical Safety Checklist" (WHO, 2009), initiated by the nonsterile support person, who follows the checklist and documents the procedure on the PC, as the team members state their names and roles. The nonsterile support person continually documents security measures on the use of sponges and sutures, estimates the loss of blood, and weighs and preserves removed organic tissue. The sponge count runs like a chain of voices through the team, where the nonsterile support person starts counting out loud how many out of five sponges there are left in each open packet s/he has in his/her zone, the sterile support counts how many s/he has on the operation assisting table, and the surgeon counts how many are in the surgery field. They are to end up with the number "Five!" for each packet of sponges that is registered as being opened. If a sponge is missing, there is the possibility of it having been left inside the patient. This is one of the greatest fears of the support people, as it can be lethal to the patient. Apart from the noise of the anesthesia equipment at the head of the operating table, the counting voices are the only sounds in the room. The operation is undertaken with silent concentration, hands in the operating field, and instruments moving back and forth between the surgeon and the sterile support, with his/her table of carefully ordered instruments. The operating field is the surgeon's domain, and the table is the sterile support's domain. Their movements back and forth in coordinated gestures are a choreography of, not dancers, but hands and instruments moving in and out of the surgical field. The operating team is dressed in identical sterile clothing. The surgeon signals with finger positions which instrument is wanted, and the sterile support indicates with gesticulations how instruments, sutures, and the like can be grasped by the surgeon without cutting or piercing any fingers. The operating team wears two pairs of gloves: a pair of green gloves closest to the skin, with white gloves over these to protect against infection caused by gloves being penetrated by a needle or sharp knife. If the green color is visible, this indicates a risk of infection, and the gloves are changed, handed in from the nonsterile zone to the sterile supporter. Instruments and materials move in and out of the operating field, on and off the operating table. Communication is close to nonverbal. The focus of the surgeon's eyes stays within the operating field, while the eyes of the sterile support follow the hand of the surgeon and the progress of the operation. The sterile support needs to be able to predict the surgeon's next move and time the exchange of instruments as fluently as possible, without interrupting the surgeon's attention to the field. It is a matter of coordination of movements and actions that make, in the words of a chief nurse, the support person "become the surgeon's eyes." What she means is that support work is not only about "handing over a petang"; it is an artistic craft. It is a technical art form in the sense that a surgeon tired from a long operation (or an inexperienced surgeon) can be supported to such an extent that the sterile support person becomes their "eyes" and, thus, can ensure safety by co-directing and co-predicting the progress of the operation. This was especially clear in relation to operations with high unpredictability: for example, in research, where new procedures and/or tools are being tried out. Here the surgeon is more dependent on having a personal sterile supporter. In routine operations with inexperienced sterile support personnel, the surgeon might prefer to assist him/herself by asking for a small operation tray of instruments to be placed directly on the patient's body. The role of the sterile supporter is then to observe that nothing is dropped or put pressure on the patient's body. Again, the performance of the surgeon and the vulnerability of the patient's body to pressure during anesthesia are dependent on the sterile support worker's experience and ability to foresee operational events.

Wordless Communication

In general, conversation is nearly absent. The surgeon's tone, in many ways, sets the mood of the team. Apart from the rituals of the Surgical Safety Checklist that start and end the intraoperative phase, all attention is directed centripetally toward the operation field, but divided among different roles, zones, and senses. Whereas eyes and tactile movements are central in the sterile zone, the nonsterile support person has his/her back turned to the sterile zone most of the time. S/he either reads or writes on the computer, answers phones, and walks back and forth between the cupboard with drugs and material of various kinds. Because his/her back is turned much of the time, s/he listens very attentively, to detect any changes that might require assistance. One nurse working in the role of nonsterile support says she can sense if something is wrong, even with her back turned. The nurse's bodily attention is horizontal and directed inward to the sterile zone of the OR, while his/her cognitive attention is mediated "outward" via the computer and phones to the surrounding hospital. S/he is communicating with the bed unit, the lab, the storage room with instruments, and so on. This ICT-mediated communication is generally carried out silently, through clicking the mouse, reading, and writing. Sometimes the nurse leaves the room to get materials or instruments for the operation.

The surgeon's attention is "vertical" in the sense that it is a focused, in-depth perception of the operation field. A surgeon explains how she concentrates so much that she does not "see the patient." This perception of the patient as a unified body and person is reserved for the nurse anesthetists with respect to the upper part of the body, vital signs, and so on, whereas the sterile support attends to the rest of the body. A surgeon also characterizes his/her attention to the operation field to be so focused, that s/he experiences, quote "verbal aphasia." Talk diverts attention and thus becomes a risk factor. The importance of the supporters' predictive skills becomes evident. Of course, talk does take place. Sometimes in an understood, self-evident manner, as when the surgeon uses a nickname for an instrument s/he wants, or simply asks for "the thingy." Here, the supports start guessing which instrument is meant. Suggestions are shown by drawing the shape of the suggested instrument in the air, and so on. These almost nonverbal interactions and multimodal communications are interesting because they reveal that these communicative work patterns are analog, and refer to a very material way of sensemaking by producing visual figures. Other kinds of talk arise at the end of the operation. A kind of merry atmosphere of relief and satisfaction that everything has gone well shows itself in humorous remarks. The surgical specialties showed some differences though, probably related to the varying risk factors, so that operations on children and on vital organs were more serious and sensitive in tone and involved less spontaneous communication than operations for such things as "tennis elbow," which is a standard procedure.

Third Phase: Postoperational Chains of Action

The open surgery operation ends after the incision has been closed with stitches, sterile pads, and/or bandages, and the instrument, sponge, and needle counts have been completed. The support workers start packing up instruments to be sent to the surgical decontamination services. The large amount of sterile clothing and plastic sheeting that created the sterile environment around the patient, machines, and so on is removed and placed in dustbins. The patient is brought back to consciousness. The nonsterile support calls a hospital porter to help move the patient from the surgery table into a hospital bed and along to the recovery room or to a ward. The cleaning staff members are informed that the OR is ready to be cleaned before the next patient arrives. As a safety and control measure, the sterile support confirms the documentation of the nonsterile support by initialing the record.

Surgical Safety as Ping-Pong

Central to this program of action to create security for the patient and safety among the team is the distribution of attention, and the many coordinated chains of action between sterile and nonsterile zones, involving a range of techniques, procedures, and embodied, tacit understandings. In total, the activity of surgery looks like one smoothly moving machine involving organs, multiple senses, and techniques, where everybody and everything seems to move according to well-rehearsed scripts for each specific role, position, and task. These complex but well-ordered socio-technically mediated interactions, where the participants are always on top of the speed of things and as such, are in control of "chance," is described metaphorically among the team members. The value of ping-pong in surgical work is a shared understanding across surgery centers and specialties that expresses and connotes how successful surgery teamwork is "played" as an elegant game of table tennis, with rapid and precise movements between the ball (the patient), the bat (the techniques), and the players (the team).

Second Program of Action: Producing Efficiency

The second program of action relates to the first; that is, the individual cases of surgery relate to the overall production plan of the OR on a daily basis. Each OR is booked for a certain number of operations, depending on the type of operation and the average performance time of the specific surgeon. This production plan is organized using an information system called ORBIT. The booking system displays in real time what operations are planned and in progress in every OR of the surgery ward. This gives an overview, and it is led by a "flow-master," or central unit, which allocates resources and plans all the activities of operations. The production plan of ORBIT is displayed on big screens in every corridor and in meeting rooms, as well as in the ORs. This reminds the staff of what is going on and what is planned. For the surgery team, the production plan plays a vital role, because it shows and measures the time they spend in the three phases of every operation, as well as showing them what operation(s) are still to be performed within the given time frame of the day. In practice, this means the team is constantly aware that they have a time schedule to keep to, and when something unanticipated occurs, they have to find the time from elsewhere. A big task for the nonsterile support is collaboration with the surrounding ward and hospital(s) on a number of issues in relation to exchange of information, materials, and tools, and coordinating patient arrivals to and from the OR. Some patient cases also require special attention in relation to contamination and the risk of infection. These risks involve extra cleaning assistance, changing the order of patients' operations, and extra aseptic precautionary measures among the team. Organizing such changes while keeping to time schedules and maintaining patient flow is, in many cases, orchestrated by the nonsterile support. Moreover, his/her success in doing so is crucial to keeping to the production plan. This becomes apparent when the team members praise each other for being "ahead of time," or when the half-awake patient is barely out of anesthesia before the porter moves his/her bed out of the OR, and the cleaning staff members enter to prepare for the next operation. This efficiency and speed is highly dependent on a whole range of human and technical actants that have to play along or be made to behave, to stick to the production plan, on the one hand, and maintain the experience of "ping-pong," on the other. In general, this is what happens, which gives the OR a magic touch of human and technological clockwork, with little virtuoso chimes sounding when disruptions are solved creatively.

To sum up, the first program of action (relating to the security of the individual patient) and the second program of action (keeping to the production program of the OR) are interrelated. They are positively related in the sense that the efficiency also benefits patients because efficiency shortens the time that patients spend anesthetized on the surgery table. From a wider perspective, efficiency also prevents delays, and possibly cancellations, in the OR's program, and shortens the patient waiting list for surgery. On the negative side, there is a risk from the pressure to increase efficiency that a high turnover rate of patients in surgery is considered a greater priority than the quality of individual patient care, as well as pushing the team's resources for preventing errors and avoiding risks to the limit.

Learning Sites: Foregrounding Context from Socio-Technical Interruptions of Flow

The unanticipated "10 percent" that is impossible to predict and plan for in advance, no matter how well the team plan, is always a threat to safety in the

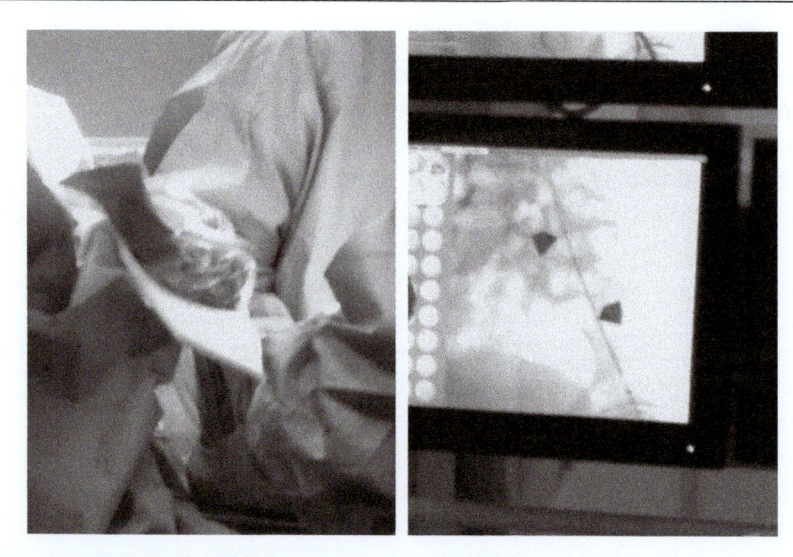

Figure 8.2 Photographs of Practical, Low-Tech Solutions

Left: Standard surgery leg holders are replaced by two soft, disposable washcloths to support the feet and legs of a small child. *Right*: The surgeon maintains focus on a vascular image in which two pieces of stocking plaster are in use.

OR. An important part of the support workers' competences, apart from nursing, is their ability to come up with new solutions to obstacles to the flow of the operation that suddenly appear. This ability to solve problems creatively can be low- or high-tech to varying degrees. Below are examples of disturbances at different levels of interaction, leading to different kinds of breakdowns that challenge the role of the surgery support in the team, its resilience, and the safety of the patient.

Disruption Caused by a "Burner with No More Lives"

This example comes from gastrointestinal surgery. In many cases, open "low-tech" surgery using a scalpel and suture is replaced by endoscopic, high-tech surgery (i.e., laparoscopy, also called keyhole surgery), where operations are performed through small incisions in the body. A burner is used instead of a scalpel inside the abdominal working space to burn, instead of cutting out, affected tissue. The burning prevents the tissue from bleeding. In this example, the burner stopped working during the operation and, thus, interrupted the flow. The nonsterile supporter had to send for a new burner from the storage room. The surgeon became annoyed with the support workers because the "knife time" of the operation was prolonged by the wait for the new burner. In the future, support staff members are expected to keep count of the burners' limited lifetime of twenty operations. This is a new task for the support workers, and they would have to agree on the development of a new "tool," a guideline to control it. Keeping systematic track of burners' lives through a guideline becomes an attempt to handle the high-vulnerability context in which surgery takes place, in a way that attempts to prevent any disruption to safety and efficiency. Technology in this context must work according to plan (see Figure 8.2).

Change of Direction in Mid Operation

The second example is also from abdominal surgery, on a patient with a gastrointestinal stromal tumor (GIST). Lack of access to the digital information system (with the patient's radiology scans) forces the surgeon to switch from the planned endoscopic operation to open surgery. In endoscopic surgery, the working and viewing space is provided by a laparoscope, a long, fiber-optic cable system, and carbon dioxide gas, which inflates the abdomen and thus makes it possible for the surgeon to see inside the patient's body. The image from the laparoscope is displayed on monitors placed above the surgery bed for the surgeon to look at and navigate by. However, they need additional information from the radiology scans to get a better overview to predict the location of the tumor and to navigate between the organs of the abdomen. But, as the digital information system remains inaccessible on this occasion, the surgeon was forced to change plans, and, thus, the whole operation was converted to traditional, open surgery, where the team members rely on their senses to observe and navigate directly inside the patient's body using their eyes and hands. This conversion of operational procedure increased safety because the nonworking ICT had made the planned procedure unsafe, but it also increased the operation time, the time the patient spent in anesthesia, and the size of the patient's operation scar.

Destabilization of Teamwork Because of an Inaccessible Information System

After the shift to open surgery, the team's spirits were low. There was no "ping-pong" between the team members, just a hostile atmosphere in the OR that was made worse by the knowledge that the patient would have a large operation scar, which in light of the events, became unavoidable—sixteen stitches for an incision of 14 cm. In the end, the surgeon, clearly dissatisfied with the support workers, stated that they were "not a team." The support workers, on the other hand, had neither the skills nor the administrative user rights to solve ICT barriers. Therefore, the resilience of the teamwork, as well as the sustainability and efficiency of the operation program of the OR, depends on ICT infrastructures, and the organizational support of these. In this example, nobody in the team had any direct power to solve ICT problems in the clinical context of interaction and dependency on ICT infrastructures. In other words, the vulnerability of surgical work is influenced by ICT in the immediate physical context of the surgery, yet the actions needed to alter these contextual conditions were located *outside* the OR and the health care staff's jurisdiction.

Risk in Technology-Driven Research

Image technologies have also opened up new research possibilities between radiology and vascular surgery. Interventional radiology in vascular surgery makes minimally invasive image-guided diagnosis and treatment of disease possible. In this example, a young woman with leg pain from poor blood circulation is diagnosed with narrow veins, using image-guided diagnosis, and is offered treatment via the insertion of a stent to increase the diameter of the troublesome vein. She received only a local anesthetic and expected to participate in the image-guided surgery, holding her breath to improve the quality of the X-ray images, and so on. The stent was inserted after 2 hours of surgery, but right after that, a blood clot (vein thrombosis) developed in the leg being operated on. The surgeon monitored developments continuously, viewing new images, and, in consultation with a radiologist, decided to continue with the operation, to prevent paralysis in the patient's foot. The stent was to be removed, after which, the blood clot would be sucked out to allow the blood to flow through the vein again. This prolonged the interoperational phase by several hours.

Ethical Patient Dilemma: "Hold Your Breath"

The patient is awake, holding her breath every time the accelerator takes an image. The X-ray radiation alarm—which monitors the amount of radiation the patient is being exposed to—goes off several times and is repeatedly turned off manually by the supporting nurse. At the same time, a team of four works intensely on finding and removing the clot by drawing out blood with a tube, called a venous access catheter. The surgeon needs total silence to concentrate. The work of the team requires fine motor skills and many coordinated movements, which are repeated in successive steps: patient holds her breath, X-ray, adjusting tube, drawing blood out, examining it for clots, cleaning instruments, and then again, holding of breath, tube adjustment, and so on, for more than 2 hours. The patient gradually becomes uncomfortable, cries quietly, starts shaking and sweating, and asks when this will be over. In the meantime, the personal assistant of the surgeon is called in, and two extra nurses come in to calm the patient. The patient complains that this was

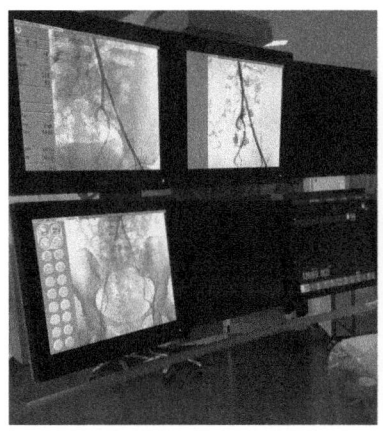

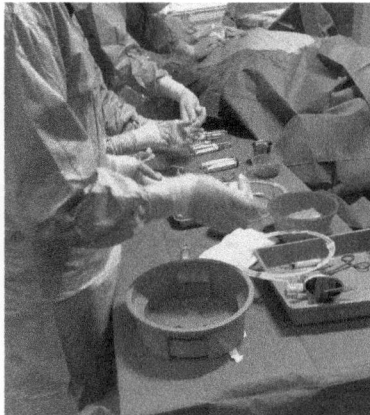

Figure 8.3 Photographs of Removing a Blood Clot, by Image Technologies in Vascular Surgery

Left: X-ray images of a venous access catheter in patient's left leg. *Right*: The surgery team with the awake patient pausing the breath to ensure the quality of the X-ray images for the surgeon to navigate by while sucking up and cleaning blood with a tube, in a chain of fine coordinated hand movements from an additional three people, a radiographer and two nurses.

not what she was informed of and consented to. She wants to go home! A senior surgeon enters the OR and tells the patient she will need to spend the night in hospital. This story about when the unplanned, the "10 percent," happens points to another level of interaction and risk, as the participation of the patient becomes a factor in the success of the teamwork. The patient, though, is placed in a double-bind situation that puts the whole intervention and team at risk, and this presents an ethical dilemma of delegating too much responsibility to the patient. On the one hand, she is uncomfortable and wants to leave but, on the other hand, she has to collaborate with the team to get the surgery completed successfully. However, the collaboration is on unequal terms, as it is her body on the table and her ability to handle the vulnerable state she is in that might determine the success of the intervention (see Figure 8.3).

Conclusion: Multilayered Contexts of Collaboration and Learning

As argued and demonstrated in this chapter, technology is highly context dependent. Context can be learned from, especially when implementing technology because technology-initiated changes of interaction, collaboration, and workflow unveil prior and tacit understandings of practice and make them negotiable. Surgery is a high-risk activity that requires as much predictability as possible. Therefore, surgery is an environment that calls for shared stable contextual understandings among participants, especially regarding modes of interaction, tasks, roles, and techniques. ORs are full of diverse forms of high- and low-tech technologies that mediate interaction at different levels of collaboration and learning. Surgery is interwoven with techniques and instruments that are essential to the outcome: patient safety. ICTs are interwoven in coordinating and planning the operation program for the OR. They are mediating artifacts that are a part of making complex operations possible. Technologies constitute an essential part of the team's communication and activities and, thereby, configure, as well as challenge, the user's skills and competences. The technically mediated teamwork is related to risk, especially when the tools do not work as expected, thereby affecting their shared understanding of context, the division of work and tasks within it, and emotional responses to unpredictability.

Learning from Contextual Knowledge

These examples of the interruptions of flow and security in the practice of surgery draw attention to the importance of context as something mediated and multilayered, which can be learned from when it breaks down, or rather "breaks open." Recalling the nine categories of unintended adverse consequences noted earlier (Campbell et al., 2006), several of these were found and demonstrated in the examples e.g., "negative emotions" and "new work" in relation to the burner "with no more lives." "Changes in communication patterns and practices," "unfavorable workflow issues," "dependency on technology," and "changes in power structures" were issues that arose from the inaccessible information system. Whereas "new kinds of errors" and risk management came into being in the example of image technology in vascular surgery that transformed the patient's role. These categories thus point to "context" as a social, technical, and politically/ethically mediated activity we take for granted and consider self-evident when everything runs smoothly, but when something breaks down, we then "see" context and how it is essential to human action.

References

Akrich, M. & Latour, B. (1992). A summary of a convenient vocabulary for the semiotics of human and nonhuman assemblies. In W. E. Bijker & J. Law (eds.), *Shaping technology/building society: Studies in sociotechnical change*. Cambridge, MA: MIT Press, pp. 259–64.

Ash, J. S., Berg, M., & Coiera, E. (2004). Some unintended consequences of information technology in health care: The nature of patient care information system-related errors. *Journal of the American Medical Informatics Association: JAMIA, 11*(2), 104–12.

Bardram, J. E. (2005). The trouble with login: On usability and computer security in ubiquitous computing. *Personal Ubiquity Computing, 9*(6), 357–67.

Campbell, E. M., Sittig, D. F., Ash, J. S., Guappone, K. P., & Dykstra, R. H. (2006). Types of unintended consequences related to computerized provider order entry. *Journal of the American Medical Informatics Association: JAMIA, 13*(5), 547–56.

Cole, M. & Engeström, E. (1993). A cultural–historical approach to distributed cognition. In G. Salomon (ed.), *Distributed cognitions: Psychological and educational considerations*. Cambridge: Cambridge University Press, pp.1–46.

Dunne, J. (1993). *Back to the rough ground: Practical judgement and the lure of technique*. Notre Dame, IN: University of Notre Dame Press.

Engeström, Y. (1986). The zone of proximal development as the basic category of educational psychology. *Quarterly Newsletter of the Laboratory of Comparative Human Cognition, 8*(1), 23–42.

Engeström, Y. (1987). *Learning by expanding*. Helsinki: Orienta-Konsultit.

Finn, R. (2008). The language of teamwork: Reproducing professional divisions in the operating theatre. *Human Relations, 61*(1), 103–30.

Gittell, J. H. (2009). *High performance healthcare: Using the power of relationships to achieve quality, efficiency and resilience*. New York: McGraw-Hill.

Havens, D. S., Vasey, J., Gittell, J. H., & Lin, W. (2010). Relational coordination among nurses and other providers: Impact on the quality of patient care. *Journal of Nursing Management, 18*(8), 926–37.

Kuutti, K. (1996). Activity theory as a potential framework for human computer interaction Research. In B. Nardi (ed.), *Context and consciousness*. Cambridge, MA: MIT Press, pp. 17–44.

Larsen, S. B. & Bardram, J. (2007). *Competence articulation: A study of the zone of proximal development in telemedical collaboration*. CHI '08 Proceedings of the SIGCHI Conference of the SIGCHI Conference on Human Factors in Computing Systems, pp. 553–62.

Latour, B. (1993). *We have never been modern*. Cambridge, MA: Harvard University Press.

Latour, B. (1994). Technical mediation: Philosophy, sociology, genealogy. *Common Knowledge, 3*(2), 29–64.

Latour, B. (2005). *Reassembling the social: An introduction to Actor-Network-Theory*. Oxford: Oxford University Press.

Lingard, L., Reznick, R., DeVito, I., & Espin, S. (2002). Forming professional identities on the health care team: Discursive constructions of the "other" in the operating room. *Medical Education, 36*, 728–34.

Mol, A. (2002). *The body multiple: Ontology in medical practice*. Durham, NC, and London: Duke University Press.

Nemeth, C., Wears, R., Woods, D., & Hollnagel, E. (2008). Minding the gaps: Creating resilience in health care. In K. Henriksen, J. B. Battles, M. A. Keyes, & M. L. Grady (eds.), *Advances in patient safety: New directions and alternative approaches*. Rockville, MD: Agency for Healthcare Research and Quality.

Nielsen, J., Dirckinck-Holmfelt, L., & Danielsen, O. (2003). From action research to dialogue design: Mutual learning as a guiding principle. *International Journal of Human–Computer Interaction, 15*(1), 21–40.

Schuback, M. S. C. (2006). The knowledge of attention. *International Journal of Qualitative Study of Health and Well-Being, 1*(3), 133–40.

Star, S. L. & Ruhleder, K. (1999). Layers of silence, arenas of voice: The ecology of visible and invisible work. *Computer Supported Collaborative Work, 8*(1–2), 9–30.

Wentzer, H. S. & Bygholm, A. (2007). Attending unintended transformations of health care infrastructure. *International Journal of Integrated Care, 7*(e41), 1–13.

Wentzer, H. S. & Meier, N. (2014). *At skabe sikkerhed, effektivitet og tryghed / Creating security, efficiency, and safety.* Copenhagen: KORA.

World Health Organization. (2009). Patient safety: Surgical safety checklist. WHO. https://www.who.int/patientsafety/safesurgery/ss_checklist/en/ (Accessed January 31, 2019).

Young, G. J., et al. (1998). Patterns of Coordination and Clinical Outcomes: A Study of Surgical Services. *Health Services Research, 33*(5, Pt 1), 1211–36.

9

Patients, Families, and Care Settings

Louise Locock, Glenn Robert, and Ninna Meier

Introduction

In this chapter, we shall discuss context from two perspectives; first, we discuss how patients understand, experience, and engage with context, and second, we consider the roles of patients in the processes by which contexts change. Our focus here is primarily at the interpersonal-relational level, although we acknowledge that patients may also shape context in collective ways. One example of the latter is how women have shaped maternity services through pressure to have particular types of birth experiences, from protests in favor of natural childbirth controlled by women in the 1970s and 1980s, through to the more recent trends of choosing elective cesarean births. Another might be the collective impact on contexts for care of the presence of increasing numbers of elderly people with dementia and physical disability in nursing homes or medical wards. However, patients are not a single, homogenous group, but rather people with variable and complex characteristics and needs, even within seemingly uniform diagnosis groups. Thus, in this chapter, we focus on the microlevel interactions and experiences of patients, their families, and health care staff.

We work from the point of view that context is not a fixed, external variable—not a passive backcloth—but is reproduced and recreated constantly by actors engaging interactively and dynamically. Both context and action are altered in the course of these interactions: context frames and constrains actions, but the actions of actors develop and amend contexts progressively. We suggest that our understanding of who these actors are must be broadened: to understand context and action in health care, we need to acknowledge patients and informal caregivers, who perform important often-neglected or overlooked informal care work (Strauss et al., 1997; Star & Strauss, 1999).

To explore this proposition we use illustrations from several of our own research studies to argue that patients and informal caregivers (often simultaneously) "see" context, "are" context, and "shape" context in health care. Finally, we reflect on how we think about context in relation to patients and families in the design of our research studies and data analysis.

Patients, Families, and Contexts

Patients and their family members often have the time and opportunity to observe what goes on around them: how different kinds of work are carried out, how people interact, and how staff members negotiate technological and material opportunities and restraints. All of these are potentially important elements of context, which may otherwise be unseen by others. Data from a research study that explored the links between patients' experiences of health care and staff motivation, affect, and well-being in a variety of health care settings illustrate how patients are able to reflect on how other patients interact with human (and nonhuman) actors. For example, a patient on a "Medicine for Older People" acute hospital ward describes seeing other patients handled roughly and in an uncaring way during a night shift (Maben et al., 2012b):

> You get one or two of the old hands do a bit of bullying. The other night one couldn't get her own way with one of the ladies and had her crying. I felt sorry. I suppose I was a bit of coward I should have said "I didn't like what I heard."

In this case, the observed context not only affects the care of the individual but also shapes the care experience of the observer.

Similarly, two patients on an Emergency Admissions Unit (EAU) describe the (contrasting) experiences of elderly patients on the unit as they observed them, highlighting the importance—and variability—of relational aspects of care, and how noticeable these are when absent (Maben et al., 2012a):

> I did observe a young, what they used to call auxiliaries in my day, nurse and an old lady couldn't feed herself. Honestly I was moved to tears. This young auxiliary nurse fed her, and was chatting away to her in such a lovely, lovely way. The old lady wasn't speaking much but they were having a really nice conversation ... they just seemed to have the time to deal with patients individually which was wonderful. It actually moved me to tears. It was so lovely ... just watching this young woman, just how she dealt with this old lady who was in a great deal of pain.

> Yeah, I remember when there was an old lady across the room from me, in sort of the EAU, and she was being sick loads, and you could see that she wasn't well. I was a bit worried about her really. No one sort of came to her and she was left there for ages with this bowl of sick under your nose. She was there for ages, and she kept shouting for help....

Patients can, of course, also reflect on their own care, and in doing so provide rich, emotive descriptions of health care contexts, as this example from a hematology-oncology ward illustrates (Maben et al., 2012a):

> The quality of the care, the regularity of observation, the courtesy, dignity and good humour of everyone was just overwhelming; it changed my life, enhanced things. I'd rather this hadn't happened rather than had happened but it was a turning point for me and the outcome at the moment is very bleak but looking back that was very positive, like a sabbatical. I was cared for, I had a beautiful room; I could relax about bodily things. I could enjoy the conversations with everyone who came in... and that must be a sign of nurse and staff wellbeing, if they can suspend whatever background they've come from and divert themselves to the benefit of the patient. That was just exhilarating. I wrote a letter to the chief executive, saying how privileged I was to be a patient there.

In watching and reflecting on such interactions, patients may have a significantly different view of the health care system than do members of staff or management. Such observations and reflections could potentially lead to new and valuable ideas for improvement and organizational change if input and feedback from patients and relatives were recognized for what they could bring to the system.

To illustrate this point further, in a participatory research project seeking to improve physical therapy for stroke patients on acute rehabilitation wards, ethnographic field notes contained numerous examples of how patients and, in particular, family members, could see (seemingly simple) opportunities for making improvements to the physical and social environment on the wards (Jones et al., 2016):

> One female stroke survivor described how the day staff would all come in in the morning and congregate around the nurses' station. She complained that by this time she was desperate for the toilet and would ask a member of staff to take her. They would refuse and make her wait 20 minutes until they had had handover (I am assuming). She found this distressing as "I'm 70 and when you get older your bladder is not as good as it was and you can't wait" – or words to that effect. She noticed that, in general, staff would not deviate from their tasks in order to help a patient at the time it was requested. In another example she said that she asked someone to simply close a window but was refused until 10 minutes later when she was "already frozen." The member of staff had been walking right past the window at the time of asking.

> A female carer said she was very upset because she was told (rudely) to leave her husband when it was teatime. She wanted to help him eat and said because she left he didn't eat anything. She said she felt that she was not allowed to care for her husband and that staff did not seem to acknowledge that "he is still my husband and we still have that bond." She was juggling visiting him, a full time job, as well as caring for her son and grand-daughter, and she needed flexibility with visiting.

She was also concerned that staff did not allow time for her husband, who has dysphasia, to communicate with them.

The organization of care around staff preference or convenience has evoked long-standing criticism. Two younger male patients on the same acute stroke ward as in the previous case labeled weekends as "soul destroying," and they coined the phrase "Sunday Afternoon Syndrome" to describe their boredom, which was largely the result of the small amount of therapy delivered on Saturdays and, in particular, on Sundays. The fact that some staff members are able to walk away from the unit and see it as a weekday "nine-to-five" environment, while patients are constrained to stay there all the time, serves to reinforce patients' sense of otherness and (literal) dislocation from the "real" world. Thus, staff and patients experience the same context very differently and for widely varying periods; patients both embody context and may encounter context in a more embodied way than do staff.

Feeling bored and isolated in a health care context can be alleviated by social contact and interaction. In a mixed-methods study exploring the impact of a move from (a) old multibed wards to (b) a newly built acute hospital with just single rooms, it was found that the wards allowed patients to engage actively or passively in the patient community (Maben et al., 2015). As the chapter on the materiality of buildings and physical infrastructure as contexts illustrates (Chapter 6), buildings *do* things: in this case, they afforded a shared visibility, co-monitoring, and potential companionship among patients. This kind of companionship can lead to engagement and attachments, which can be not only emotionally rewarding, but also potentially difficult. Below, a patient on a hematology-oncology ward describes how she felt about other patients there, and specifically after the death of another patient (Maben et al., 2012a):

> I love them, yes. And berate they're lost. It's unthinkable; there's a young woman with two children, apparently she didn't make it. I'm just devastated.

Patients in shared accommodation wards reported enjoying the security of being very visible to staff and to each other, which resulted in good patient camaraderie for some:

> In the bed I was in, you had a nice little community of us, all within talking distance... It's good for morale... [it] created a wonderful atmosphere between... we got on well with one another. And we all knew what each other had got wrong with them. -*Patient, surgical ward*

However, the disadvantages of shared patient accommodation included exposure to confused and disruptive patients, lack of privacy, and lack of physical comfort (Maben et al., 2016):

> The man who was opposite...he'd got dementia and he was in the shouting stage...shouting out "Help" all the time...they tried everything to help him; they were terribly, terribly patient...most of us, well I think all of us, understood, but it was a nuisance, because in the end it took over, you couldn't do anything else but listen, and see how they were getting on with him.

Although in this study two-thirds of patients expressed a clear preference for single rooms, lack of interaction with other patients led to strong feelings of isolation in some cases:

> It would have been nice to have been able to see other people, or maybe just to chat with other mothers...If you're in an open ward, you just see people coming and going...you can chat to people across the ward...you can see other people going through what you're going through...I just wanted to get home...because there isn't anyone to chat to and I just felt a little bit isolated being in the room on my own.

> Once you're on the mend and you can get up out of bed that's when it seems to be very lonely in a way, and isolated, I suppose...and the days and the nights seemed very, very long...If you're alone in a room you tend to think about your illness more than if you're chatting to somebody about the weather or your car, or something like that. That's how I felt.

> I don't like it here...It's boring sitting indoors all day either watching [TV] or reading [the paper] and looking at four walls. You can talk to [other patients on an open ward/bay]. Who are you going to talk to here? There's nobody to talk to. The staff, you do talk to them sometimes but they're busy, they've got their work to do.

Thus, patients and families are an integral component of context for other patients and for staff: the way in which patients in multibed wards are able to benefit from each other can become included in the organization of work on such a ward. For example, in elective hip and knee replacement surgery, early mobilization is key: in a multibed ward, staff may organize patient information and training seminars to this effect, facilitating patients who share a multibed ward to motivate each other, actively or through example, to become active as soon as possible.

All of the examples so far have been drawn from studies undertaken in the acute hospital setting. Yet most care is home self-care; a smaller proportion happens in GP surgeries or pharmacies, and even less in hospital. Thus, patients' homes become increasingly important sites for health care services, and the roles of patients and relatives in delivery of treatment and care changes. Focusing on the hospital sector obscures this much wider and more variable context, particularly the way in which the fabric of health care work is interdependent across different settings, and how events that occur in one setting may have unintended or overlooked consequences for patients and staff in other contexts. When we apply a micro perspective on context, we may explore the unpredictable and complex ways in which practices and interactions are connected across time and place, as demonstrated by practice scholars (Schatzki, 1996; Berg & Mol, 1998; Law & Mol, 2002; Nicolini, 2012). Examples drawn from studies of patient experiences disseminated on www.healthtalk.org show how family and patients together perform care work in the home, completely outside the remit of health care professionals, as this person with Type 2 diabetes explains:

> The family have been incredibly supportive of what I'm trying to do. Even through my rattiest moments, bless them. They are now actually more strict with my diabetes control than I am. If, if I eat something that they think I shouldn't eat you know, they, they will keep an eye on the clock and poke me to test an hour later, and if I do test and it's gone up too high, they'll be shoving me out the door for a walk, occasionally coming with me, but they are very supportive.

A person with asthma explained how she had shaped her home and work environment (and even her car) as a site of self-care, describing herself as an "organized asthmatic":

> I was given a very good piece of advice, which was that the best way to be asthmatic was to be an organized asthmatic. And that means keeping a note of your medication near your telephone or in your mobile phone or in the glove compartment of your car, or in your purse or something.... The other thing was to keep a peak flow meter about your person. So I have one in my office and I have one at home and I have one in the car and I have one in the holiday home, which probably sounds a bit excessive, but if you wake in the night and you're having difficulty breathing, yeah.

To understand context in health care form a micro perspective, we also need to attend closely to patient and staff interactions. On the one hand, what patients and families do can affect staff and services through subtle "under the radar" changes to context:

> *Louise (Peggy's daughter):* I put pictures all around the walls just so people would get to know my mum as the person not just the stroke sufferer—that gave her a distraction so she could look at her favourite cards and photos.
>
> *Peggy:* It just felt like a little bit of home—there's nothing like home—and it had a coming home feeling – it was new as I was able to talk about them to the staff, and when you are lying there so dehumanised, and unlike yourself you can't really respond. If I could talk about my children it made me feel better.[1]

On the other hand, a mixed-methods case study undertaken over 8 months in a "Medicine for Older People" acute hospital service in England highlights how a series of contextual factors (a high-demand/low-control work

Patients, Families, and Care Settings

environment, poor staffing, ward leadership, and co-worker relationships) shaped staff and patient interactions (Maben et al., 2012 b). The findings suggest that poor ward and patient-care climates often lead staff to seek job satisfaction through caring for "poppets," leaving less favored—and often more complex patients ("parcels")—to receive care that is less personalized. The "poppets" were those patients for whom staff felt particular sympathy, those with no frequent visitors or who reminded them of a close relative: "(they've) got something that just endears to you and you just feel, 'Oh, she's gorgeous.' You just click with them as well" (HCA 3). Staff were aware of the difficulties this presented, and tried not to show favoritism or get too close to patients but said they often "could not help it." The implications of resulting contextual changes on other patients or families and staff were that staff might not simply favor some patients but—through "discretionary care"—offer good care selectively to them, thus enhancing staff satisfaction in an otherwise unsatisfying work environment. Such good care was undertaken at the expense of time and attention shown to the less favored patients with less rewarding direct care needs.

This study also found that, in a high-demand patient-care environment, patients are cognizant of their vulnerability to becoming seen by staff as "difficult or demanding," and they seek to manage their relationships with nursing staff (in particular) accordingly. The researchers saw patients being extremely polite and grateful to staff, offering treats and almost "courting" staff favor—both potentially as a way of giving back to staff and perhaps trying to manage the relationships to gain good or better care for themselves. On the whole, patients did not wish to complain for fear of care worsening—a clear example of power dynamics at work—yet one patient noted that "making a nuisance" could be used as a strategy to improve care delivery:

> there's always one that doesn't want to work and turns away, and unless you make them do it by being a nuisance, it doesn't get done ... none of them really helped me [get back into bed] and I said "I'm sorry you think I'm a nuisance" and then he was alright....

In this example, the embodied context of the patient is ignored until he engages in strategies of micro resistance to assert some power, despite his vulnerability. The study findings suggest that the emotional labor involved in being a patient is greater in poor-care climates, where the quality of care is unpredictable and patient experience variable; patients need to "manage" relationships with a plethora of staff, as well as their own responses, so as not to be seen as a nuisance or a "problem" patient.

By contrast, in long-term conditions where most care is self-organized, the impact of staff on context is inevitably limited. Here, a senior civil servant with Type 2 diabetes describes, on www.healthtalk.org, how dietitians' advice to manage blood sugar levels by eating in a meeting failed to engage with her working environment and, as a result, was disregarded. Thus, the patient's wider context wins out over narrow clinical advice.

> I found that, when I went to the dietitians... Lovely women, but had no concept of my lifestyle... I mean I go to meetings (and they're quite senior level meetings)... and I said, "But sometimes they overrun or whatever." And somebody suggested I ate a yoghurt in the meeting. Now, yes, I could do, you know – women can breastfeed if they want to – but on the whole you don't. There's a bit of a credibility issue. And it also highlights that you have a condition and do you want people to know that you have a chronic condition? I don't as a whole mind, but I don't think I necessarily want, you know, the Director General of the Department of Health R & D to know that I'm a diabetic. And sort of some of the suggestions were quite inappropriate.

Discussion

We have argued that patients and informal caregivers (often simultaneously) "see" context, "are" context, and "shape" context in health care. We have shown that being a patient (being *patient* in a fast-paced system) affords the possibility of a unique vantage point on central elements of health care contexts, and that the feedback and input from patients and their families should be recognized as a resource. We demonstrated how patients and their families are contexts for other patients and for staff: this is hardly surprising, as we are all part of each other's context. However, the level of complexity that this point brings with it when studying and analyzing contexts in action is often ignored. We discussed patients and their families as being actively engaged in shaping contexts for themselves and others, offering a few examples of how brief, seemingly mundane everyday actions of patients can be strategically aimed at altering, for example, the physical environment of care, how they are perceived by staff, or the quality of care they receive.

We have also sought to demonstrate the potential of adopting a microlevel approach, as well as the need for further explorations of patients and families in health care contexts. Even with such an approach, we see several methodological and theoretical challenges ahead. Specifically, the question of how to study emotional and relational aspects of contexts in various illness settings strikes us as particularly challenging. Often, the unit of analysis for research refers to parts of peoples' subjective experiences and understandings of a situation or an event. Not all of the elements of such experiences can be expressed through language (e.g., embodied or tacit aspects). Comparing such phenomena across actors or illness settings will require systematic attention being paid to how both researcher and participants understand the phenomena, and what constitutes their context.

Several methodological considerations arise. First, there is scope for greater attention to studying how patients and relatives engage with the different aspects of the system, such as the physical buildings and artifacts, geographical distribution of work, health IT, staff, or other patients and relatives, *and* how such actions, in turn, reshape the context for other patients and relatives, as well as for health care staff. This would be highly relevant in several under-researched areas: in studies of patients, not just as recipients of care but also in terms of self-care and caring for others during or after their treatment, and in exploring patients, their families, and their home environment as central elements of the larger health care system. To contribute here, we suggest further detailed empirical analysis of who does what when providing care in different settings, and by which means interactions between patients, families, and staff are more or less successfully integrated across these. Particularly in the case of long-term conditions, May et al.'s (2014) reflections on the "burden of treatment" are relevant, as, here, patients become the providers of their own care, and their home becomes the care setting. There is work involved in shaping this care context that often remains invisible to professionals and systems, and, indeed, to researchers interested in studying context in health care.

Second, more could be done to enlist "patient and family ethnographer" observations as an alternative and supplementary perspective on important questions such as how teams function, how care decisions are made, why mistakes and miscommunications happen, and what happens to other patients. We acknowledge that patients can see contexts in ways that are different from staff, and they may be able to offer important feedback the health care system needs. However, we stress that enlisting patient and family ethnographers should be done with due attention to issues of power relationships, negotiations of perspective and knowledge, and ethics. This would require a more participatory stance to research, and a continuous and relational engagement with the field, characteristics of qualitative methods such as shadowing (Czarniawska, 2007), or engaged scholarship (Van de Ven, 2007). These methods may allow researchers to capture the complexity of contexts in action: the physicality the embeddedness, as well as the interactions, actions, and actors (human and nonhuman) that constitute the lived experiences that make up the material of contexts.

Finally, our challenge to organizational research is to focus on the continual and changing interplay between context and how a wider range of actors "see," "are," and "shape" it, as neither can be viewed satisfactorily in isolation. The perspective of those for whom health care is provided has been almost entirely absent in research discussions of context, with potential detrimental effects on how we understand and research organizational issues in specific health care contexts such as cancer care, mental health, and chronic diseases, where quality of care also rests on patients' and relatives' abilities to play an active part in their own care process. The turn to patient-centeredness means that researcher-led definitions and demarcations of what context is and how it should be studied are no longer sufficient.

Note

1. The extract here is from is from an NIHR HS&DR study in stroke services, in which one of the authors is participating (Jones et al., 2016). The names are pseudonyms.

References

Berg, M. & Mol, A. (eds.). (1998). *Differences in medicine: Unraveling practices, techniques and bodies*. Durham, NC, and London: Duke University Press.

Czarniawska, B. (2007). *Shadowing and other techniques for doing field studies in modern societies*. Malmö: Liber AB.

Jones, F., et al. (2016). *Using co-production to improve patient carer and staff experiences in health care organizations: A multi-centre, mixed methods evaluation in inpatient stroke units (CREATE)*. National Institute for Health Research Health Services and Delivery Research program. https://www.journalslibrary.nihr.ac.uk/programmes/hsdr/1311495/#/. (Accessed 14 March 2017).

Law, J. & Mol, A. (eds.). (2002). *Complexities: Social studies of knowledge practices*. Durham, NC: Duke University Press.

Maben, J., Adams, M., Peccei, R., Murrells, T., & Robert, G. (2012b). "Poppets and parcels": The links between staff experience of work and acutely ill older peoples' experience of hospital care. *International Journal of Older People Nursing, 7,* 83–94.

Maben, J., et al. (2015). Evaluating a major innovation in hospital design: Workforce implications and impact on patient and staff experiences of all single room hospital accommodation. *Health Service Delivery Research, 3*(3), n. pag.

Maben, J., et al. (2016). One size fits all? Mixed methods evaluation of the impact of 100% single-room accommodation on staff and patient experience, safety and costs. *BMJ Quality and Safety, 25,* 241–56.

Maben, J., et al. (2012a). *Exploring the relationship between patients' experiences of care and the influence of staff motivation, affect and wellbeing*. Final report. National Institute for Health Research Service Delivery and Organisation Programme.

May, C., et al. (2014). Rethinking the patient: Using burden of treatment theory to understand the changing dynamics of illness. *BMC Health Services Research, 14,* 281.

Nicolini, D. (2012). *Practice theory, work, and organization: An introduction*. Oxford: Oxford University Press.

Schatzki, T. R. (1996). *Social practices: A Wittgensteinian approach to human activity and the social* (digitally printed edition). Cambridge: Cambridge University Press.

Star, S. L. & Strauss, A. (1999). Layers of silence, arenas of voice: The ecology of visible and invisible work. *Computer Supported Cooperative Work, 8*(1–2), 9–30.

Strauss, A., Fagerhaugh, S., Suczek, B., & Weiner, C. (1997). *Social organization of medical work* (2nd ed.). Piscataway, NJ: Transaction Publishers.

Van de Ven, H. A. (2007). *Engaged scholarship: A guide to organizational and social research*. Oxford: Oxford University Press.

10

Place Matters in Context Analysis

Understanding Patients' Experiences of Context

Ninna Meier

What Is the Problem and How Can a Different Approach to Context Help?

In this chapter, I discuss the question of how patients might experience context for their illness in a multiorganizational health care system. Across modern health care sectors, the organization of health care work is changing, with growing attention to coherence and integration across the health care system. Here I focus on the organizational fragmentation and geographical distribution of work in cancer care, specifically how these issues relate to collaboration with and involvement of patients. These interactions between patients and health care professionals are central to each individual patient's process, and they are increasingly important to the overall health care system because patients are "partners" in the co-production of care, a point I will unfold below. The traditional monitoring of a patient's body during a process of illness by health care professionals takes place when patients and professionals are colocated, typically during the patient's admission to hospital. When admitted, patients are in the same physical location as the specialized knowledge of health care professionals, who have the responsibility to act if the illness develops unexpectedly. When patients are *not* admitted, they must engage in self-care activities and follow instructions regarding side effects or complications; therefore, the involvement of patients is essential. From a health care system's perspective, patients (and relatives, if possible) need to be involved in their treatment and care. For this to happen, the health care system's approach is to transfer information from health care professional to patient for instance via patient information leaflets. These knowledge transfer approaches are potentially problematic because they tend to overlook social and situated aspects of knowing in practice (see for instance Greenhalgh and Wieringa 2011 for a discussion). Such practice based contextual approaches can shed light on the interplay between three main elements: the ways in which work is organized (distributed organizationally and geographically), the movements of patients' bodies between their homes and different parts of the system (patients' perspective), and how these two influence the conditions for interaction between patients and health care professionals.

Drawing on traditional approaches to context as external elements in the "outer" layers of the health care system, we tend to miss at least two important elements of the relationship between patient and health care system. First, patients' experiences of being ill (and thus of being the object of organization or the subject of involvement) are situated in time and place, *where* the patient is. Second, as patients move physically from place to place during their illness, they move in and out of sight of and colocation with the different health care professionals that treat them. As a result, most patients are part of *many* different health care professionals' contexts, while the patients' contexts are still much less visible from a system's perspective.Considering the centrality of patients to health care systems, their experiences in and with the system are curiously under-researched, as discussed in Chapter 8, by Locock et al. The problem with this is that we lack a solid empirically based foundation for understanding this crucial aspect, and this has potential implications for research and practice. Because the collaboration between patients and health care professionals is increasingly important and because patients carry out important (albeit informal) health care work, organization scholars, in general, and health care researchers, in particular, can benefit from exploring patients' experiences of context. A systematic approach to researching patients' experiences of context can benefit research in several areas, but I would especially like to see the questions of vantage point (which perspective is context studied from?) and representation (whose context is studied?) integrated into contextual analyses of health care systems.

So how can a more nuanced and systematic approach to context, and patients' experiences of context, help? A common distinction in the usage of context is the distinction between focal event or phenomenon and background (Fetzer, 2004), also discussed in Chapter 2. Additionally, several approaches to context highlight the distinction between general social context and particular or individual social contexts, by some understood as (outer and inner) levels of context, which are often said to differ. In such approaches, outer layers are made up of objective elements of context that are not understood as a question of individual perception (Johns, 2017). However, as I will argue here, the question of context is less a matter of layers or objectivity and more a matter of approach: in this case, a matter of vantage point (which also relates to location) and representation as also discussed in Chapter 3. Thus, the approach I pursue in the discussions below is related to the second question in this book: *how do actors make sense of and engage with context?* In anthropological or ethnographic terms, this question deals with the challenge of how we (researchers) can know what others perceive (for a discussion, see Geertz, 1993 pp. 56–8). When we use an approach to context such as the one presented above, we see that patients' experiences of context may simultaneously be particular and individual, as well as containing common, shared features. Additionally, such an approach allows us to see how patients and health care professionals are essential elements of each other's context for action in the health care system.

Reorganization of Work: Examples from Cancer Care

The temporal ordering of health care work has changed, simultaneously compressing and extending time through an acceleration in the pace of work *and* prolonging the duration of treatment. Additionally, increasing economic pressure on health care systems has led to shorter lengths of stay in the hospital and more outpatient treatment. Moreover, cancer has evolved from being primarily a terminal disease toward being a chronic condition, with technologies and therapies emerging to improve diagnose and treatment, thus prolonging the life of many cancer patients. As a result, many cancer patients receive treatment for longer periods of time (American Cancer Society, 2015).

Until recently, welfare was regarded as a service provided to citizens by public or private organizations. However, there is now an important shift in the role of the citizen, from being a passive recipient to becoming an active coproducer of welfare across nations. In line with this, patient involvement is high on the agenda as an approach to engage patients to participate actively in and contribute to their own treatment. Health care work is increasingly organized around this premise. For this system to work, patient involvement is crucial: patients need to be informed about complications and side effects, and they need to be instructed in what to do should they exhibit signs of, for example, an infection. However, research into patient nonadherence to instructions demonstrates that such knowledge-transfer models seem to import a range of challenges for both health care practitioners and patients (see, e.g., Martin et al., 2005). These challenges are linked to the way work is organized because increasing centralization and specialization of medical knowledge also brings with it increasing organizational fragmentation and geographical distribution of work. In a way, patients' and relatives' active participation in the treatment and care process can be seen as a necessity to enable this style of organization to work. In policy papers[1], it is widely assumed that a systematic approach to patient involvement applied throughout the health care system will make patients more satisfied and empowered, and provide better clinical outcomes. Accordingly, professionals should inform patients about both their condition and what they need to know in order to be engaged in their own treatments. Patients, in turn, should inform professionals about their preferences and needs. This dialogue takes place in the consulting room through professionals' communication aimed at including patients and relatives in the treatment and care. However, traditional roles of general practitioners and internists are changing: having one primary doctor who is responsible for and thoroughly acquainted with each individual patient's history, condition, and preferences is no longer common. Therefore, while the relational continuity that comes with having one designated doctor is weakening, the need for coherence across organizational and geographical boundaries is increasing. In this, the relationship between patients, health care practitioners, and system is crucial.

Fragmentation and Distribution of Work

To elaborate, I will use cancer care as example. In several modern health care systems, geographically centralized and professionally specialized wards have been established for oncology and other high-cost conditions to increase the quality and efficiency of care. The treatment and care these places provide are part of a larger network of care components provided by different health care professionals; a process whose content can only be specified fully after the treatment of the patient's illness has been concluded. This is because of the high level of variation and unpredictability in each patient's illness trajectory as it unfolds over time (Strauss et al., 1997). Standardization of care into clinical guidelines, such as cancer pathways or "packages," may specify content, timing, and the sequence of events in cancer diagnostics and care.[2] These contain information in the formal steps in a general treatment process: GPs refer patients for investigation (typically diagnostic imaging or biopsy) on suspicion of cancer; the specialized oncology wards perform surgical and medical cancer treatment and care, while the patient's local hospital provides treatment and care for the majority of side effects and complications. If the patient suffers from any comorbidities, these are handled within that specialty. Physiotherapy is offered as a municipal service, often in health centers, while palliative care is delivered by mobile teams affiliated with the oncology wards, often in the patient's home.

Components of care are practiced in a network of different places or action nets (Czarniawska, 2004), by people in a range of formal and informal capacities or functions. In a simplified manner, Figure 10.1 illustrates this for a generic cancer patient who receives cancer treatment according to a specialized cancer package, e.g., breast cancer.

As Figure 10.1 illustrates, cancer care consists of several elements, which the patient receives in different locations and organizational units. The gray lines between the patient's home and each location represent potentially multiple visits to the chemotherapy unit, the radiology ward for control scans, or the local hospital's emergency department in case of complications. However, in the case of complications or unexpected developments in the patient's illness, standardized pathways are not sufficient to specify all the work that needs to take place. Additional organizing and practice of health care work steps in to handle the situation at hand, suited to the temporary, ad hoc nature of the event and the fragmentation of the system (Bohmer, 2009; Meier, 2015). If this is not in place, patients and their relatives may need to coordinate efforts and share knowledge with health care professionals from different sites to compensate for a lack of coherence in the system. In figure 10.1, coherence is illustrated by the lines connecting each site for treatment and care.

There are at least three main problems with this organization of work: first, the general lack of prolonged colocation of patients and health care practitioners potentially creates an "out of sight, out of sync" situation, where misunderstandings and coordination challenges may proliferate, which we also see in relation to distributed work (Hinds & Bailey, 2003). Second, this lack of colocation and the increased pace of health care work resulting from economic pressure on health care systems, in general, leaves time as a scarce resource in patient–health care practitioner encounters. Third, this organization of work separates the specialized knowledge of health care practitioners from the patient's body and personal experience of the development of the illness. This is potentially very problematic because the patient's situated knowledge and responsibility for action is located with the patient, while the professional and highly specialized knowledge and professional responsibility to act with regard to symptoms and developments is located in the hospital.

Moreover, with cancer, time is a vital factor: when cancer patients develop side effects or complications (e.g., a fever), infections can develop into sepsis within hours because the treatment given compromises the immune system (Williams et al., 2004). Cancer patients are instructed repeatedly in *what* to be aware of at home and *how* to react in a scenario of cases. They are expected to know and act in very specific ways, based on highly specialized knowledge they are expected to have acquired via "patient involvement." The logic seems to be that we can assume a shared or common context for cancer care across patients, relatives, and health care practitioners, and that in this context,

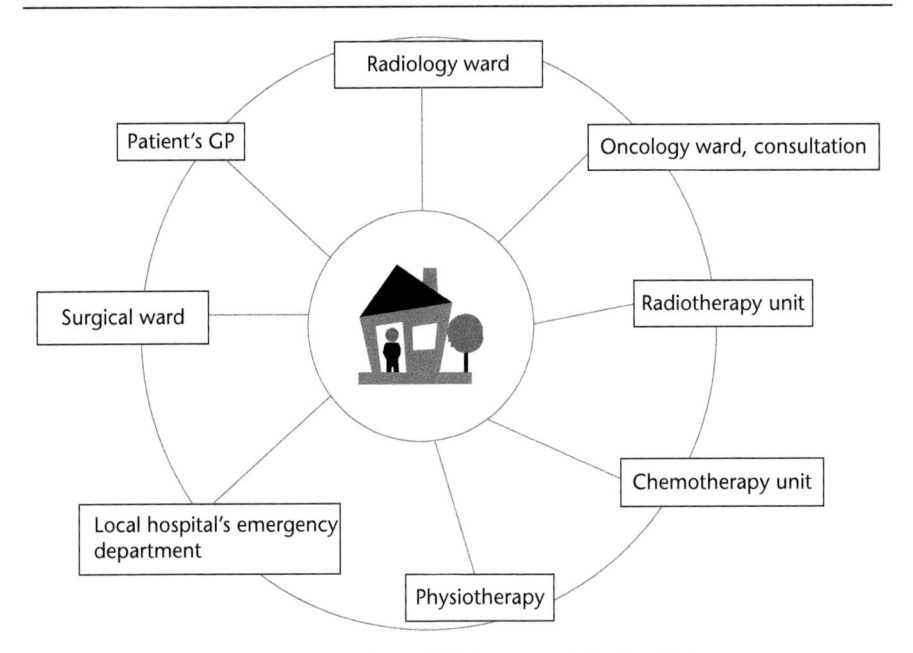

Figure 10.1 Continuity and Coherence in Patient Pathways

everyone knows what action needs to be taken, when and how. But patient involvement is not only a matter of shared decision-making or discussions of options and preferences. Before I discuss this challenge, I shall present a short vignette (Miles & Huberman, 1994) with the purpose of illustrating what being a cancer patient typically includes.

Vignette: In a Patient's Shoes

Imagine you have cancer. You are sitting in an office in the Cancer Ward with an oncologist, a nurse, and your spouse, assuming you are one of the fortunate cancer patients who are married, and thus have significantly better clinical outcomes and survival rates.[3] Since your first visit, you have been given a mass of information that is crucial to your treatment and care. As your surgery is over, you will now have outpatient radiation and chemotherapy treatment; thus, you are mainly at home. However, to keep the treatment on track you need to know where to go for regular blood tests, for consultations with nurses and oncologists, for radiation therapy and chemotherapy ("chemo") treatment, the planned control scans, and your physiotherapy, which prevents edema from building up around your surgical scars. You also need to know who to talk to, and about what. You need to know about effects of the radiation on your body, particularly, on your skin, and whom to go to for advice on lotions that will alleviate such symptoms. You may have questions about your diet, what to expect in terms of hair loss, or feelings of despair or anxiety, what pills you need to take, and when, and who will help you with the renewal of your prescription for your hypertension medication. At times, you may also need to know if it is possible to postpone a chemo treatment, so you can make it to your aunt's 85th birthday. On top of that, and perhaps most important of all, you need to know what to do in case you develop side effects or complications, such as diarrhea or a fever, which may be life-threatening as a result of the toxic treatment to your immune system. You were advised to bring your spouse with you, and you are glad you did; the amount of information you receive is overwhelming, and when you get home and talk about what the doctor said, you realized there are things you have already forgotten or just didn't register at the time. This is well-established in the literature and one of the reasons why patients are encouraged to bring a relative or friend with them to consultations. Once you have left the hospital, you and your spouse are tasked with monitoring your condition and reacting in the right way should you develop a fever, rash, or sudden pain. As a cancer patient, your life may depend on the right action at the right time. In other words, patient involvement and your adherence to treatment and guidelines for self-monitoring of side effects or complications are essential to both the quality and safety of your process.

This is what one element of being a cancer patient might look like: keeping track of all the things patients and relatives need to know to perform their part of the work that goes into the treatment and care of a cancer patient. Why is this relevant for how patients' experience context? Is this not just a case of exchanging information and distributing tasks? Well, yes and no. The way health care is changing, patients and their relatives expect—and are expected—to be actively involved in, and to assume a certain responsibility for, their part in the process of treatment and care and the front-line staff and managers are expected to make sure this happens (Holm-Petersen & Navne, 2013; Holm-Petersen & Navne, 2015). Yet, as research into nonadherence demonstrates, this does not always happen. Patients may leave the consulting room and *not* know or act according to the agreed treatment regimen. Patients are "always already elsewhere" as they navigate between the many different geographical locations in which they interact with health care professionals, often in brief intervals of time; in short, they move in and out of sight of the health care professionals, who treat them. W patients are not in one of the many organizational units, they are present in electronic records, in booking systems, and in health care professionals' conversations in meetings, morning conferences, and so on. Most of this is "backstage" work (Strauss & Corbin, 1988) and patients may be virtually present in IT systems or standardized procedures, while their bodies are located at home or in another department.

Patient Involvement as Compensation Mechanism?

There are good reasons for wanting to involve patients. Research has shown that involvement may simultaneously heighten both patient satisfaction and patient safety, but also that this is especially challenging when patients are severely ill (Andersen et al., 2011). However, *patient involvement* is not a term that is theoretically well-defined in the literature, and usage of the concept usually overlaps with, and is linked to, other terms such as *patient engagement, patient empowerment, patient safety, patient adherence,* and *patient engagement* (Martin et al., 2005; Coulter, 2012). The assumption is that successful patient involvement makes it more likely that patients and relatives know their roles and tasks in the treatment and care processes. In this vein, patient involvement becomes a tool that health care staff must use to ensure patient compliance with guidelines for how to behave at home, away from the view and guidance of specialized physicians and nurses. Involvement—and in particular the knowledge exchange elements of involvement—is treated as something that can be achieved relatively unproblematically and be transferred between professionals and patients through dialogue techniques such as "shared decision-making" tools. As a safety strategy, it can engage patients and relatives in their own treatment and care, so they will be vigilant and react if additional actions are needed. This can increase patient safety in the traditional sense (Ekstedt & Ödegård, 2015) and perhaps also increase the sense of security a health care professional feels when sending patients home and "out of sight." Further, it might also increase patients' satisfaction and sense of engagement in their own process, as prior research has shown (Coulter, 2012). However, all of these elements rest on a certain conceptualization of knowledge that fails to explain why patient involvement does not always lead to these outcomes. Although there is ample evidence of the potential benefits of interventions to engage patients (Coulter & Ellins, 2007), implementation in practice shows repeated challenges that are found in other cases of "transferring knowledge into action" in health care (Dopson & Fitzgerald, 2005; Greenhalgh & Wieringa, 2011; Holm-Petersen & Navne, 2015).

Patient Involvement as Integrative Mechanism

Patient involvement is also a central political and organizational instrument, with several aims and potential outcomes, and a certain set of practices that goes into performing and sustaining it. I have argued that patient involvement must be seen in the light of changes in health care in which work is increasingly specialized, organizationally and geographically fragmented, and distributed across time and space. This specialization and distribution of health care work calls for other measures to ensure coherence across sites and situations, which Figure 10.1 illustrated. The involvement of patients (users and citizens) is one such measure (European Commission, 2012; Danish Ministry of Health, 2014; Agency for Healthcare Research and Quality, 2015). One important integrative mechanism in this system is the collaboration between patients and health care professionals through practices of patient involvement. This takes place primarily in health care consultations, and these are managed places, where lived experiences of patients are put into paper form and electronic records. Here, knowledge is categorized in classification systems ordering experiences and knowledge into, for example, diagnoses, comorbidities, symptoms, or side effects. In this process, certain things are left out or placed in residual categories ("other") if they are not part of the classification system. Certain knowledge may be deemed to be relevant by professionals (and stored in their notes or memories) even if the system does not have a place for it, or the knowledge may leave the consultation room with the patients and relatives, who carry it with them. Star and Bowker, in discussing the knowledge that comes with lived experience, reflect, "to experience, to undergo, is to be certain; to hear of someone else's experience is to be uncertain" (2007 p. 277). In relation to organization or work and the patient involvement it entails, this underscores some of the potentially problematic consequences of detaching place and practice from knowledge. Thus, it seems information cannot just be handed over by the professional to the patient, and carried to another place to be unpacked by the patient when symptoms or complications assert themselves in the patient's body in ways that require action.

When Patient Involvement Does Not Work

For a variety of reasons, patients may not follow the instructions given: "failure to adhere to treatment is a common patient response in the context of serious illness such as cancer" (DiMatteo & Haskard-Zolnierek, 2011 p. 102). But what does "in the context of serious illness" mean here, and whose context are we talking about: the patients' contexts? The health care practitioners' context? Or the researchers' contexts? I shall return to the importance of stating this at the end of the chapter, and move on now to what we know from current research.

The literature on patient adherence points to the many situations in which patients do not undertake the required actions. This is caused by either not knowing or not acting in line with what was discussed and decided in the consulting room. In other words, the success of patient involvement depends largely on what happens when the patient leaves the room. Studies of patients' nonadherence have tied it to huge economic costs, increased risk factors for poor health outcomes, and even death. In their review, Martin et al. (2005) mention several elements of nonadherence: for example, patients' ability to remember instructions and information; the level of complexity of the condition and treatment; trust in the patient–physician relationship; patients' anxiety; and the amount of information included in an exchange. Indeed, research has shown that "Under the best of circumstances, many patients forget what they have been told by their physicians. One study found that patients forgot 50% of what they were told by the time they exited the medical visit" (DiMatteo & Haskard-Zolnierek, 2011 p. 109). What is happening here? Are patients being given potentially life-saving information and then just forget it? Martin et al. (2005 p. 192) offer additional evidence: "Even when information is communicated effectively and comprehension is initially high, much of what is conveyed during the medical visit is forgotten within moments of leaving the doctor's office." According to this, patients knew and understood during the consultation what they needed to do in order to adhere to the treatment schedule, yet once they had left the situation, they apparently forgot what they had been told. This raises an important question: why do some patients *not know* and *not do* the right thing despite being involved and having received this information from the outset? The empirical evidence suggests a range of explanations, but at the same time, it raises a caution: "our current interventions aimed at increasing health literacy to improve patient adherence have, so far, been disturbingly ineffective" (Martin et al., 2005 p. 191).

Knowing What to Do and Where and When to Do It

Rather than viewing knowledge only as mental transfer or translation processes, I suggest we expand the unit of analysis from the individuals' ability to contain, deliver, and receive and use knowledge and to include embodied, emotional, and socio-material interactions in practice. From such a situated perspective of knowing, we can offer an alternative explanation: knowledge is not merely something someone *has*; rather it is practiced in events and activities and may be embedded in buildings, tools, and artifacts. Importantly, it is always altered or repositioned in use (Czarniawska & Sevón, 2005; Fischer et al., 2016). For some patients, practicing the knowledge needed to be a patient outside the consulting room is difficult, and the knowledge does not seem to move easily with the patient from place to place, from one context related to their illness to the next.

In this approach to knowledge, which emphasizes knowing in practice, knowing is conceived of largely as a form of mastery expressed in the capacity to carry out a social and material activity (Nicolini, 2011, 2012). In this approach, it is "a way of knowing shared with others, a set of practical methods acquired through learning, inscribed in objects, embodied, and only partially articulated in discourse" (Nicolini, 2012 p. 5). Learning is something people *do*, and knowing is an active process (Blackler, 1995) we carry out with our physical bodies. Such a conceptualization links knowledge, body, and place. Knowledge is most easily shared among people who share practices or ways of knowing, as, for example, in a community or a network of practice (Brown & Duguid, 2001) as it is tied to experience, to the body, and to situated, embedded cognition (Robbins & Ayede, 2009). Brown and Duguid (2001) argue that knowledge, learning, and identity are tied together, and that identities are dynamic, changing as practices change. For the purpose of this chapter, I propose that knowing what to do as a patient is something learned, something that changes from place to place, for example, "in the consulting room" or "at home." In this sense, learning and knowing are understood as actions and activities embedded in complex social and cultural contexts, which can be experienced quite differently by the actors involved.

Different Places, Different Experiences of Context?

If we explore the link between body and place, we can open for further scrutiny the set of practices inherent in the current understanding of "patient involvement." This allows us to investigate what types of knowledge in practice are assumed on behalf of patients and health care professionals, how this knowledge is tied to certain locations and potentially absent in others, and to discuss potential reasons why such knowledge may not be enacted in practice (patient nonadherence).

During the consultation, the patient is a listening and talking body, as well as the object of a certain kind of knowledge. This knowledge is specialized medical knowledge regarding the fields of oncology and infectious diseases; it is complex knowledge, which builds on accumulated scientific research; and it is codified, subject to classification and the foundation of diagnosis. Taken together, it forms the basis of written communication such as information leaflets. This knowledge is supposed to be something that can be possessed and exchanged. The consulting room is a managed place; there are rules, protocols, and routines, and everyone involved expects certain behaviors from others, and, in turn, are expected to behave according to their role. Identities are fixed and clear: the oncologist, the nurse, the patient, and the relatives, all have their roles. Here, a person is told that s/he is a patient, and what dealing with the illness requires him/her to know and to do. Inside the consultation, professionals and patients are colocated, and within this managed place, professionals have the clinical responsibility to act based on their specialized knowledge and the state-sanctioned right to practice. However, as the patient moves outside consulting room, the monitoring of his/her body, and thus the practical responsibility to act, moves with it; it is now the patient's and the relative' task and responsibility to react according to the specialized knowledge that the professionals' shared during the consultation and in leaflets. Outside the consultation, the patient's body is a moving, acting body. It is the subject of emotions and experiential, personal, embodied knowledge particular to the individual and situation at hand. "Outside the consultation" refers to all the places where patients go about their everyday life. Here, a person needs to learn how to be a patient outside the hospital. This means that the place for learning as an involved patient and enacting patient involvement is "all over the place," a classic example of a residual category (Star & Bowker, 2007).

Accordingly, cancer patients need to be vigilant about their bodies and alert as patients everywhere they go, as symptoms may develop fast. Within the complex health care system, the patient's body moves across a patchwork of places: as a patient, the patient is expected to self-manage and monitor his/her condition after returning home, based on the information given at the consultation—and failure to do so may be lethal. This means that while the patient is at home, going about his/her life, s/he needs to monitor actively his/her body and know what signs to act upon, when, how, and whom to inform. The patient needs to act with the knowledge of effects and side effects of oncological treatment, symptoms of the most common complications, relevant elements of how cancer care is organized (Do I call my GP for this, or my oncologist?), and the timeframe within which to react (Should I call now, or can it wait till morning?). This displacement of knowledge and responsibility for action and the patient's body holds one potential explanation to the challenge of both patient involvement and what has been researched as "patient nonadherence." Current instrumental approaches to knowledge and patient involvement leave potentially significant situations out of sight from a practitioner's vantage point and perception of context. I unfold this proposition below.

An examination of the place dimension of patient involvement puts an emphasis on the problems of conceptualizing patient involvement as simple knowledge transfer during the consultation. The general context-free approach to patient involvement that is found in policy documents, and in much of the research literature on patient involvement, does not correspond to the complexities and variety of what patients may experience as "contexts" for their illnesses. Nor does it take into account the contextualization of knowledge that patients must perform on a daily basis: they need to have knowledge about their condition, *and* they need to know and act *in the situation* on this.

Because health care work is interdependent across sites, as patients and relatives play increasingly important roles, they become knowledge and coordination resources for the health care professionals across the system. This resource view is echoed in discussions of patient involvement, but I propose that researchers and practitioners should approach it with caution. The relationship between patients and professionals is unequal: the professionals have years of specialized education and training, a state-sanctioned monopoly to practice, and a professional medical responsibility toward their patients. Patients have their preferences and their experiences of a body that is unwell. Indeed, patient involvement is simultaneously important *and* challenging, because practices—and thus conditions for learning, knowing, and being a patient—change from place to place. Each time a patient moves physically to a new location, his/her body and what s/he knows and can do is altered and must be understood with a sensitivity toward how this sets a slightly different context for being ill and, therefore, also for being involved in one's own illness.

Discussion and Implications for Theory and Practice

To sum up, in this discussion of the place and knowledge elements of patients' contexts for illness, the body surfaces as a site for knowing and, thus, for being involved as a patient and/or relative. In the network of different actors carrying out work in different places, the patient's body becomes the common denominator between all the places in a treatment and care process, and the mediating object among all the people involved. This body is always immersed in a web of relationships and specific practices that patients must negotiate locally because situations often occur at the patient's home and out of sight of health care professionals. At the same time, all the involved actors construct their own understandings of the situation (e.g., in a patient's illness process) and their own understanding of the context for their current and future actions and interactions.

I have shown that the current organization of health care work creates multiple places that patients' bodies must move between (illustrated in Figure 10.1 above). However, I also demonstrated how the organization of the health care system requires patients and relatives to know very specific things about bodies, treatment regimens, and how their health care system is organized, so they can act in certain ways if the patient becomes acutely ill as a result of complications or side effects. This is required because the organization of treatment results in a fragmentation of work (both formal and informal), which, in turn, means that the specialized knowledge of health care practitioners, the traditional prerequisite for responsibility and action, is practiced in certain locations, while patients and relatives operate from their homes. Through discussing knowledge, knowing, place, and body in patient involvement, I have shown that patient involvement is a practice that entails considerable effort from professionals, patients, and relatives, but also that this effort is distributed over a range of locations in which participants are essential parts of each other's contexts for action. Currently, most contextual research in health care does not engage in the difficult task of exploring patients' experiences and engagement with contexts for their illnesses. However, because of the way health care work is organized toward increasing patient involvement, I argue that this needs to change: patients and their immediate communities are becoming such important actors in health care systems that we should adopt a far more systematic approach to exploring both the differences and similarities in how patients make sense of and engage with contexts for their illnesses.

This book calls for approaches to contexts in action that are more systematic, especially how these phenomena are studied and analyzed. Here I have discussed a specific element of the health care system that is often ignored: the relationship between the location of the body and knowledge in the organization of cancer care. Moreover, I have considered place in relation to how we can conceptualize patients' experiences of context. Thus, to theorize the important concept of context further, I suggest two immediate avenues for future development of contextual research into the role of patients and relatives in the larger health care system. The first is a question of representation: whose context is being represented? The second is a question of vantage point: from which perspective is context being explored? Additionally, I have argued for more research into how patients and relatives experience and engage with the contexts of illness and how these experiences can change from one situation to another. Both avenues have the potential to yield new theoretical insights and important contributions for scholars and practitioners working in the health care system.

Notes

1. The chapter discusses cancer care primarily based on studies in a Danish health care system and thus the policy papers references here are mostly Danish. However, the general tendencies are likely to be recognizable beyond this national context.
2. See., Danish Health and Medicines Authority (2016).
3. Aizer et al., (2013).

References

Agency for Healthcare Research and Quality. (2015). *Patient involvement*. http://www.ahrq.gov/patients-consumers/patient-involvement/index.html. (Accessed February 16, 2017).

Aizer, A. A., et al. (2013). Marital status and survival in patients with cancer. *Journal of Clinical Oncology, 31*(31), 3869–76.

American Cancer Society. (2015). *Cancer facts & figures 2015.* http://www.cancer.org/acs/groups/content/@editorial/documents/document/acspc-044552.pdf. (Accessed 31 October 2016.)

Andersen, V., Lipczak, H., & Ammundsen, N. I. (2011). *Involving patients in patient safety: A literature review 2005–2010.* Copenhagen: Danish Society for Patient Safety, Trygfonden, and Danish Cancer Society (*Involvering af patienter i patientsikkerhed. Litteraturgennemgang 2005–2010*. Dansk Selskab for Patientsikkerhed, TrygFonden og Kræftens Bekæmpelse, Kvalitet & Patientsikkerhed).

Blackler, F. (1995). Knowledge, knowledge work and organizations: An overview and interpretation. *Organization Studies, 16*(6), 1021–46.

Bohmer, R. M. J. (2009). *Designing care: Aligning the nature and management of health care.* Boston: Harvard Business Press.

Brown, J. S. & Duguid, P. (2001). Knowledge and organization. *Organizational Science, 12*(2), 198–213.

Coulter, A. (2012). Patient engagement—What works? *The Journal of Ambulatory Care Management, 35*(2), 80–9.

Coulter, A. & Ellins, J. (2007). Effectiveness of strategies for informing, educating, and involving patients. *BMJ, 335*(7609), 24–7.

Czarniawska, B. (2004). On time, space, and action nets. *Organization, 11*(6), 773–91.

Czarniawska, B. & Sevón, G. (eds.). (2005). *Global ideas: How ideas, objects and practices travel in the global economy.* Copenhagen: Copenhagen Business School Press.

Danish Health and Medicines Authority. (2016). *Diagnostic pathway for patients with unspecific symptoms of severe illness, potentially cancer.* Copenhagen: Danish Health and Medicines Authority. (Sundhedsstyrelsen 2016: Diagnostisk pakkeforløb for patienter med uspecifikke symptomer på alvorlig sygdom, der kunne være kræft).

Danish Ministry of Health. (2014). *Increased involvement of patients and relatives.* Copenhagen: Danish Ministry of Health. (Ministeriet for Sundhed og Forebyggelse (2014): Dialogpapir om øget inddragelse af patienter og pårørende).

DiMatteo, M. R. & Haskard-Zolnierek, K. B. (2011). Impact of depression on treatment adherence and survival from cancer. In D. M. Kissane, N. S. Maj, & N. Sartorius (eds.), *Depression and cancer.* Oxford: Wiley-Blackwell, pp. 101–24.

Dopson, S. & Fitzgerald, L. (2005). *Knowledge to action? Evidence based health care in context.* New York: Oxford University Press.

Ekstedt, M. & Ödegård, S. (2015). Exploring gaps in cancer care using a systems safety perspective. *Cognition, Technology & Work, 17*(1), 5–13.

European Commission. (2012). *Patient involvement.* European Commission. https://ec.europa.eu/health//sites/health/files/systems_performance_assessment/docs/eurobaro_patient_involvement_2012_en.pdf. (Accessed February 16, 2017).

Fetzer, A. (2004). *Recontextualizing context: Grammaticality meets appropriateness.* Amsterdam: John Benjamins Publishing Company.

Fischer, M. D. et al. (2016). Knowledge leadership: Mobilizing management research by becoming the knowledge object. *Human Relations, 69*(7), 1563–85.

Geertz, C. (1993). *Local knowledge: Further essays in interpretive anthropology* (2nd ed.). London: Fontana.

Greenhalgh, T. & Wieringa, S. (2011). Is it time to drop the "knowledge translation" metaphor? A critical literature review. *Journal of the Royal Society of Medicine, 104*(12), 501.

Hinds, P. J. & Bailey, D. E. (2003). Out of sight, out of sync: Understanding conflict in distributed teams. *Organization Science, 14*(6), 615–32.

Holm-Petersen, C. & Navne, L. E. (2013). *Leadership of user involvement: Three case based examples.* (Ledelse af brugerinddragelse—tre casebaserede eksempler). København: KORA.

Holm-Petersen, C. & Navne, L. E. (2015). *What is management of user involvement? A review of aims and three individual user involvement models.* (Hvad er ledelse af burgerinddragelse? En review a mål og tre individuelle brugerinddragelsesmodeller). *Tidsskrift for Forskning i Sygdom Og Samfund/Journal of Research in Sickness and Society, 22*, 103–33.

Johns, G. (2017). Incorporating context in organizational research: Reflections on the 2016 AMR Decade Award. *Academy of Management Review, 42*(4), 577–95.

Martin, L. R., Williams, S. L., Haskard, K. B., & DiMatteo, M. R. (2005). The challenge of patient adherence. *Therapeutics and Clinical Risk Management, 1*(3), 189–99.

Meier, N. (2015). Collaboration in healthcare through boundary work and boundary objects. *Qualitative Sociology Review, 11*(3), 60–82.

Miles, M. B. & Huberman, A. M. (1994). *Qualitative data analysis: An expanded sourcebook* (2nd ed.). Thousand Oaks, CA: Sage Publications.

Nicolini, D. (2011). Practice as the site of knowing: Insights from the field of telemedicine. *Organization Science, 22*(3), 602–20.

Nicolini, D. (2012). *Practice theory, work, and organization: An introduction.* Oxford: Oxford University Press.

Robbins, P. & Ayede, M. (eds.). (2009). *The Cambridge handbook of situated cognition.* Cambridge: Cambridge University Press.

Star, L. S. & Bowker, C. G. (2007). Enacting silence: Residual categories as challenges for ethics, information systems, and communications. *Ethics and Information Technology, 9*(4), 273–80.

Strauss, A. & Corbin, J. M. (1988). *Unending work and care.* San Francisco: Jossey-Bass.

Strauss, A., Fagerhaugh, S., Suczek, B., & Weiner, C. (1997). *Social organization of medical work* (2nd ed.). Piscataway, NJ: Transaction Publishers.

Williams, D. M. et al. (2004). Hospitalized cancer patients with severe sepsis: Analysis of incidence, mortality and associated costs of care. *Critical Care, 8*(5), 1–5.

11

How Researchers Understand, Construct, and Bound Context

Liminality and the Integration Space

Eleanor Murray

Introduction

In this chapter, I take a conceptual perspective on context, offering the metaphor of context as constituted through constructions of liminal transitional spaces. The research question that guides this chapter asks how researchers understand, experience, and engage with context. I examine how, as a researcher studying the highly complex process of integrating care services, I need to understand where to direct my focus to understand context. Integrating care is recognized as a multidimensional, complex process of combining siloed services to create seamless care delivery to patients. Researchers face several challenges in studying complex change processes, such as how best to understand the contextual setting of a multilevel, multiagency change, the nature of context in a process of continuous change, and the interdependency between action and context. These challenges highlight an important problem, which is discussed in several other chapters in this book: that traditional ways of conceptualizing and using context do not seem to address adequately the interdependencies that characterize these settings. Increasingly, as we study complex, heterogeneous, contested, and dynamic phenomena, such as the integration of care, we need a more sophisticated way of conceptualizing context that offers greater insights into socially constructed and dynamic systems.

To explore how researchers may understand context in this setting, I conceptualize it as an instance of liminality. The concept of liminality denotes a ritual of transition, and it can be used metaphorically to provide a temporal and spatial perspective on processes of change (Czarniawska & Mazza, 2003). Organizationally, liminality represents the inversion of normative, hierarchically structured, and boundaried social systems; a relatively unstructured, undifferentiated, and equal community (Turner, 1969). I draw on this application of liminality to offer a perspective on how researchers can understand and analyze context during systems change, through insights into the transitional space of "integrating care" and the transitional people who inhabit that space. I adopt documentary analysis as my method. Documentary analysis is an effective and valuable tool, as it enables a detailed overview of the formal system landscape of routine care delivery overlaid with integrating care services (Bowen, 2009). Through this, I contribute what I have learned as a researcher, struggling to understand context through the actions and involvement of actors in integration activities. I offer researchers analytical hooks and hinges from which to explore context within their own work.

My contribution focuses on showing how, as a researcher, I act as a boundary constructor. I "bound" context through the analysis, identifying the thresholds and activities within the liminal space, by forging connections between elements across levels and organizations to produce not only actors' understandings of what is happening but also, based on this, researchers' understanding of what is happening. Thus, the focus is primarily on Question 2 in Figure 1.1 in Chapter 1: "How do actors understand, experience, and engage with context [in a given situation or phenomenon]?"

Understanding and Bounding Context as a Researcher

To explore how researchers understand context as it relates to strategic and organizational change first requires a definition of *context*. In this chapter, I draw on the Latin derivation of the word, *contexere*, meaning "to weave," as I reflect on the interweaving of the concepts of context, meaning and action, from both the perspective of the researcher and that of the actors being observed (Burke, 2002). I build on the definition of *context* offered in Chapter 1 as a relational construct. I aim to reflect on my sensemaking as a researcher, bounding the context for my work and contextualizing my object of study as I continually weave the background and foreground together, using the documents as materials. I start by exploring how the conceptualization of context in relation to organizational change has undergone a transition since the 1980s. I examine the implications of this transition for the researcher understanding context from two perspectives: first, the reconceptualization of context from "static" entity to "dynamic" interactions, and second, the transition from a structural interpretation of context to one that encompasses the role of agency.

Traditionally, context for organizational change has been perceived as static, where the researcher's role is to assess objectively a stable background environment from a distance (see, e.g., Chapters 2 and 4 in this book), capturing a snapshot of the external forces that influence how foreground planned change in the organization occurs. Challenged for failing to take into account temporal, historical, or processual characteristics of change, this static approach was superseded by an emergent framework outlined by the "contextualists"—academics who emphasized the antecedents or postcedents to change (Pettigrew, 1990). This framework focused on the researcher's role in understanding the interplay between content, process, and context, and appreciating the dynamic tension between change and continuity (Child & Smith, 1987; Pettigrew, 1987; Pichault, 2007). Despite this development toward a processual understanding of context, much of the language used by the contextualists to define and operationalize *context* still points to relatively stable features "out there," often described as the "inner" and "outer" contexts (Armenakis & Bedeian, 1999; Pettigrew, 1987), where the latter describes the firm or organization that is the focus of study, and the former describes the wider competitive environment (Sminia, 2016). There is less emphasis on *how* these features have been "made stable" by researchers. A further issue is that definitions of *context* as agency or micro concerns are noticeably absent.

The transition to an interpretation of context that recognized agency challenged this structural approach, which assumed a unidirectional effect, where changes identified by the researcher in the outer context acted as forces for change in the inner. *Agency* (narrowly defined as corporate leaders in these studies) is given less weight than the structural determinants of strategic change. Leadership is underemphasized because of an overemphasis on contextual forces and incrementalism of process where change is shaped by legacy (Caldwell, 2005). Insufficient emphasis was placed on the importance of multidirectional interrelationships and interactions (Caldwell, 2005). More recently, the structural approach inherent in institutional theory recognizes the role of changing institutional dimensions, where context is understood as broad changes in often-competing institutional fields and institutional logics. Within this paradigm, structure constrains and enables action.

Alongside these structural developments, researchers were theorizing as to how agency elucidates a more dynamic understanding of context, one where human agency alters and shapes social structures (Barley & Tolbert, 1997). The micro foundations of institutional theory have been reconsidered, particularly the role of agency. This shift acknowledges the nature of agency as generating action and influencing context, thus shaping future actions and contexts for other actors, with a transition from rationalization to reinforcing micro processes (Cardinale, 2018; Dopson, Fitzgerald, & Ferlie, 2008). Researchers may conceptualize context "bottom-up," through such micro processes as microlevel interactions that instantiate macro structures (Gray, Purdy, & Ansari, 2015; Smets, Morris, & Greenwood, 2012). The challenge for researchers in multistakeholder environments is understanding context as a contested phenomenon, because contexts can be experienced, understood, and enacted differently, as discussed in Chapters 1–3 of this book. More recently, the focus has shifted from an assumption that context is "out there," and measures on one level can be linked to measures on another, to an appreciation that contexts are constructed and as such, set the frame for what we and others can see and act on/with. Researcher have an important role: first, in recognizing that contexts are constructed by them; second, in applying that approach to multilayered, complex, and interdependent change processes; and third, in experiencing how individuals and groups shape actions by continually influencing existing contexts and creating new contexts for action (Dopson et al., 2008).

Liminality as a Lens on Context

I examine the concept of liminality to shed light on how researchers bound contexts in certain ways in their work; exploring how the metaphor of liminality can help the understanding of change in social systems and the role of actors within them, and reflecting on how, as a researcher, I am constructing/bounding "the context"—and thus the center and the periphery and the liminal spaces. Liminality, a concept with anthropological roots, describes the second of three distinct sequential phases within a rite of passage. Preceded by the rites of separation and concluded by the rites of incorporation, the second transition or "liminal" phase describes a temporary stage characterized by ambiguity, uncertainty, and blurred boundaries that is bounded by a literal and metaphorical "limen" (Latin, meaning "threshold") (van Gennep, 1960). The identification by van Gennep of this pattern across the rites associated with human life, whether birth, adulthood, marriage, or death, offers a metaphor for understanding the relationship between social order and change, and the state of transition between them (Szakolczai, 2014). Drawing on the early work of van Gennep (1960), the later work of Turner (1969, 1982) and more recent explorations of liminality by Szakolczai (2009, 2014), I explore the potential the concept offers for understanding how a researcher might understand context in organizational settings. Liminality offers an insight into our roles as researchers, as in effect, we occupy liminal spaces, in that we should not be separate from, nor fully incorporated into, what we study, but should be in a position from where we can bound context for our object of study. Addressing the first issue, liminality offers a new way of understanding contexts during complex change processes, as researchers construct the change process from liminal (transitional) space and understand the relationships between the liminal space and the incumbent social system. The liminal space, described in van Gennep's work as a "symbolic and spatial area of transition" (1960 p. 18), is an important temporal and spatial ritual sequence considered separate from the space inhabited by the established social system, often comprising a journey, a geographical change, or a physical separation from the social order (Turner, 1982). As a researcher, I can use this metaphor to forge connections between the temporal and spatial boundaries of the liminal space and the incumbent system.

Recently, in organizational studies, scholars have challenged the separation of the established social order from the liminal space, suggesting that liminal activities may serve as a catalyst for change in the incumbent social system. In her study of consulting as a liminal space, Czarniawska inverts the traditional rite-of-passage function, assessing whether, in the process of changing the community, consultants also change themselves (Czarniawska & Mazza, 2003), suggesting that the effects of liminality are multidirectional. Szakolczai reflects on the ambivalent influence of the transitional activities on the social order, remarking that, "while liminal situations and positions can contribute to creativity or the renewal of institutions and structures that have become oppressive or simply tired, liminality also implies deep anxiety and suffering," (2009 p. 166). Developing this argument further, I propose that liminality offers a metaphor for change in social systems through the existence of a two-way relationship, where activities occurring in the liminal space elicit changes in the incumbent social system and vice versa. I suggest that this multidirectional relationship occurs when structural, relational, and political upheavals in the incumbent social system initiate dynamic shifts in the liminal space, causing the liminal space and the actions of those operating within it to expand or contract accordingly. I can understand and engage with contexts by exploring and articulating the transitioning boundaries that define the interaction between this fluctuating liminal space and the changes in the incumbent system. I propose that, as researchers, we do our work from liminal spaces, and this vantage point influences us, as the research we do will always be shaped in myriad ways by each piece of research we engage in and every context we construct to understand a phenomenon of study.

Liminality also offers researchers insights into the social interactions of actors within the liminal space and that of the incumbent system. Those that participate in a ritual of transition—the liminars (i.e., or actors involved in change activities)—offer an insight into the role of agency in generating action and shaping context. Liminars are considered to function beyond the normative social structure and are liberated from social obligations, acquiring a special freedom. They are considered outside the reach of society, and their actions are untrammeled by societal obligations and duties (Turner, 1982). As I adopt liminars as a conceptual lens, I am able to identify those actors who are freer from incumbent system obligations and have greater scope to introduce systems changes in the liminal space than are their counterparts. Through their activities within the fluctuating liminal space, I observe these actors constructing and enacting contexts for action.

As a researcher, a substantial part of my time is spent on making sense of my unfolding research, but in the case of researching complex systems change, the challenge is where to focus my attention to understand context, given the dynamic temporal and spatial nature of this work. I propose that my role is as boundary constructor, exploring and articulating the transitioning boundaries of the center and the periphery and how they are continually and recursively reconstituted through a liminal space. Liminality is a useful analytical tool to better understand the changing agent–structure relationships in this dynamic process, as it has the capacity to explain apparently unstructured situations and activities in contemporary organizational settings (Pace & Pallister-Wilkins, 2018). Through this metaphor, the role of agency is explicated via the actions of liminars, or "intermediaries," as boundary spanners, as they command the liminal space, yet also engender authority in the incumbent social system.

Methodological Reflections on Bounding Context

Research Context and Design

To explore how researchers can understand and thus "bound" context for change in a study, I have drawn on my experience of undertaking documentary analysis of two health, social, and voluntary care systems that were integrating care services. Integrating care services represents an appropriate research context because it serves as an example of complex systems change across organizational boundaries, which means that as a researcher, I have to take into account core concepts such as *action, process,* and *context* at multiple analytical levels. This setting is also appropriate because it is a highly regulated domain in which documentation of meetings and events is mandatory and services are held accountable through the publication of these records, thus making documentary analysis a useful means of understanding context.

First, I chose a research setting in which understanding and constructing what counts as context was evidently important. This enabled a temporal and spatial observation of agency and structure at macro, meso, and micro levels, across different governance regimes, under varied conditions, and across organizational boundaries. Second, I chose to explore two comparative cases, constituting a "matched pair" based on similar geography and demography. This choice enabled comparability of case contexts, as I constructed these, and a broadening of the generation of insights from this work (Pettigrew, Ferlie, & McKee, 1992).

Background Study

As a researcher interested in processual cases, I focused on more than a decade of integration activities from 2007, as this period encompassed iterative, centrally led government programs of integration named pilots, pioneers, and vanguards. In addition, a documentary analysis at the national level was completed to understand the progression of integration policy over this time. Over 500 publicly available documents for each case were reviewed between June and September 2017. Documentation for each case included minutes of regional and local meetings, and internal reports including plans, frameworks, intentions, and newsletters. In analyzing the data, I adopted a three-phase approach. In the first phase, I generated an initial understanding of the data through a temporal analysis of the chronology of integration activities. At regional and local levels, I analyzed key events, integration focus, organizations, actors, and outcomes to direct my inquiry. I noticed the presence of key actors, instances where information was missing, or "the trail went cold." At the national level, I analyzed key policy developments that were located chronologically. In the second phase, my attention was drawn to repetitive occurrences of actors, events, issues, or organizations in single documents, or across multiple documents, either longitudinally or cross-sectionally. I generated preliminary themes through the initial coding of these activities. As the third phase, which serves as the primary material upon which this chapter is built, I reflected on the process by which I understood context, generating a further set of categories.

Discussion

The research question that guides this chapter asks how researchers come to, or can, understand, experience, and engage with context. For the purpose of this chapter, I address the question through a visual portrayal of my approach to bounding context, drawing on the metaphor of transitioning liminal spaces (see Figure 11.1). I reflect on how I constructed the context for change and in this process, acted as a boundary constructor/analyst of the liminal space I propose as being central for my analysis.

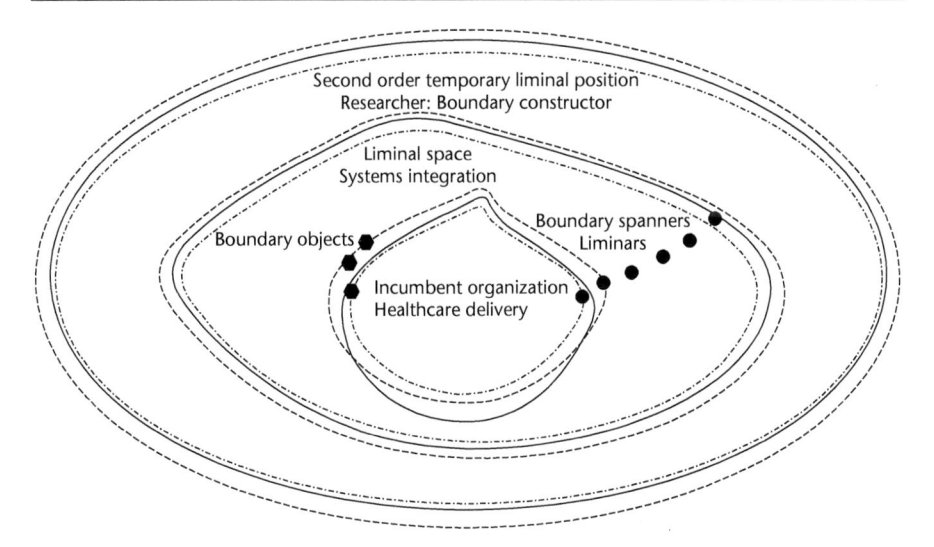

Figure 11.1 The Researcher's Bounding of Context through Transitioning Liminal Spaces

Delineating the Contextual Spaces as a Boundary Constructor

I aim to reflect on how, as a researcher, I "bound" context through my analysis. Figure 11.1 presents a model of context construction, reflecting how, as a researcher, I act as boundary constructor, delineating the context for change, including the boundaries of the transitioning liminal space and incumbent system. I delineate the thresholds and the nature of these spaces through: (1) the materiality of boundary objects that groups act toward and with, and (2) the actions of key actors operating as boundary spanners (Star, 2010), drawing on spatial and temporal analysis to achieve this. I approached my research with an interest in making sense of the process of change in health systems, in particular, to learn more about the relative interplay between structure and agency, and the extent to which this influenced integration outcomes in comparative health systems. This focus enabled me to construct the outer contextual boundary for my research—the outer solid line that can be seen in Figure 11.1. However, as I progressed with the research and I deepened my knowledge of integration activities through the analysis of documents, the boundaries I had initially delineated as representing the context for change shifted, sometimes expanding and other times contracting as I broadened or deepened my lines of enquiry. In effect, I occupied a second-order temporary liminal position, as I was not trying to "enter" the system I was studying, but was in a transitory phase, neither fully outside nor inside the system, but close enough to it to enable me to construct and bound my analysis.

Demarcating a Transitioning Liminal Space through Boundary Objects

As a researcher, I demarcated the liminal space temporally and spatially through analysis of my data, particularly the materiality of boundary objects that groups acted with and toward. *Boundary objects* can be defined as "objects which both inhabit several intersecting social worlds...and satisfy the informational requirements of each of them" (Star & Griesemer, 1989 p. 393). This liminal space was constructed from documents that I found constituted boundary objects, as they formed "the boundaries between groups through flexibility and shared structure" (Star, 2010 p. 603) and represented the intersection between organizations. With sufficient interpretive flexibility to legitimize the system (integration process) over organizational causes, at other times these boundary objects were used to promote organizational (incumbent) causes over the system needs (Weick, 1995). I redrew the thresholds of the liminal space iteratively as I explored these boundary changes, as shown in Figure 11.1. At certain times, an expanding liminal space was demarcated, as groups progressed and developed the systems-level integration projects and programs, while at other times, particularly in the light of structural constraints (e.g., finances), a contracting liminal space was differentiated, as groups focused on incumbent organizational causes over systems integration. A reciprocal context in the incumbent space was constructed, where at times, integration activities were incorporated into daily health care delivery, and I reflected this in an expanding incumbent space but at other times, I contracted the incumbent space as a result of structural pressures. Using boundary objects and associated documents, I was able to trace the process of fluctuation between integration programs of work at the systems level (liminal) and organizational health delivery (incumbent). These boundary objects provided punctuation points on a complex, ambiguous and changing landscape, and I was able to join the points to construct the changing boundaries of liminal and incumbent spaces. From a temporal perspective, I propose that what we call context is constructed by us as researchers as we explore, articulate, and delineate the transitioning boundaries that define an evolving liminal space.

Articulating a Transitioning Liminal Space through Boundary Spanners

Insights from liminars have been drawn on to explain how I construct context through the actions and articulation of pivotal individual actors or boundary spanners. Just as liminars make the transition across the threshold from established society to liminal space, so boundary spanners transition into the liminal space between agencies. However, liminars are not required to hold a multidirectional relationship with the incumbent system. Once liminars are in the liminal space, they are protected from the obligations of the incumbent society. Conversely, boundary spanners are "key agents managing within inter-organizational theatres," who are required to maintain "a balancing act between inclusion and separation, dependence and autonomy" (Williams, 2002 pp. 103, 111). As Williams acknowledges in relation to integrated care, boundary spanners are "a valuable and distinctive class of actor, operating within intra- and inter-sectoral collaborative environments" (2011 p. 27). These individuals play a key role in articulating integration, using interpretation, communication, coordination, and innovation to achieve changes, thus constructing context through their actions. Through my analysis, I have identified pivotal actors with boundary-spanning roles who are central to progressing integration agendas across organizations and agencies, and are able to create and maintain the thresholds of this often-fluctuating liminal space. These actors were highly visible in the documentation, which facilitated my construction of context through their differing roles and increasing levels of seniority over time. In certain cases, these actors occupied joint roles that straddled the incumbent and liminal spaces, so as their actions across these spaces were traced, I was able to articulate a recursive and nuanced context. From a spatial perspective, I identified the thresholds and activities within the liminal space by stitching together elements derived from boundary objects, to produce both actors' understandings of what was happening and, based on this, my own understanding of events.

This study confirmed that, as a researcher, I can improve my conceptualization of context through the metaphor of liminality. I identified the nature of my own role as boundary constructor through which I delineated the research liminal and incumbent space. I demarcated and articulated the nature of the liminal space through boundary objects and boundary spanners. I integrated my findings into a model and explored how, as a researcher, I was able to construct context so that I could understand, experience, and engage with it from a liminal perspective.

Contributions and Future Research

Drawing on my experiences of constructing context for a specific study, I have illustrated how the concepts of context and action can be understood through the lens of transitional liminality. The core contribution I make is to propose the role of researchers as "boundary constructors," actively interpreting and bounding context through the analytical process. By combining the metaphor of liminality with boundary work, I have attempted to make the role of the researcher explicit, exploring and articulating their role as a participative actor in a dynamic process.

Unlike the anthropological perspective on liminality that suggests it represents a transition from one state to another, I have extended the conceptualization of the term, arguing that the liminal space fluctuates back and forth over time. Much literature focuses on the characteristics of a defined liminal space that can be understood as a distinct stage of a transitionary process. I argue that, in the case of integrating services, temporal transitions of the liminal space occur iteratively as actors react and respond to structural challenges, causing liminal activities to shrink and expand, leading to threshold movement. These shifts cause a continual extension and contraction of the liminal space, requiring the researcher to stay attuned to the changes and delineate and redelineate the changing context. This line of thinking transfers attention from a defined liminal space to a fluctuating interrelationship between the incumbent space and the liminal space, offering a more nuanced perspective on context.

A limitation of this study is that while documentary analysis serves as a useful tool to see *what* is constructed, this particular type of empirical material does not allow us to investigate *how* the phenomenon (here integrative care) is constructed. As a result, the social, cultural, behavioral, and cognitive elements of context were less evident, unless they were referred to explicitly through the actors' use of boundary objects. Further research is required to explore how researchers construct context in different settings, and using a broader range of methodologies. I hope this chapter has provided readers with reflections on the implications of the constructed nature of context for their own methodological and analytical work.

References

Armenakis, A. A. & Bedeian, A. G. (1999). Organizational change: A review of theory and research in the 1990s. *Journal of Management, 25*(3), 293–315.

Barley, S. R. & Tolbert, P. S. (1997). Institutionalization and structuration: Studying the links between action and institution. *Organization Studies, 18*(1), 93–117.

Bowen, G. A. (2009). Document analysis as a qualitative research method. *Qualitative Research Journal, 9*(2), 27–40.

Burke, P. (2002). Context in context. *Common Knowledge, 8*(1), 152–77.

Caldwell, R. (2005). Things fall apart? Discourses on agency and change in organizations. *Human Relations, 58*(1): 83–114.

Cardinale, I. (2018). Beyond constraining and enabling: Toward new microfoundations for institutional theory. *Academy of Management Review, 43*(1), 132–55.

Child, J. & Smith, C. (1987). The context and process of organizational transformation—Cadbury Limited in its sector. *Journal of Management Studies, 24*(6), 565–93.

Czarniawska, B. & Mazza, C. (2003). Consulting as a liminal space. *Human Relations, 56*(3), 267–90.

Dopson, S., Fitzgerald, L., & Ferlie, E. (2008). Understanding change and innovation in healthcare settings: Reconceptualizing the active role of context. *Journal of Change Management, 8*(3–4), 213–31.

Gray, B., Purdy, J. M., & Ansari, S. (2015). From interactions to institutions: Microprocesses of framing and mechanisms for the structuring of institutional fields. *Academy of Management Review, 40*(1), 115–43.

Pace, M. & Pallister-Wilkins, P. (2018). EU–Hamas actors in a state of permanent liminality. *Journal of International Relations and Development, 21*(1), 223–46.

Pettigrew, A., Ferlie, E., & McKee, L. (1992). *Shaping strategic change: Making change in large organisations, the case of the NHS*. London: Sage.

Pettigrew, A. M. (1987). Context and action in the transformation of the firm. *Journal of Management Studies, 24*(6), 649–70.

Pettigrew, A. M. (1990). Longitudinal field research on change: Theory and practice. *Organization Science, 1*(3), 267–92.

Pichault, F. (2007). HRM-based reforms in public organisations: Problems and perspectives. *Human Resource Management Journal, 17*(3), 265–82.

Smets, M., Morris, T., & Greenwood, R. (2012). From practice to field: A multilevel model of practice-driven institutional change. *Academy of Management Journal, 55*(4), 877–904.

Sminia, H. (2016). Pioneering process research: Andrew Pettigrew's contribution to management scholarship, 1962–2014. *International Journal of Management Reviews, 18*(2), 111–32.

Star, S. L. (2010). This is not a boundary object: Reflections on the origin of a concept. *Science, Technology, & Human Values, 35*(5), 601–17.

Star, S. L. & Griesemer, J. R. (1989). Institutional ecology, "translations" and boundary objects: Amateurs and professionals in Berkeley's Museum of Vertebrate Zoology, 1907–39. *Social Studies of Science, 19*(3), 387–420.

Szakolczai, A. (2009). Liminality and experience: Structuring transitory situations and transformative events. *International Political Anthropology, 2*(1), 141–72.

Szakolczai, A. (2014). Living permanent liminality: The recent transition experience in Ireland. *Irish Journal of Sociology, 22*(1), 28–50.

Turner, V. W. (1969). *The ritual process: Structure and anti-structure*. New Jersey: Transaction Publishers.

Turner, V. W. (1982). *From ritual to theatre: The human seriousness of play*. New York City: Performing Arts Journal Publications.

van Gennep, A. (1960). *The rites of passage*. M. B. Vizedom & G. L. Caffee (Trans.). London: Routledge.

Weick, K. E. (1995). *Sensemaking in organisations*. London: Sage.

Williams, P. (2002). The competent boundary spanner. *Public Administration, 80*(1), 103–24.

Williams, P. (2011). The life and times of the boundary spanner. *Journal of Integrated Care, 19*(3), 26–33.

Part III
Change

How Do Contexts Change, and What Is the Role of Actors in Such Processes?

12

Analyzing Context in Health Care Organizations

Some Reflections on Past Work and Contemporary Research Challenges

Ewan Ferlie

Introduction

The invitation to write this chapter provides an interesting opportunity to reread and reflect on a monograph I coauthored some years ago (Pettigrew, Ferlie, & McKee, 1992). The text analyzed major service change processes occurring in the late 1980s in the National Health Service (NHS) in England from a contextualist and processual perspective, based on a set of eight comparative and longitudinal case studies of management teams in English District Health Authorities attempting to accomplish large-scale service-level change.

This book poses three main questions, which the chapter authors have considered: the specific theme among these three that will be explored in this chapter is the processual nature of context and action, and in particular, how "context" can evolve over time. "Time" is defined over a long duration (say, 30 years) rather than over the life of a single government (4 to 5 years), often the time-frame taken within UK health policy analysis. Theoretically, most attention is paid to how we might study the evolving "outer context" (which includes, but goes beyond, the national political economy) and best analyze how it is changing over the longer term. This chapter draws out some possible implications for the (re-)specification of the outer context of contemporary health care organizations.

After reprising the design, methods, and key findings of the earlier study, the chapter will locate the monograph in the broader academic and health policy context of the late 1980s, and the broader implications of its findings then will be discussed. As the original book came from an earlier period, the chapter will end by suggesting research challenges for progressing contextualist research within contemporary health care settings. How might the "context" for UK health care organizations have changed since the late 1980s?

Pettigrew, Ferlie, and McKee's *Shaping Strategic Change* (1992): Background and Research Design

Pettigrew, Ferlie, and McKee's *Shaping Strategic Change* (1992) represents a worked attempt to apply contextualist ideas and methods in a large-scale empirical study of significant strategic service change (e.g., the closure or merger of hospitals and the reprovision of services on a community basis, the building of new hospitals, or significant innovation in new services) in the health care sector in England in the late 1980s. Many such service changes (notably the politically contentious question of hospital closures) were the result of long-standing national policies, supported by the Department of Health, while other service changes unfolded in a more decentralized and innovative fashion, driven by local clinical leaders and teams (e.g., two case studies from Inner London about developing new services for the unexpected HIV/AIDS epidemic).

The research team (namely Andrew Pettigrew as Principal Investigator, Lorna McKee, and myself as the project researchers) was based in the Centre for Corporate Strategy and Change (CCSC) in Warwick Business School at the University of Warwick, UK. CCSC had already developed a research "genre" based on Pettigrew's earlier work, which was broadly sociological in nature and with an interpretive rather than a positivistic approach based on intensive organizational case studies. However, comparative designs were typically preferred to single case studies. The case study approach adopted tended to be longitudinal, tracing the way that events and processes unfold over an extended period.

The CCSC was distinctive in pursuing large-scale, theoretically informed but empirically grounded management research, funded through major research contracts from external funders. These projects were staffed by full-time senior research staff, usually at the postdoctoral level (as was the case here). The CCSC was unusual within UK business schools (and more so now) in according equal attention to public agencies as to private firms. Indeed, the text considered (Pettigrew, Ferlie, & McKee, 1992) replicated the design of an earlier study of variation in the competitive success of pairs of UK private firms (Pettigrew and Whipp, 1991). While there were big differences between these two sectors, as it was easier to develop success indicators in private compared with public sector settings, nevertheless it was argued that in both sectors, large organizations were struggling with significant change agendas, which could be studied within the same broad analytic framing. In the NHS study, the assessment of the extent of the implementation of desired strategic service changes (as expounded in national and local strategy documents) was taken as a (perhaps contestable) performance indicator.

This concern for exploring organizational "performance" in implementation signals that this study was based in a business school, rather than (say) a Department of Sociology. The focus was on strategic and large-scale service change, rather than microlevel or incremental change more apparent in the developing literatures on quality improvement or service improvement.

The monograph by Pettigrew, Ferlie, and McKee (1992) synthesized and theorized the findings of an earlier 3-year empirically based study tracking strategic service change processes in eight English health care organizations. The then District Health Authority (DHA) was the unit of analysis, with a typical population of about 300,000 people. The sample consisted of four matched pairs of DHAs progressing similar service change agendas, and it traced their decision-making and implementation processes. Variation in the pace of change was assessed and explained inductively through developing a model of Receptive and Non-Receptive Contexts for Change (discussed later in the chapter). The study was funded by a consortium of eight English Regional Health Authorities (RHAs) interested in exploring implementation gaps they had experienced locally. The study was not funded through a specialist NHS Research and Development function, as, at that period, these were still poorly developed. One case study was selected in each supporting region, and local feedback workshops were offered at the end of the project. Its empirical breadth and ambition remains unusual in the broader corpus of English health management research.

The receptive national policy background helped to secure significant funding for health management research (an unusual occurrence both before and since). The traditionally low profile of management research had been boosted temporarily by the new role of the general manager, following from the Griffiths report (1983). General managers were given a brief to increase "drive" and ownership of national policies locally. For example, policies to close small hospitals and concentrate services in fewer, larger, hospitals or in the community had been implemented only imperfectly. The picture of "immobolisme" painted in Griffiths was also recognized in some social science research (Smith, 1981). It was thought that the study might shed light on the role of general managers in service change, and assess whether they had accelerated it. In the end, the analysis explored processes of strategic service change more holistically, as they were found to be only one of a range of influential actors that still included clinicians and local politicians/authority members.

Analyzing Change Processes in Context: The Pettigrew Triangle

Pettigrew, Ferlie, and McKee (1992 p. 6) adopted a contextualist perspective, noting that too much organizational change research was "ahistorical, aprocessual and acontextual in character. There are remarkably few studies of change that allow the change process to reveal itself in any kind of substantially temporal or contextual manner." The heuristic device of the "Pettigrew triangle"(Pettigrew, Ferlie, & McKee, 1992 pp. 6–7) was invoked as an analytical framing: "theoretically sound and practically useful research on change should involve the continuous interplay between ideas about the context of change, the process of change and the content of change, together with skill in regulating the relations between the three." Here was an attempt to move away from linear accounts of the implementation process and an over-reliance on rational analysis as a driver for change (while not discarding reason and data altogether).

Within this triangular model, the first dimension—*content*—refers to the nature of the particular area of service transformation. At the most basic level, this category highlights the substantive nature of the service (e.g., acute or hospital-based services versus community services) that might then bring in different actors. Senior doctors within acute sector medicine, for example, might be more powerful and more capable of antimanagerial resistance than might nursing staff in community health services. More abstractly, health care–change issues might display different characteristics that could affect their adoptability, such as incremental (easier) versus radical (more difficult) forms of change. Staff role-based changes may be more complex than technologically based changes, where there is also evidence of premature and non-evidence-based diffusion, as well as blocks on desired change.

The second dimension—*context*—includes both the inner and outer context. The *inner context* refers to the features of the focal health care organization, here the DHA (Pettigrew, Ferlie, & McKee, 1992 p. 7):

> inner context, by contrast, refers to the ongoing strategy, structure, culture, management and political process of the District which help the processes through which ideas for change proceed. Perhaps a weakness of much of the generic organizational change literature is an over reliance on the inner context, which has led to a neglect of wider issues.

As this quote indicates, the model draws strong attention the *"outer context"* at a national level:

> outer context refers to the national economic, political and social context for a District Health Authority as well as the perception, action and interpretation of policies and events at national and regional levels in the NHS. The changing national political economy has clearly exerted major top down pressures on the NHS in the 1980s. (Pettigrew, Ferlie, & McKee, 1992 p. 7)

Other outer contextual forces identified included background trends in the 1980s toward (de)professionalization and a challenge to traditional professional dominance. The rise of identity politics and related social movements was also bringing new actors into some aspects of the health policy process (e.g., HIV/AIDS, mental health, and maternity services).

This openness to the macro context and political economy is a characteristic feature—and I would argue, a strength—of the approach, when compared with the apolitical approaches of other schools of strategy, such as rational planning. Chapter 3 (Top Down Restructuring) in Pettigrew, Ferlie, and McKee (1992) developed this analysis of the effects of the changing political economy in more detail. Working in the late 1980s, management researchers certainly needed to be aware of major changes occurring in the wider UK political economy, reflecting the "Thatcher shock" in both the UK private (Pettigrew, 1985) sector and the public services. Indeed, the national introduction of general management (Griffiths, 1983)—which formed the policy background to the book considered here (Pettigrew, Ferlie, & McKee, 1992)—represented an early intervention in an attempt to disturb the existing professionalized and trade unionized order in the health care sector.

The late 1980s were a period in which these major changes in the outer context of the UK political economy needed to be captured within a politically aware form of organizational analysis, especially in the politically charged and visible arena of health care organizations. This early work on general management and its effects (Pettigrew, Ferlie, & McKee, 1992) sparked a personally enduring interest in wider New Public Management (NPM) reforms, which became the central theme of a later monograph (Ferlie et al., 1996), again placing the Thatcherite political economy of health care restructuring at center stage.

The third dimension of the triangle is *the process of change,* which refers to the "actions, reactions and interactions of the various interested parties as they negotiate around proposals for change" (Pettigrew, Ferlie, & McKee, 1992, 7). This processual stance had strong methodological implications: a choice for interpretive rather than positivist social science; a concern for the intensive and longitudinal examination of organizational behaviors as revealed in action and within a contained set of cases; and an awareness that different stakeholders may have different agendas, interests, and, indeed, varying power bases. Thus, powerful groups may be more able to push through their own change agendas or to resist successfully alternative agendas being advocated by others.

Inductively Derived Model of Receptive and Nonreceptive Contexts for Change

The set of eight comparative case studies produced by the study inductively produced a model of receptive and nonreceptive (RNR) contexts for change. Each case was initially written up as a single, stand-alone document, but in a common broad format to facilitate later cross-case analysis and the induction of higher order concepts. The RNR contexts model sought to explain the observed variation within the case studies in the ability of matched pairs of DHAs to progress similar espoused strategic change objectives. It has similarities with Peters and Waterman's (1982) earlier and so-called 7S model (as each indicator began with the letter S) of organizational excellence derived from their study of excellent American private companies, except the cultural dimension is not given any privileged status here.

The model (Pettigrew, Ferlie, & McKee, 1992 ch. 9) is presented as a pattern of eight interrelated features and a series of loops rather as a causal path between independent and dependent variables. These factors are given equal importance rather than any one being accorded a central status. The factors are seen (Pettigrew, Ferlie, & McKee, 1992 p. 275) as:

> providing a linked set of conditions which produce high energy around change. This energy and the capabilities which underpin it cannot be conjured up over a short period of time through the pulling of a single lever. The past weighs a heavy hand in determining local perceptions and layers of competence emerge only slowly to enable and protect champions of change.

We shall now recap briefly the eight features of the model in Figure 12.1, which is discussed below.

Factor 1: The Quality and Coherence of "Policy"—Analytical and Process Components

The quality of locally crafted health policy (e.g., a reconfiguration strategy) was found to be important, as seen from both an analytic and a process perspective. It was not enough to take, perhaps dated, national policy "off the shelf," and the content of local policy, as well as managerial process, was

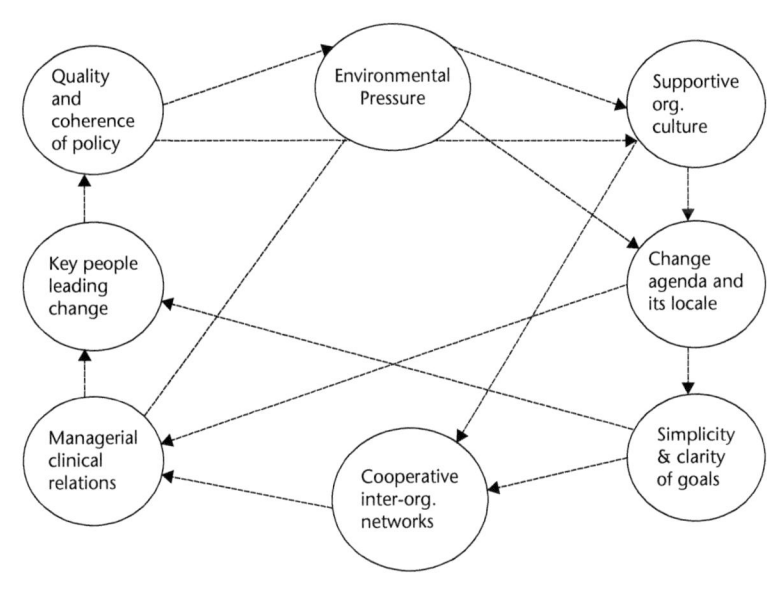

Analyzing Context in Health Care Organizations

Figure 12.1 Model of Receptive and Non-receptive Contexts for Change, from Pettigrew Ferlie, and McKee (1992)

important, where solid data and clear analytical framing (e.g., population-level data from the local public health department) helped to frame complex issues and make them more legitimate in the eyes of the scientific public (Pettigrew, Ferlie, & McKee, 1992 p. 277) such as clinicians. This finding rowed back somewhat from the highly action-oriented finding of "paralysis by analysis" apparent in other influential studies (Peters and Waterman, 1982) by leaving open a role for data and formal analysis.

These analytical considerations perhaps represented necessary conditions to achieve service change, while sufficient conditions related to processes of negotiation and change (Pettigrew, Ferlie, & McKee, 1992 p. 277): "here the starting point was critical: a broad vision seemed more likely to generate movement than a blueprint. Such broad visions were found to have significant process and implementation benefits in terms of commitment building and allowing interests to buy into the change process."

Factor 2: Availability of Key People Leading Change

This factor clearly brought in a more subjective and leadership-related dimension as a further facilitating force in service change. But it did not refer to individualistic or charismatic notions of a single heroic managerial leader so popular then (as now), but rather took a more subtle and pluralist view. The small mixed leadership group—which critically included clinical and nursing members, as well as general managers—was found to be an effective vehicle. They might also include frontline health workers with core expertise, especially where a rapid service innovation process was under way (for example, HIV/AIDS services): (Pettigrew, Ferlie, & McKee, 1992 p. 279) "the need appears to be for not boldness nor decisiveness, as much as for a combination of planning, opportunism and the adroit timing of interventions."

There was found to be an important role for senior figures in the sites (e.g., the non-executive chair) in selecting leading individuals, building the leadership team, and keeping it together. We found an important role for team continuity (Pettigrew, Ferlie, & McKee, 1992 p. 278): paradoxically, there was a requirement for some stability in the management of strategic service change, which could be eroded by excessive staff turnover. Such unplanned turnover could lead to a rapid regression in a locality's change capability as the core leadership team was hollowed out, perhaps leaving a soured context for change. The NHS later became well- known for its high turnover of senior management staff, as part of a "targets and terror"—oriented performance-management regimes (Bevan & Hood, 2006).

Factor 3: Long-Term Environmental Pressure—Intensity and Scale

Studies of strategic change outside the NHS (e.g., Pettigrew, 1985) have highlighted the role of environmental or financial crisis in triggering a radical burst of intense change in a firm. The picture in the NHS seemed more complex, as such a financial crisis—often evident—could drain purpose and energy out of a system, leading to denial, the scapegoating of the management team, or even a collapse of decision-making capacity. Moderate and predictable levels of financial pressure on a local system played a more positive role in increasing incentives for action.

Factor 4: A Supportive Organizational Culture

The cultural domain was found to be important, as some aspects of the DHAs' managerial culture appeared to be associated with a higher rate of service change. These included a style of flexible working using purpose designed structures rather than a formal hierarchy, along with a nonrepresentational mode of working with a focus on skill rather than on rank and status. Positive cultures also demonstrated an open, risk-taking approach, an openness to research and evaluation, a strong value base, and a strong, positive track record and sense of collective achievement.

Factor 5: Effective Managerial Clinical Relations

As expected, the quality of relations between managerial and clinical constituencies was found to be an important factor, but more unexpectedly, the nature and tone of managerial and clinical relationships was found to vary strongly by locale. In other words, there was not a universal and structurally determined pattern of conflict, but in some cases, cooperation appeared to have been built up, which then acted as a strong, positive feature. Where clinicians had gone into opposition (Pettigrew, Ferlie, & McKee, 1992 p. 282), they could exert a powerful block on what were seen as managerially dominated proposals for service reconfiguration. Perhaps more surprisingly, the cadre of general managers varied in the extent to which they saw relationship building and trying to agree bargains with clinicians as a core part of their brief.

Managerial clinical relations were easier to develop where negative stereotypes had broken down, perhaps as a result of the emergence of mixed roles or perspectives. Experienced NHS managers who were semi-immersed in the world of clinicians knew what to offer them to win support on other matters within a balanced package (this inside knowledge was an advantage possessed by the former NHS administrators who were often ultimately reappointed as general managers). As an example, general managers who could acquire large-scale capital investment in a major redevelopment for their district quickly built up clinical credibility.

On the clinical side, in addition, a small but important group of clinicians (Pettigrew, Ferlie, & McKee, 1992 p. 283) had come up through the medical advisory machinery but thought more managerially and strategically. This emergent cadre of clinical directors could develop as a second linking group: "such strategic clinicians are critical people for management to identify, foster and encourage and under no circumstances should they be driven into opposition by trivia" (Pettigrew, Ferlie, & McKee, 1992 p. 283).

Factor 6: Cooperative Interorganizational Networks

This factor is the only one that explicitly considers the role of non-NHS organizations in jointly coproducing large-scale service change. Some major changes in the nonacute sector (e.g., in the fields of mental health and learning disabilities) required effective joint working with local government (Social Services) and nongovernmental organizations (NGOs) as services moved across organizational boundaries. So the building of interorganizational networks across different agencies emerged as an important capability. Health organizations had little direct power in these settings, but rather had to win influence and build trust through repeated interactions. Various features could enrich these networks, such as the presence of dedicated boundary breakers, who crossed agency divides, plus clear referral and communication pathways. The best networks kept a sense of purpose rather than being self-absorbed and inward looking, which was a danger.

This factor subsequently became even more important, as the awareness and prevalence of so-called wicked problems (Ferlie et al., 2011, 2013) in health policy that crossed conventional agency boundaries increased. A NPM markets/management mix of governance modes seems ill-suited to such issues, which may be better tackled by using a network governance model (Ferlie et al., 2013). Examples of wicked problems in health care settings include responding to an aging society and, in particular, the pressures on social care; and Type 2 diabetes and obesity.

Factor 7: Simplicity and Clarity of Goals and Priorities

This focusing issue arose from the observation that general managers varied greatly in their ability to narrow the vast and ever shifting NHS change agenda down into a set of key long- term priorities. Given this question of change overload and fatigue, "rather, persistence and patience in pursuit of objectives over a long time period seemed to be associated with achieving strategic change" (Pettigrew, Ferlie, & McKee, 1992 p. 285). A culture of panics, issue succession, and crises seemed to be strongly evident in the NHS, which meant that a protective competence in focusing and protecting important long-term agendas was vital.

Factor 8: The Fit between the District's Change Agenda and the Locale

This structural dimension incorporates strongly the notion of the inner context. The observation is made that some local contexts are structurally simpler and more tractable in terms of effecting desired strategic change. For example, the redevelopment of a hospital might be easier where a DHA included one large center of population rather than two rival towns. The presence of a powerful medical school might offer an institutional constraint. The number of agencies involved in a strategic change process, their differential power bases, and the way in which agency boundaries were drawn (affecting the so-called degree of interagency coterminosity) was also important. The nature and degree of unionization of the local NHS workforce also varied, and reflected the nature of the local political culture: there was a left-wing and oppositionist culture in one district studied that manifested itself in strong, politically motivated campaigns against proposals for hospital closures.

While many of these factors were beyond direct management control, awareness of them might be important in anticipating possible obstacles to change proposals. Some might also be reshaped in the long run by higher tiers, as in the redrawing and simplifying of boundaries.

On Rereading the Text: Wider Discussion

On rereading the text, what broader observations can be made? Pettigrew, Ferlie, and McKee (1992) clearly represents a worked attempt to apply contextualist ideas and methods to the study of large-scale changes in the English health care sector. It is rooted in a substantial empirical set of comparative case studies of such changes in eight District Health Authorities. Its main formal contribution is the inductive model of RNR contexts for change, presented in the final chapter of the text. Its acknowledgment of the role of the political economy and of the outer context in UK public services reform in the 1980s is important and distinctive in the management literature. There have been few subsequent studies of such empirical ambition in UK health management research.

However, the book was published in 1992, and it clearly reflects the interests of the time, in both a public/health policy and an academic sense. Its policy focus is mainly on general management, and it precedes the major, market-driven reforms evident from 1990 onward. In terms of academic emplacement, Pettigrew, Ferlie, and McKee (1992) is part of a broader "process wave" that occurred in late-1980s management research. Most obviously, the text largely replicated the design of another CCSC-based and recently completed process-based study (Pettigrew and Whipp, 1991) of UK private firms. It was also influenced by an earlier longitudinal analysis of strategic change processes at ICI, conducted by Pettigrew (1985).

Pettigrew's own processual work contributed significantly to the nascent discipline of UK management research, which was, at that stage, still developing an academic research base. Previous well-known UK management research had often been quantitative and contingency theoretic in nature, such as the Aston School's exploration of formal organizational structures and dimensions (Pugh et al., 1968). The developing process school was, by contrast, influenced by alternative and the more interpretive social science disciplines (including sociology and anthropology), and its longitudinal emphasis also gave it some affinity with the discipline of history in the humanities. Pettigrew's (1987) broader reflections on the relation between context and action in corporate change processes, for instance, suggests affinities with Giddens's (1979) sociological concept of structuration, and it challenges simple notions of transformational leadership exercised by charismatic individuals. It also explicitly brings in theories of background social power (Lukes, 1974) from sociology to explore how these may affect major organizational closure decisions in the UK (another good theme coming from the 1980s!) (Hardy, 1985). This broader tradition of process research in health care organizations is considered more fully in Chapter 4 in this volume, by Louise Fitzgerald.

Pettigrew, Ferlie, and McKee (1992) can also be seen as a relatively early text that helped to identify longer-term research questions picked up in later work by the wider CCSC team and other health management researchers. Three examples of later streams of work consistent with these initial findings can be given. First, Pettigrew, Ferlie, and McKee (1992) challenged currently fashionable charismatic and transformational leadership theories, arguing instead for a quieter, team-based, and multidisciplinary form of leadership that, in turn, was set in its context. This theme has been developed recently by Fitzgerald and McDermott (2017), who argue that transformational theories of change and leadership fit badly within highly politicized contexts.

Second, Pettigrew, Ferlie, and McKee (1992) stressed the continuingly salient role of clinical professionals alongside the new general managers in leading major service change. Hence, their representation was still important in mixed leadership teams, as was their career and educational development. In addition, the differing roles and identities of clinical managerial hybrids who straddled these two worlds were explored in recent writing (McGivern et al., 2015).

Third, the focus on the outer context brought in a concern for the operation of the political economy, and for processes of top-down restructuring. The implementation in the mid-1980s of new general management roles recommended by Griffiths (1983) had helped to create a policy climate in which management-oriented research projects had become fundable. With the benefit of hindsight, general management can be seen analytically as an early and significant NPM-inspired reform. While an examination of the wider NPM narrative of reform was not explored deeply in Pettigrew, Ferlie, and McKee (1992), it sparked an interest explored more deeply in a later project (Ferlie et al., 1996) on major changes introduced in 1990 to NHS corporate governance on lines similar to those of private firm. And other, later work (Ferlie et al., 2013) explored a possible post-NPM narrative of UK public management reform developing under the period of New Labour governments (1997–2010), namely network governance. The NPM versus post-NPM debate was also picked up as a question of interest in the later text. So Pettigrew, Ferlie, and McKee (1992) sparked an enduring interest in the analysis of wider narratives of public management reform that apply in the health care sector as in other public services, as opposed to a focus on single, narrow, or technical organizational changes limited to the health care sector (e.g., the many reorganizations of the primary care sector).

Of course, the Pettigrew, Ferlie, and McKee (1992) text explored change processes in health care settings, rather than in private firms (Pettigrew and

Whipp, 1991). This sectoral location brought it closer to the strongly embedded and institutionalized scientific and clinical research traditions within the health care sector. Methodologically, contextualism represents an alternative research stance to the tradition of scientific randomization, so dominant in the biomedical research domain and influential in the developing health services research (HSR) tradition. In these more scientific approaches, there is often a methodological preference for experimental or quasi-experimental designs over case-based studies, which are then expressed in implicit or explicit "hierarchy of evidence" models. Within this randomization tradition, context is treated as an "effect modifier" rather than a major force in its own right, and there is more interest in assessing the effects of a discrete "intervention" and trying to "control out" other variables. So there is some tension between contextualism and other strongly embedded research traditions in the health care domain.

What might now—with the benefit of perfect hindsight—be seen as the major gaps in the text? It paints a picture of a relatively simple world with a largely "closed" NHS economy (albeit with a recognition of the role of local government and voluntary organizations in providing care in the community) and run on hierarchical lines. There is little consideration of the financialization of the health sector that was to become increasingly evident in the 1990s with the growth of the private finance initiative and public–private partnerships (PPPs). The downsizing of the physical estate and of hospital bed numbers, for example, may be driven by the desire to reduce long-term annual repayments due in exchange for the private-sector capital investment secured to refurbish dilapidated estate. Nor was the role of private-sector providers explored in any depth. Of course, the fieldwork for the study (just) predated the 1990 Health and Community Care Act, which brought in a quasi-market, along with a new organizational form of autonomized provider units (NHS Trusts). The old District Health Authorities were simply abolished.

Nor was there any sustained concern in Pettigrew, Ferlie, and McKee (1992) for exploring the organizational effects of new technology, notably including information and communication technology (ICT), which was just beginning at that stage to develop as a major force. Contextualism would be likely to take a socio-technical perspective on new ICTs, as they would be seen as interacting with current work practices and existing organizations rather than exerting a form of crude technological determinism. It was, however, possible that they could reinforce new modes of organizational control going beyond line management hierarchy and the physical presence of a manager.

Studying private-sector firms, Zuboff's prophetic book (1988) explored new electronically based control and surveillance systems at a time, when Castells's (1996) influential work on the "network society" still lay in the future. Dunleavy et al. (2006) subsequently developed a distinctive model of "digital era governance" (DEG), which analyzed the reintegrating effects of ICTs within public agencies. Some later work has seen the diffuse and invisible control mechanisms associated with ICT-based performance-management systems in health care organizations (as in other settings) from a Foucauldian or govermentality perspective (Ferlie et al., 2013). So there may now be a rich seam to explore in future work on the organizational effects of ICTs in health care organizations.

Finally, the definition of *performance*—the faster implementation of desired policies in relation to service reconfiguration—used in Pettigrew, Ferlie, and McKee's 1992 study was a crude proxy and in any case, contestable. For example, community care for those with mental health problems had indeed been a long-standing national and regional policy, but was it right? Did it have perverse and unintended effects on patients and their families? So any future studies may wish to consider the whole area of performance assessment, and how it should be made with some caution in relation to health care organizations.

Some Challenges for Future Contextualist Research in Health Care Organizations

How might the contextualist analysis of UK health care organizations usefully be developed in the future? Here, we first address the specific questions of how best to specify the "context" and analyze changes over a longer duration.

There are well-known frameworks that can help in assessing an organization's external environment, such as a PESTELI (that is, political, economic, sociological, technological, legal, environment, and industry) analysis. *Socially*, for example, the gradual aging of the population evident since the 1980s may well pose significant challenges for health care organizations, and lead to attempts to change patterns of service delivery. A long-term and major *technological* development has been the rapid growth of powerful new ICTs since the 1990s, leading to a distinct narrative of DEG (Dunleavy et al., 2006), where the new ICTs can help to reintegrate NPM-style fragmented organizations and service processes. DEG principles could affect UK health care organizations as much as other public agencies, leading to the ICT-driven redesign of complex care pathways.

The *political* dimension of the "outer context" is of great interest, at least in largely publicly funded health systems (such as the NHS), where it assumes great importance. The assessment of this dimension—and of significant but perhaps only occasional changes in it—requires interpretive skill and cannot simply be read off from a conventional PESTELI trends analysis.

Pettigrew, Ferlie, and McKee (1992) helpfully acknowledged some major changes that had occurred in the UK's outer political context in the late 1980s. These changes expressed themselves through top-down managerial reforms, of which the new general management role recommended in Griffiths (1983) was the first major example. Griffiths (1983) was in fact the policy-related trigger for the research project, and later the book discussed here. However, these NPM-related health management reforms were at that stage analyzed more empirically than theoretically, and then only rather briefly (Pettigrew, Ferlie, and McKee 1992). With the benefit of hindsight, these general managerialization processes were only a localized symptom of a wider NPM "narrative" of public management reform, which was analyzed more fully in later work (Ferlie et al., 1996).

The notion of a broad "narrative" of public management reforming is an important one. It goes beyond a focus on one particular reform (here, general management) to consider linked bundles of reforms and moves beyond technical analysis to recognize the importance of political and ideological elements.

They can be seen as an expression of the dominant version of the political economy as it seeks to find a language and set of reform doctrines that enable it to influence the management of public services organizations where it is a political priority.

So a key question that arises is whether the NPM paradigm of the 1980s has survived within the management of the NHS, or whether it has been displaced by a later so-called network governance (NG) paradigm, associated with later New Labour governments (1997–2010) (Ferlie et al., 2013), introducing distinctive non-market-based reforms, including managed networks as a governance mode. While there is some evidence for enduring NG reforms, other studies (Trenholm & Ferlie, 2013) show the resilient and embedded nature of NPM reforms in NHS management, even if they are dysfunctionally so. There is thus a major debate in the academic literature about whether health organizations in the UK are still operating in a NPM mode or have moved to a post-NPM mode. The view one takes on this question influences individuals' judgment about whether there has been a major shift in the UK political economy since the 1980s or not.

Other long-term changes in the "inner context" of health care delivery system organizations should also be considered. The notion of "inner context" in UK health care organizations, however, has become more complex since the initial study. The focus in Pettigrew, Ferlie, and McKee (1992) was largely on the role of the then focal DHA which had—at least in formal terms—hierarchical control over "its" hospitals (although a couple of chapters on the reprovision of mental health and learning disability services did consider the role of non-health agencies). The introduction and long-term survival of the purchaser/provider split, of the internal market and of autonomized NHS Trusts in 1990, further weakened the assumption that a DHA was in control of health services delivery within its territory. Private and not-for-profit providers have also taken on an enhanced role in what is now a more fragmented service delivery system.

So there is now also increased interest in so-called wicked problems in health policy, which are complex, multifaceted, and beyond the jurisdiction of any single agency (Ferlie et al., 2013). The field covering the care of older people is a good example, as health, social care, and voluntary agencies will need to improve their interagency coordination if hospitals are not to be overwhelmed by increasing demand. Yet earlier NPM reforms, which created inward-looking, operationally focused, and self-contained agencies (NHS Trusts, cost pressured local government, and voluntary organizations operating to narrow performance-oriented contracts with public funders) may well fail to tackle these laterally facing problems effectively (see Trenholm and Ferlie's (2013) study of the flawed multi-agency response to resurgent tuberculosis across London), as each agency faces local incentives to meet its own targets, but also to shunt costs on to other agencies.

Thus, the level of systemic capacity at the subregional level represents an increasingly important aspect of the inner context. Therefore, future contextualist work might well look further at how these health and social care systems operate (or not) as systems in relation to such wicked problems, and where it is that stronger joint working has been built up, and why. This switch of focus from the single organization to the local system may also require new basic ideas from systems and complexity thinking to be explored (Trenholm & Ferlie, 2013).

Resource and funding issues in relation to future health management research also need to be considered. Was the Pettigrew, Ferlie, and McKee (1992) study a "one-off" product of its time? Clearly, the original study required considerable resources to be invested in managerial and organizational research—as opposed to the usual focus on clinical research—in health care settings. These demanding studies further required experienced qualitative researchers to be in post for a considerable time (the project was funded for 3 years and employed two postdoctoral researchers). There was a post-Griffiths (1983) moment when significant investment in UK health management research became possible, but that moment appears to have passed. There has since been a significant growth of funding for the National Institute for Health Research, created in 2006, but mainly in the biomedical or HSR domains.

Since the 1990s, there has been a growth in HSR and service-improvement-oriented research. Highly applied evaluations of particular (often-transient) policy initiatives have been evident, often highly multidisciplinary in focus and strongly directed at practitioner audiences. But there has also been an eclipse of funding for single discipline and basic organizational research within UK health care. The big RHAs that funded the Pettigrew, Ferlie, and McKee (1992) study have long ago been abolished. In part, this decline has been because the health management community in the field found it difficult to articulate, support, and win funds for the management research agenda. There may also be a suspicion that such long-term management research takes too long, comes up with equivocal findings, and has low real-world impact (as Weiss (1979) argued in her authoritative article on the limited impact of classic American evaluation studies). So the long-term and basic mode of health care management research in Pettigrew, Ferlie, and McKee (1992) has not flourished recently, with negative effects on theory building.

There are supply-side issues about who would undertake any new large-scale research projects. Where would the researchers be based academically? The CCSC was a freestanding and self-funding research center at Warwick Business School. Given the changes in the research-funding climate considered above, one question is could it generate significant health management research contracts now?

A wider institutional question for many current UK business schools is whether they indeed wish to champion such health/public management research as part of their research mission, or whether they have since become too narrow and "siloed" (Currie, Davies, & Ferlie, 2016). A major change in many business schools since the 1980s has been the rise of large finance groups, with their own, distinctive research concerns and common use of quantitative and technical methods. Many business schools now appear to be focused on the study of a relatively narrow range of private-sector settings (notably shareholder-owned public limited companies—PLCs), despite the political, economic, and societal importance of public service organizations, certainly including the health care sector. While there is growing public and academic disquiet about the role and future of the private corporation, such important concerns have too infrequently influenced the research agendas of many business schools.

So, finding an academic and institutional base for progressing theoretically informed contextualist research in UK health care organizations may not be easy. Existing writing networks and learned societies (e.g., the Society for the Study of Organizing in Health Care) may have an important facilitating role to play in forming supportive links across the relevant academic community.

References

Bevan, G. & Hood, C. (2006). What's measured is what matters: Targets and gaming in the English public health care system. *Public Administration, 84*(3), 517–38.

Castells, M. (1996). *The information age: Economy, society, and culture, vol. I: The rise of the network society*. Oxford: Basil Blackwell.

Currie, G., Davies, J., & Ferlie, E. (2016). A call for university-based business schools to "lower their walls": Collaborating with other academic departments in pursuit of social value. *Academy of Management Learning & Education, 15*(4), 742–55.

Dunleavy, P., Margetts, H., Bastow, S., & Tinkler, J. (2006). New public management is dead—Long live digital-era governance. *Journal of Public Administration Research and Theory, 16*(3), 467–94.

Ferlie, E., Ashburner, L. Fitzgerald, L., & Pettigrew, A. (1996). *The new public management in action.* Oxford: Oxford University Press.

Ferlie, E., Fitzgerald, L., McGivern, G., Dopson, S., & Bennett, C. (2011). Public policy networks and "wicked problems": A nascent solution? *Public Administration, 89*(2), 307–24.

Ferlie, E., Fitzgerald, L., McGivern, G., Dopson, S., & Bennett, C. (2013). *Making wicked problems governable? The case of managed networks in health care.* Oxford: Oxford University Press.

Fitzgerald, L. & McDermott, A. (2017). *Challenging perspectives on organizational change in health care.* Abingdon: Routledge.

Giddens, A. (1979). *Central problems in social theory.* London: Macmillan.

Griffiths, R. (1983). *NHS management enquiry.* London: Department of Health.

Hardy, C. (1985). *Managing organizational closure.* Aldershot: Gower.

Lukes, S. (1974). *Power: A radical view.* London: Macmillan.

McGivern, G., Currie, G., Ferlie, E., Fitzgerald, L., & Waring, J. (2015). Hybrid manager–professionals' identity work: The maintenance and hybridization of medical professionalism in managerial contexts. *Public Administration, 93*(2), 412–32.

Peters, T. & Waterman, R. (1982). *In search of excellence.* New York: Harper & Row.

Pettigrew, A. (1985). *The awakening giant: Continuity and change in imperial chemical industries.* Oxford: Basil Blackwell.

Pettigrew, A., Ferlie, E., & McKee, L. (1992). *Shaping strategic change.* London: Sage.

Pettigrew, A. & Whipp, R. (1991). *Managing change for competitive success.* Oxford: Basil Blackwell.

Pettigrew, A. M. (1987). Context and action in the transformation of the firm. *Journal of Management Studies, 24*(6), 649–70.

Pugh, D. S., Hickson, D. J., Hinings, C. R., & Turner, C. (1968). Dimensions of *organization structure. Administrative Science Quarterly, 13*(1), 65–105.

Smith, J. (1981). Conflict without change: The case of London's health services. *Political Quarterly, 52*(4), 426–40.

Trenholm, S. & Ferlie, E. (2013). Using complexity theory to analyse the organisational response to resurgent tuberculosis across London. *Social Science & Medicine, 93,* 229–37.

Weiss, C. H. (1979). The many meanings of research utilization. *Public Administration Review, 39*(5), 426–31.

Zuboff, S. (1988). *In the age of the smart machine: The future of work and power.* New York: Basic Books.

13

Context and Work Organization in an Acute Health Care Setting

Ian Kessler

Introduction

The relationship between context and work organization in health care is a topic of compelling interest to researchers of health care policy, management, and practice. In a sector where, despite technological advances, service delivery continues to center on the direct and unmediated relationship between the patient and the health care worker (Dubois, McKee, & Nolte, 2006 p. 13), work organization—defined as the distribution of tasks and responsibilities across the workforce, and between occupations—is likely to have significant consequences for the nature and outcome of service provision.

The influence of context on work organization in health care, indeed, in most sectors, derives from a well-established literature presenting the allocation of work tasks and responsibilities as being a socially and politically driven process. Attention has, for example, been drawn to the profession as an occupational construct emerging from the competitive pursuit of closure over the performance of "expert" tasks (Larson, 1977; Friedson, 2001), with ongoing institutional work often being required to protect the fragile occupational jurisdictions established (Abbott, 1988; Lawrence & Suddaby, 2006). Indeed, the sensitivity of task allocation to context is deepened by the indeterminate nature of the employment relationship (Marsden, 1999). Thus a formal specification of the tasks associated with an occupation, such as an employment contract or job description, is unlikely to capture the full range of emergent activities required by the employer and from the employee, in the invariably dynamic and unpredictable workplace environment. Such indeterminacy lends the enactment of work roles a situated quality, contingent not only on social and political influences but also on a wider range of economic, historical, and cultural factors.

Contextual influences over the allocation of work tasks and responsibilities assume a distinctive form in the health care sector, given the range of occupations comprising the workforce. The nature of the services delivered in health care generate a myriad of tasks and responsibilities performed by a uniquely sophisticated workforce, extending from the hospital cleaner and porter to the highly trained medical consultant and senior hospital manager responsible for a multimillion-pound budget. There are, for example, over 300 different occupational groups in National Health Service (NHS) England, with the process of allocating tasks and responsibilities to occupations informed by an unusual degree of uncertainty and fluidity.

As a means of highlighting the potency of context, this chapter focuses less on the distribution of tasks *between* occupations in the health care workforce, and more on the factors shaping the contours of a *single* health care role: the health care support worker (HSW) in NHS England. Adopting a critical realist perspective, the chapter argues that a shared HSW job title masks considerable variation in the configuration of tasks undertaken by those holding the post. This configuration is sensitive to contextual influences at different levels of the health care system, which both facilitate and constrain the tasks performed by those in the role.

The chapter is divided into three main parts: the first outlines how the notion of "context" is viewed and used here; the second sets out the approach adopted in exploring the influence context on the distribution of tasks to the HSW role; and the third presents research findings to illustrates this influence.

Approaching the Relationship between Context and Work Organization in Health Care

The influence of context has been implicit but sometimes weakly articulated in the literature on health care management (Bate et al., 2014). This weakness in part derives from conceptual imprecision, a difficulty in characterizing and placing a boundary on the notion of context. As Pollitt (2013 p. xvii) notes, context can "become a vague, catch-all concept that, by containing almost everything, ends up with little discriminating power," suggesting the need for greater specificity and detail on those substantive features of context interfacing with aspects of health care management. Nonetheless, conceptual difficulties have subdued rather than negated an interest in context (Johns, 2006), with a limited but noteworthy stream of research relating work organization to context in the health care sector. In this section, the work organization–context relationship is examined through a critical realist lens, providing an opportunity to define key terms, review previous research, and elucidate an analytical framework for the chapter.

Critical realism is a meta-analytical framework based on a set of principles and assumptions, applied by social scientists from various disciplines and to different substantive research issues (Archer et al., 1998). In this discussion, three tenets of the framework are highlighted. The first is an emphasis placed by critical realists on the stratified nature of social entities, with influential policies, practices, and rules emerging in a layered, often- cascading fashion. This tenet connects to definitions of context, which suggest that context is influential at different societal levels. Thus, Griffin (2007 p. 260) defines *context* as, "The set of circumstances in which phenomena (for example events, process or entities) are situated. The context typically exists as a unit of analysis above the phenomena being investigated and the context can explain some salient aspects of the phenomena." Similarly, Pettigrew's (1987) distinction between the inner and outer context recognizes the layered nature of environments, found in and beyond the organization.

Various studies on work organization in health care draw on a layered notion of context. For example, Abbott (1988) suggests that the process by which professions establish and maintain their occupational territories is played out through engagement with actors at different societal levels: at the national level, as an occupation seeks state endorsement of and protection for its professional status; at the level of public opinion, as the occupation seeks a broader legitimacy for its privileged labor market position; and at the workplace level, as occupations battle to secure the exclusive right to perform discrete tasks. More specifically, Reay, Golden-Biddle, and Germann (2006) focus on the emergence of a new work role, the nurse practitioner, at different levels of a Canadian provincial health care system. This role is seen as being opened-up to health care providers by the introduction of a dedicated nurse practitioner training program at the provincial level. However, the institutionalization of the nurse practitioner role at the system level is presented as achieved through the enactment of microprocesses at the workplace level.

While the first tenet of critical realism encourages a focus on the locus of context, the second centers on its properties. Thus, for the critical realist, institutional structures at different societal levels are characterized by their dualism. On the one hand, structures are observable and influence attitudes and behavior, while, on the other, structures are sensitive to actor agency over time. Thus, structures frame and shape actions, but they do not determine them. The actor retains scope to engage in what Archer (1983) refers to as structural elaboration.

This dualism has much in common with Johns's (2006) definition of *context* as "the situational opportunities and constraints that affect the occurrence and meaning of organizational behavior, as well as functional relationships between variables." Thus, Johns is presenting context as a permissive or restrictive influence on agency. In viewing context and process as an interactive field, Pettigrew (1987) similarly suggests a close, ongoing relationship between structure and agency. Indeed, Pettigrew is keen to draw on Giddens's structuration theory, which breaks down the analytical distinction between structure and agency, with structure being presented as enacted (Whittington, 1992). Such an approach, however, moves beyond critical realism, which regards structures as being ontologically and epistemologically distinct from action (Archer et al., 1998).

The interaction between context and agency is reflected in various studies on work organization in health care. For example, Nelsen and Barley (1997) plot the development of the emergency medical technician role in the USA as an interactive process by which volunteers and paid employees, both transporting patients to hospital, competed for a cultural mandate from the public essential to the exclusive performance of this role. Currie et al. (2012) and Kitchener and Mertz (2012) reveal how shifts in the health care context at system level—for example, revisions in workforce regulations and the introduction of new medical technologies—opened the way for the emergence of new work roles, which challenged established health care professions: in the former case, the specialist doctor confronting new generic nurses and consultants, and in the latter, the registered dentist facing the dental hygienist.

Critical realism's third tenet rests on a preoccupation with generative causal mechanisms. Real structures moderate agency to produce socioeconomic patterns, begging questions about how and why these (demi-) regularities emerge. This interest in causation is reflected in calls from those championing contextual analysis to theorize the relationship between context and individual and collective outcomes. As Rousseau and Fried (2001 p. 9) argue, "When contextual factors are an integral part of the theory and research method, organizational research can directly address the impact a setting has on the participants and the participants' impact on the groups and firms of which they are a part."

A focus on theorization prompts a consideration of the substantive dimensions of context: the contextual features at different societal levels are likely to influence individual and collective attitudes and behaviors. This is not a straightforward task. In searching for a definition of *context*, Hood (2013 p. 117) notes that "structure is too limiting. I prefer to view context as meaning the larger historical context including ideals, policies and social currents, within which structures operate and within which they are subsumed." Indeed, with context viewed in such catholic terms, there are grounds for arguing that an inductive or retroductive approach is better suited than a hypothetico-deductive one to revealing such influences.

The remainder of this chapter uses the tenets of critical realism to explore the relationship between context and the allocation of tasks and responsibilities to the HSW role in a hospital setting. The principal organizing device for the discussion is critical realism's first tenet, which allows for the exploration of contextual influences at different societal levels, in the case of the HSWs:

- The sector, NHS England level;
- The health care provider, NHS Trust or hospital(s) level; and
- The workplace—that is, the clinical-area and ward level.

A focus on levels ensures that the analysis can connect to critical realism's second tenet, examining whether and how the structures and institutions at these levels constrain or facilitate the allocation of tasks and responsibilities to the role. To the extent that patterns emerge in the allocative process at these levels, finally it becomes possible to explore context as a causal mechanism, pinpointing those contextual features that regulate task allocation, and why they acquire this functional capacity.

In the main, the discussion draws on primary data, and, before moving to a presentation of the findings, the next section sets out the research approach.

Research Design

The research design adopted for the work presented in this chapter was based on a multi-method case study approach. The research was explicitly informed by an interest in the influence of context on the shape of the HSW role, and the case study has long been recognized as a research design well-suited to examining a "phenomenon in-depth in a real-life context" (Yin, 1984). Four acute NHS health care providers, or Trusts, were selected purposely by location, being drawn from different parts of the country (London, South, North, and Midlands—henceforth, the terms used here in referring to the cases). These fell into pairs: two of the Trusts (London and Midlands) were medium-sized, single-site district general hospitals, whereas the other two (South and North) were large, multisite teaching hospitals. However, in each case, attention focused on the same two clinical areas: in-patient surgical and medical wards.

Such a research design generated questions that allowed us to probe the influence of context at different levels:

- *How diverse were the forms assumed by the HSW role across the four Trusts?*—the greater the diversity, the more permissive the national context, and the greater the scope for agency at the organizational level.

- *If organizational context was active in shaping the HSW role, what properties were influential at this level?* In selecting Trusts from different regions, the impact of local labor markets could be discerned. More significantly, the emergence of diverse HSW- role types would encourage an interest in the contextual effect of bespoke Trust policies and practices.
- *How permissive or restrictive was the organizational context, and what residual scope remained for the HSW role to be shaped by the workplace context?* Just as diverse HSW roles at the Trust level would suggest a permissive national context, so would diverse HSW role types across clinical areas and wards point to a permissive organizational context. This would encourage the search for aspects of the workplace context shaping the HSW role.

While broadly focused, a central theme of the research was the nature and shape of the HSW role: the range and character of the tasks performed and the responsibilities held. This issue was explored by interviews with almost one hundred HSWs, evenly spread between the cases, and with a similar number of nurses and nurse managers. Interviews were complemented with a total 275 hours of observation of HSWs (and nurses) on morning shifts, again evenly distributed across the Trusts. Finally, all HSWs in the four Trusts were surveyed, with close to 500 returns, a response rate of almost a half for each Trust. The survey included a question on the regularity (daily, weekly, monthly, annually, or never) with which around a dozen tasks were performed. The tasked ranged from basic health care tasks such a feeding and washing the patient to more complex activities, including taking vital signs, cannulation, and catheterization.

These primary data are used in discussing contextual influences at the organizational and workplace levels. In first examining context at the system or sector level, we draw on secondary sources.

Findings

The Sector Context: NHS England

The HSW is an unregistered individual working alongside, and often assisting, the registered nurse (RN). The role has long been part of the health care workforce, emerging with "modern nursing" in the mid-nineteenth century (Abel-Smith, 1960). In June 2017, there were almost 150,000 nursing support workers in NHS England—around 11 percent of the total workforce—with around half of these located in acute care settings (https://digital.nhs.uk/data-and-information/publications/statistical/nhs-workforce-statistics/nhs-workforce-statistics-december-2017). However, numbers have varied over the years, particularly relative to the volume of nurses employed, prompting debate over safe staffing levels, and, more specifically, over the skill mix: the ratio of RNs to HSWs. It is broadly recognized that safe staffing is sensitive to clinical circumstances: the more acute the patient's condition, the richer the requisite skill mix. This has not, however, deterred the UK nurses' professional body, the Royal College of Nursing (RCN), from recommending a 65:35 nurse-to-HSW ratio in acute care (2006), while noting that, in practice, this ratio has fallen—from 62:38 in 2009 to 58:42 in 2017 (2017).

This significant fall in the RN-to-HSW ratio is broadly indicative of a permissive national context for the organization of nursing work. Indeed, various contextual features at the sector level have combined to construct a light-touch national framework for work organization in acute nursing across NHS England. The first feature is associated with the statutory regulation of the nursing workforce. Clearly, nursing is a registered profession in England, functioning under the auspices of a regulatory body, the National Nursing and Midwifery Council (NNMC). However, the very existence of the HSW role is a testament to the failure of nursing to secure full occupational closure over the performance of care tasks.

This failure draws attention to a crucial distinction between, on the one the hand, the statutory regulation of entry requirements into a role based on accredited qualifications, and, on the other, the statutory regulation of substantive work tasks. In NHS England, nursing is certainly regulated in the former sense: the "registered nurse" is a "protected title," which can only be used by someone with approved qualifications at a graduate level. In the latter sense, however, there are few tasks beyond the narrow provision of controlled drugs that are performed exclusively by the RN. The weak statutory regulation over the allocation of nursing tasks is brought into sharp relief by comparisons with midwives, who not only have a protected title, but also a protected function, which allows only those with this title (or a medical practitioner) to "attend a woman in childbirth." In nursing, the absence of broad-based functional protection has opened the way to considerable fluidity in the distribution of tasks between nurses and HSWs.

The second, closely related, national contextual feature concerns the unregistered status of HSWs, limiting constraints on how health care providers might use the role. Over the years there has been much debate about whether the HSW should be subject to statutory regulation, typically revolving around the balance to be struck between cost, flexibility, and risk. In the absence of registration, there are no formal, minimum entry requirements or performance standards to be met by the HSW, inevitably raising concerns about the risks associated with performance of the role. Indeed, as a Report commissioned by the NNMC noted (Griffiths & Robinson, 2010 p. 26), "It cannot be unequivocally concluded that unregulated support workers present a risk to public safety; it is likely that they do but not an absolute certainty." At the same time, regulation inevitably introduces costs and undermines flexibility, arguably reducing the perceived value to the health care provider of the HSW as a resource. Thus, it has been argued by Thornley (1996) that HSWs have often been used by policy makers and practitioners as a source of "cheap labor," and deployed to address periodic financial pressures.

Over the years, governments of different political complexions have been swayed more by the latter than the former argument, seeing the risks associated with use of the HSW as being too low to justify the high costs associated with the introduction of a statutory model of registration. As a Department of Health paper concluded: "For groups such as healthcare support workers full-scale statutory regulation is likely to be disproportionate to the risks involved and risks overly constraining roles and functions that are often designed to meet the needs of patients and the public" (2009 p. 35).

The third national contextual feature centers more narrowly on the allocation of nursing tasks as managed by sector-based pay and grading systems. In many industries and organizations, such systems underpin the allocation tasks by attaching pay rates or scales to an ordered and evaluated hierarchy of work roles. As a nationally funded and delivered service, the NHS has long been governed by a national agreement with employee representative organizations, which establishes a sector-wide pay and grading system. The most recent agreement, Agenda for Change, signed in 2004, establishes two main pay bands for HSWs (Bands 2 and 3 in a nine-band pay structure), reflecting notional differences in the size of the support role performed. Each of these respective pay bands is tied to a formal national job profile, setting out the tasks and responsibilities associated with it.

The agreement, however, has no statutory basis, with health care providers abiding by it voluntarily. The job profiles underpinning the pay structure are generic and, notwithstanding the collective efforts of resource-limited and stretched trade unions, they remain difficult to enforce. For a variety of reasons, the national agreement has been resilient (Kessler, 2012), the most severe challenge taking the form of only a few of NHS England's 250 Trusts periodically threatening to break away (Nursing Times, 2012). Yet this very resilience may well reflect the agreement's limited capacity to constrain the behavior of health care providers, particularly in the domain of work organization.

The final contextual feature at the national level relates to general policy developments, which over the years have created scope for an extension of the HSW role and, therefore, for greater variation in its shape. In the mid-1980s, the government implemented the recommendations of a Report, Project 2000 (United Kingdom Central Council, 1986; Bradshaw, 2001), produced by the nursing regulatory body, calling for a shift from a workplace to a "classroom" model of nurse training. The result was the withdrawal of student nurses on placement as the main source of frontline support for nurses, with the HSW being given an opportunity to fill the space vacated. Indeed, over the succeeding years this space has widened, not least as a consequence of the European Working Time Directive, implemented in 2009, which reduced junior doctors' hours of work. Nurses began to withdraw from the bedside delivery of basic care to take on the more specialist, clinical tasks formerly performed by junior doctors, further enhancing opportunities for HSWs to develop their roles.

In combination, the four features outlined above have created a largely permissive or enabling national context for the distribution of tasks and responsibilities to the HSW role. The failure of RNs to achieve full closure over tasks performed weakened occupational boundaries with HSWs and, as nurses began to retreat from the bedside, opened the way for an extension of HSW relatively unhindered by systems associated with registration or by enforceable national job descriptions. However, the test of permissiveness is practice at the organizational level, and the shape of the HSW role within Trusts.

The Organizational Context: The Health Care Provider

Drawing on the case study material, the opportunities for and constraints on Trusts in shaping the HSW role are manifest in two sets of findings. The first relates to the relationship between pay grades and the tasks performed by HSWs. In all four of the Trusts examined, this relationship had largely broken down. As Table 13.1 highlights, the overwhelming proportion of HSWs, 80 percent or more in each case, were concentrated in pay Band 2, the lower of the two bands. Rather than HSWs undertaking a similar set of tasks within the case Trusts, this pattern was more a reflection of HSWs performing very different sets of tasks within the same pay band. Thus, the range of tasks performed by a Band 2 HSW was found to range from basic care tasks such as washing patients to complex technical tasks such as cannulation.

Certainly, this shared disconnect between pay and tasks performed in the four Trusts suggests aspects of the national context may have retained some influence. It is not insignificant that all four Trusts had chosen to corral their HSWs into the lower pay band, regardless of tasks they performed. Operating within the context of a centrally funded health care system under financial pressure in a period of austerity, it might be argued that the Trusts were

Table 13.1 The Pay Banding of Health Care Support Workers (%)

	South	Midlands	North	London
Band 2	80	82	90	82
Band 3	18	18	8	16

similarly driven to control labor costs by placing HSWs in the lower of the two available pay bands. At the same time, it is clear that a national pay and grading structure had ceased to reflect or regulate organizational practice as it related to the allocation of HSWs tasks. Indicative of the picture across the Trusts, nurse managers in London and the North noted:

> You haven't got any difference between a Band 2 and a Band 3, they're doing the same job. There are not clear boundaries on some wards, so the Band 2s and Band 3s are all doing the same. (London)
>
> We'd looked at skilling some [HSWs] up to Band 3s and to be honest some of them do bloods and do ECGs now, but the Trust still just pays them Band 2s. (North)

The permissiveness of the national context was more apparent in the varied forms assumed by the HSW role at the Trust level. Cluster analysis of the tasks performed by HSW, as reported in the survey, revealed five types of HSW role. Presented in Table 13.2, these types of roles are labeled and characterized as:

- *The Bedside Technician*, not only performing direct care tasks such as feeding, bathing and bed making, but also some low-level clinical tasks such as observations and blood sugars.
- *The Ancillary*, undertaking only a limited range of relatively routine tasks, such bed making.
- *The Citizen*, regularly performing not only direct care and low-level clinical tasks, but additionally team-centered tasks such as stocking stores and escorting patients.
- *The All-rounder*, carrying out a wide diversity of tasks, even those that involve higher levels of technical skill, such as taking bloods.
- *The Expert*, concentrating on the performance of a narrow range of complex clinical tasks, such as performing ECGs.

The incidence of these HSW types varied, with beside technicians most in evidence, and the all-rounder and expert found less commonly. More striking, however, are the differences in the development and take-up of these HSW types by each Trust, as shown in Table 13.3. There is, for example, a notable concentration of the ancillary HSWs in the South, comprising close to a third of its HSWs, while the proportion of bedside technicians, at well under a third, is relatively low. Midlands has a significant concentration of citizen HSWs—over a third—markedly higher than in any other Trust, but also having a comparatively low proportion of bedside technicians. North has very few ancillaries, but a noteworthy proportion of bedside technicians, over half of its HSWs, along with a significant concentration of experts. London also has a high proportion of bedside technicians, close to half of its HSWs falling into this category, alongside a concentration of citizens.

Context and Work Organization in an Acute Health Care Setting

Table 13.2 The Distribution and Performance of Tasks by Health Care Support Workers

Task	Bedside technician (n=205)	Ancillary (n=100)	Citizen (n=132)	All-rounder (n=38)	Expert (n=63)
Bathing	Daily	Weekly	Daily	Daily	Weekly
Feeding	Daily	Weekly	Weekly	Daily	Weekly
Bed making	Daily	Daily	Daily	Daily	Daily
Collecting tablets	Monthly	Weekly	Daily	Weekly	Weekly
Escorting patients	Monthly	Monthly	Daily	Weekly	Weekly
Stocking stores	Monthly	Daily	Daily	Weekly	Daily
Vital signs	Daily	Monthly	Daily	Daily	Daily
Blood monitoring	Daily	Yearly	Daily	Daily	Daily
Simple dressings	Monthly	Yearly	Monthly	Daily	Weekly
Taking blood	Never	Never	Never	Weekly	Daily
Female catheterization	Never	Never	Never	Monthly	Never
Complex dressings	Never	Never	Never	Monthly	Never
ECG	Never	Never	Monthly	Weekly	Weekly
Cannulation	Never	Never	Never	Monthly	Yearly

Table 13.3 Health Care Support Worker Type by Trust (%)

	South (n=164)	Midlands (n=133)	North (n=141)	London (n=100)
Bedside technician	29	26	55	46
Ancillary	34	18	2	17
Citizen	25	36	13	25
All-rounder	9	5	9	5
Expert	4	16	21	7
Total	100	100	100	100

This idiosyncratic distribution of HSW types by the Trusts examined points to the possible influence of organizational context, though establishing causal linkages remained difficult. Certain organizational policies and practices could plausibly be related to the character of the respective HSW workforces. For example, there was a marked contrast between the Trusts in the take-up and systematic use of formal vocational qualifications. Such qualifications arguably act as a signaling device to managers regarding HSW skills, with their greater use allowing Trusts to deepen, extend, and then draw on HSW capabilities. Thus, it is noteworthy that in South, with its relatively high proportion of ancillary HSWs, with their narrow span of activities, the use of such qualifications had largely broken down:

> (HSWs) have not been given much opportunity to do national vocation qualifications: the Trust can't financially afford it so it's a very selective procedure and only a very few (HSWs) every year are allowed to do them. (Ward Manager, South)

This contrasts with North and London, where the wider availability and more robust encouragement of vocational training had led to a higher proportion of HSWs in roles such as experts and bedside technicians performing clinically more complex tasks.

However, a comparison of the distribution of HSW types between the matched case study Trusts cautions against overstating the influence of organizational context. The size and type of Trust—reflecting the range of services and patient profiles—might have been expected to produce similarities in the profile of the HSW workforce within the matched pairs, but Table 13.3 suggests few similarities. The two large teaching Trusts (North and South) have very different HSW workforces, while the contrast between the smaller district general hospitals (Midlands and London) is similarly marked. It is a finding that suggests some weakness in the organizational context as an influence on the allocation of tasks to HSW, and the need to drill-down to the workplace level to reveal the more direct and potent influences. As one of the interviewees in London noted:

> Although there are some generic job descriptions, you'll find across the Trust different [HSWs] doing different things and working in different ways. Some are more autonomous than others and have a wider skill set. HCAs are a resource some people maximize and others don't. (London)

Workplace Context: Clinical Areas and Wards

The tasks performed by HSWs emerged as being particularly sensitive to the workplace context, both the clinical area and the ward. Figure 13.1 highlights the influence of clinical context on the tasks performed by the HSW. Drawing on the observational data, this figure maps the proportion of time devoted to different tasks by HSWs on medical and surgical wards, bringing into sharp relief significant differences. The differences can plausibly be related to the care needs of patients in the respective clinical areas. Thus, the HSWs on the surgical wards were much more likely to undertake technical tasks than those on medical wards, as pre- and postoperative patients required close and frequent monitoring. Surgical HSWs were also more likely than medical HSWs to undertake indirect care tasks such as escorting, admitting, and discharging associated with the shorter stays and quicker turnaround times of surgical patients. On the other hand, medical HSWs spent over a third of their shift time on direct care—patient washing and feeding, compared with barely a quarter of their time being devoted to these tasks by surgical HSWs—a reflection of the relatively high dependence of patients on such wards as elderly care and stroke.

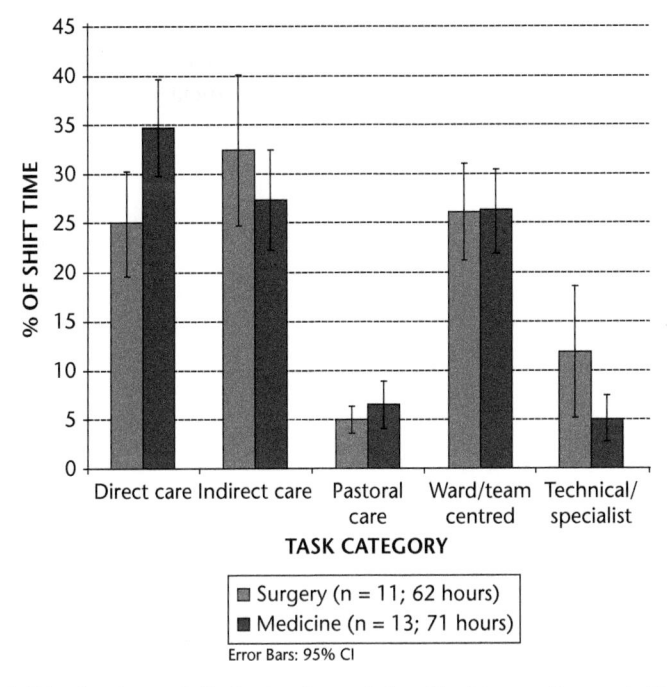

Figure 13.1 Distribution of Tasks Performed by Healthcare Support Workers by Clinical Area

Yet even within these clinical services areas, the form assumed by the HSW remained subject to a series of more refined, often ward-based, contextual influences, including:

- *The shift*: The shape of the HSW role was closely associated with the shift worked, reflecting the rhythms of the day and related patient needs. A HSW working on an early shift would be heavily involved in washing and getting patients out of bed. A HSW working a late shift would overlap with visiting hours, involving intensive interaction with patients' friends and families. A HSW working a night shift would interact less with patients and visitors, keeping a watching brief and monitoring patient well-being:

    On a late shift you have got all the relatives and they'll come up and say "Have you heard what treatment's been going on with my mum?"' (HSW, Midlands)

- *Management style*: Ward managers varied in their propensity to engage HSWs in the delivery of care. Some managers were cautious, seeing the HSW role as being limited to basic care, while others saw the role in a more expansive light, as an opportunity to develop the role's potential and the capabilities of the post-holders:

    A lot of wards don't allow their healthcares to do observations, but we trust our healthcares to do it. (Nurse, North)

- *Nurse relations*: Similarly, and perhaps in more direct terms, the orientation of RNs as the HSWs' co-workers influenced the range of tasks performed. Within the context of the daily work routine, RNs supervised HSWs and were responsible for delegating tasks to them. The NNMC code of practice for RNs (and midwives), often reinforced by Trust policies, sets out a procedure for appropriate delegation. Nonetheless, nurses varied in their confidence and willingness to delegate, sometimes retaining a degree of uncertainty about their accountability for the actions of HSWs:

  > [HSWs] need some sort of regulatory body because at the moment it's like if they do take bloods or they do plastering, as a registered nurse we are overall accountable for that. Even though they've gone through the course, we have to constantly monitor them because it's our registration on the line.
  >
  > (Nurse, London)

- *The ward team*: Within the same Trusts, there was an uneven take-up of certain specialist roles at the ward level, with implications for the distribution of tasks and responsibilities. For example, in the absence of a ward housekeeper, the HSW would often be required to take on more cleaning and catering tasks. With a phlebotomist on the ward team, the scope for the HSW to extend his or her role by training to take bloods was naturally limited.

Given the sensitivity of the role to these contextual clinical and ward influences, the final issue to address is whether HSWs retained a residual degree of discretion to shape or craft their role. There were occasions where HSWs, typically driven by career aspirations, were keen to push the boundaries of the role. The potency of workplace context in constraining this activity is highlight by the example of an HSW thwarted by a ward manager keen to ensure that the HSW remained focused on what the manager felt were the role's core care activities:

> Recently we had a healthcare assistant who got very keen to do the cannulation and blood-taking bit, but I was saying like you need to go and do that commode and strip that empty bed first, and you're kind of thinking, it's all very well learning these things but actually you're here to go and empty the skips and keep the trolleys stocked up. (Nurse manager, South)

However, our study did find that those HSWs with aspirations to become RNs were disproportionately more likely to be performing an "all-rounder" role, in other words, seeking to shape the role as a means of preparing for and signaling career intentions.

Conclusions

In drawing on the main tenets of critical realism, this chapter has sought not only to describe but also to explain how context at different societal levels either constrains or facilitates the allocation of tasks and responsibilities to the HSW. The permissiveness of a national context that weakly regulated the distribution of nursing tasks, leaving HSWs in an unregistered role to take on an increasing range of activities, as RNs withdrew from the bedside, appeared to allow health care providers considerable discretion in their use of these workers. The disconnect between national pay banding and the tasks performed by HSWs in the four case study Trusts was seen as being indicative of this permissiveness, though a shared reliance on the lowest pay band in grading HSWs might well be seen to reflect shared financial pressures in the context of austerity.

More striking were differences in the form assumed by the HSW role at the organizational level and, in particular, the variation among the Trusts in how they combined and used different HSW role types. It was tempting to view these differences in workforce profile as reflecting the influence of organizational context, and, indeed, this influence was plausibly traced to certain Trust policies and practices, specifically those associated with vocational training. However, with our matched case Trusts displaying very little similarity in how they combined HSW types, we urged caution in overstating the influence of organizational context, arguing that the workplace was perhaps a more likely source of direct influence over the HSW role.

At the workplace level, most noteworthy was the effect of clinical area on the tasks performed by HSWs, an influence meaningfully related to distinctive patient conditions and needs on medical and surgical wards. However, the significance of clinical influence was qualified in two respects. First, even at the ward level, contingent factors could shape the HSW role: for example, the shift worked, the management style of the ward sister, or relations with nurse co-workers. Second, the potency of contextual influence should not detract from a residual degree of agency, with the HSWs retaining some scope to shape their roles, often in pursuit of career goals.

As a coda to this chapter, it is worth highlighting important changes to the national context following the completion of our research, and with implications for the shape of the HSW role. Following the Francis (2010) report into service failures at the Mid Stafford NHS Foundation Trust, and, as one of the many follow-up actions, a dedicated review of the HSW role (Cavendish, 2013), the national regulatory framework for the HSW role was tightened. While this regulation fell well short of statutory registration, a Care Certificate was introduced, setting out fifteen care standards that "patient-facing" support workers had to meet before taking up their role. This significant development can be seen to reflect the dynamism inherent in the context–process–action field highlighted by Pettigrew (1987), and in particular, how contextual influences at different societal levels interact. In this case, regulatory changes at the national level directly and demonstratively fed through to encourage greater standardization of the HSW role at the organizational and workplace levels.

References

Abbott, A. (1988). *The system of professions: An essay on the division of expert labour.* Chicago: University of Chicago Press.

Abel-Smith, B. (1960). *A history of the nursing profession.* London: Heinemann.

Archer, M. (1983). Morphogenesis verses structuration: on combining structure and action. *British Journal of Sociology, 33*(4), 455–83.

Archer, M., Bhaskar, R., Collier, A., Lawson, T., & Norrie, A. (eds.). (1998). *Critical realism: Essential readings.* London: Routledge.

Bate, P., Robert, G., Fulop, N., Ovretveit, J., & Dixon Wood, M. (2014). *Perspectives on context.* London: Heath Foundation.

Bradshaw, A. (2001). *Project 2000.* London: Whurr.

Cavendish, C. (2013). *A review of health assistants in the NHS and social care.* London: Department of Health.

Currie, G., Locket, A., Finn, R., Martin, G., & Waring, J. (2012). Institutional work to maintain professional power: Recreating the model of medical professionalism. *Organization Studies, 33*(7), 937–62.

Department of Health (2009). *Extending professional and occupational regulation.* London: Department of Health.

Dubois, C., McKee, T., & Nolte, E. (2006). *Human resources for health in Europe.* Maidenhead: Open University Press.

Francis, R. (2010). *Independent inquiry into care provided by Mid Staffordshire NHS Foundation Trust: Report.* London: Stationery Office.

Friedson, E. (2001). *Professionalisation the third logic.* Cambridge: Polity Press.

Griffin, M. (2007). Specifying organizational contexts: Systematic links between contexts and processes of organizational behaviour. *Journal of Organizational Behavior, 28*(7), 259–63.

Griffiths, P. & Robinson, P. (2010). *Moving forward with the regulation of healthcare support workforce.* London: King's College.

Hood, C. (2013). Can cultural theory gives us a handle on the differences context makes in management by numbers. In C. Pollitt (ed.), *Context in public policy and management: The missing link?* London: Edward Elgar, pp. 115–23.

Johns, G. (2006). The essential impact of context on behaviour. *Academy of Management Review, 31*(2), 386–408.

Kessler, I. (2012). *National pay determination in the NHS: Resilience and continuity.* Oxford: Templeton.

Kitchener, M. & Mertz, E. (2012). Professional projects and institutional change in healthcare: The case of American dentistry. *Social Science and Medicine, 74*(3)372–80.

Larson, M. (1977). *The rise of professionalism*. Berkeley: University of California Press.

Lawrence, T. & Suddaby, R. (2006). Institutions and institutional work. In S. Clegg, C. Hardy, T. Lawrence, & W. Nord (eds.), *Sage handbook of organizational studies*. London: Sage, pp. 215–54.

Marsden, D. (1999). *A theory of employment systems*. Oxford: Oxford University Press.

Nelsen, B. & Barley, S. (1997). For love or money: Commodification and construction of an occupational mandate. *Administrative Science Quarterly, 42*(4), 619–53.

NHS England. (n.d.). www.jobs.nhs.uk/about_nhs.html.

Nursing Times. (2012). Local threats to agenda for change continue. *Nursing Times, 19*, 5–6.

Pettigrew, A. (1987). Context in action in the transformation of the firm. *Journal of Management Studies, 24*(6), 649–70.

Pollitt, C. (2013) (ed.). *Context in public policy and management: The missing link?* London: Edward Elgar.

Reay, T., Golden-Biddle, K., & Germann, K. (2006). Legitimizing a new role: Small wins and micro processes of change. *Academy of Management Journal, 49*(5), 977–98.

Rousseau, D. & Fried, Y. (2001). Location, location, location: Contextualizing organisational behaviour. *Journal of Organizational Behavior, 22*, 1–13.

Royal College of Nursing (2006). *Setting appropriate ward staffing levels in acute trusts*. London: Royal College of Nursing.

Royal College of Nursing (2017). *Safe and effective staffing: Nursing against the odds*. London: Royal College of Nursing.

Thornley, C. (1996). Segmentation and inequality in the nursing workforce. In R. Crompton, D. Gallie, & K. Purcell (eds.), *Changing forms of employment*. London: Routledge, pp. 160–81.

United Kingdom Central Council (UKCC) for Nursing, Midwifery and Health Visiting (1986). *Project 2000*. London: UKCC.

Whittington, R. (1992). Putting Giddens into action: Social systems and managerial agency. *Journal of Management Studies, 29*(6), 693–717.

Yin, R. (1984). *Case study research: Design and methods*. London: Sage.

14

How Context Shapes the Experience of Staff and Residents in Residential Long-Term Care Settings

Carole A. Estabrooks and Stephanie A. Chamberlain

Introduction

In the late 1990s and early 2000s, relatively little robust health literature addressed the role of context in influencing knowledge translation (KT), implementation, or quality-improvement (QI) success (Dopson & Fitzgerald, 2005; Glisson, 2002; Glisson & Hemmelgarn, 1998; Greenhalgh et al., 2004; Kitson, Harvey, & McCormack, 1998; Rycroft-Malone et al., 2002). Extensive bodies of work in other fields made their way very slowly—*if at all*—into the health literature or the research of implementation scientists (Martin, 1995, 2002; Pettigrew, 1979; Schein, 1983, 1986; Smircich, 1983a, 1983b). Much of this work in organizational and anthropological areas focused on organizational climate or organizational culture. A few researchers considered climate and culture as being part of an organization's social context (Glisson, 2015; Glisson & Williams, 2015). Recently, Schneider et al. (2017) have argued for research that clarifies the coexistence of these elements. We now see arguments that are far more rigorous in the literature for the importance of organizational context. It is seen as a key element in implementation efforts to both increase the use of best practices (research use) and improve the success of QI initiatives (Harvey & Kitson, 2016, 2015; Kaplan et al., 2010; Kaplan et al., 2012). The role and influence of context in the use of research or best practices, and on the success of QI initiatives, have been argued theoretically (Berta et al., 2010; Damschroder et al., 2009; Estabrooks et al., 2009b; French et al., 2009; Grol et al., 2007; Harvey et al., 2002; Kaplan et al., 2012; Kitson et al., 2008; McCormack et al., 2009; Ward et al., 2012); examined empirically (Barnett et al., 2011; Cummings et al., 2007; Estabrooks et al., 2007; Estabrooks et al., 2008; Janssen et al., 2012; McCullough et al., 2015; Pepler et al., 2005; Scott et al., 2008; Yamada et al., 2017); and been the subject of several reviews (Berta et al., 2005; Estabrooks, 2003; Glisson, 2007; Greenhalgh et al., 2004; Kaplan et al., 2010).

The other construct that has received attention in the health literature, particularly the nursing literature, is the work environment (Aiken et al., 2011; Choi, Flynn, & Aiken, 2012; Stalpers et al., 2015; Stalpers et al., 2017; Zúñiga et al., 2015). Authors often include the elements of staffing numbers and the skill mix of existing staff when addressing the work environment. However, the work environment construct has even less consistency or precision. Despite conceptual tangles among terms such as *context, culture, climate*, and *work environment*, some elements do emerge across disciplinary and professional boundaries (e.g., resources, leadership support, or a supportive work setting). Still, operationalization of concepts varies considerably, making it hard to understand what various authors are discussing, and how it may differ or be similar (Kaplan et al., 2010; Squires et al., 2015a; Squires et al., 2015b). While intensive efforts are ongoing to rectify this (Squires et al., 2015a; Squires et al., 2015b), the field remains somewhat murky, and conclusions are difficult to draw. The only sure assertion seems to be that (somehow and in some ways) *context matters* (Dopson & Fitzgerald, 2005). How it matters depends on its conceptualization, operationalization, and the setting under consideration. Before beginning TREC in 2007, we focused our efforts largely on KT and the individual: how do we encourage clinicians, managers, and policy makers to use research findings in their practices? Several years of frustration and exploring the extant literature convinced us of the limitations of focusing on the individual. We decided, based on our experiences, and on an emerging literature related to KT, to conceptualize *context as a modifiable and important feature of organizations*. Our focus on organizations led us to examine context in relation to care units, and the teams that comprise those units. In our organizational approach, optimizing context would foster more research use and eventually more successful QI initiatives at the unit level. Over time, our team has come to understand that QI is a powerful tool in the KT arsenal, sharing many similarities with it and offering action-oriented designs of interventions for change (Shojania & Grimshaw, 2005).

With this as a general backdrop, we designed our initial research program in 2006, using the PARiHS framework (Promoting Action on Research Implementation in Health Services), whose developers argued that successful implementation (of research evidence) depends on the interplay among context, facilitation, and evidence (Harvey & Kitson, 2016, 2015; Kitson, Harvey, & McCormack, 1998; Kitson et al., 2008; Rycroft-Malone et al., 2002). They expanded the concept of context to encompass leadership, culture, and evaluation. More recently, they have advanced the framework and renamed it the "integrated PARiHS" (i-PARiHS). Core constructs of the revised framework are facilitation, innovation (replacing evidence), recipients, and context (Harvey & Kitson, 2016, 2015). The three core concepts of PARiHS (leadership, culture, and evaluation) were the guiding elements of our conceptualization and operationalization of context.

Measuring Context: The Alberta Context Tool

We struggled with the absence of a valid measure of context. Consequently, we undertook to develop, pilot test, and validate a pragmatic tool to assess organizational context: the Alberta Context Tool (ACT) (Estabrooks et al., 2009b). We used the PARiHS framework to conceptualize our research program because it offered a useful framing device and heuristic for understanding context and implementation (Helfrich et al., 2010). During the initial PARiHS conceptualization, three instruments with origins in the framework were developed to measure context: the Context Assessment Instrument (McCormack et al., 2009), the Consolidated Framework for Implementation Research (Damschroder et al., 2009), and the ACT (Estabrooks et al., 2009b). In developing the ACT, a fifty-six-to-fifty-eight-item measure, we defined *context* as "the environment or setting in which people receive healthcare services, or in the context of getting research evidence into practice, the environment or setting in which the proposed change is to be implemented"(Rycroft-Malone et al., 2002).

We relied largely on the PARiHS framework for guidance in developing the three core elements of the ACT (leadership, culture, and evaluation), though guidance was limited. Moving beyond the three core elements, we brought in other work, such as a transformational perspective on leadership and a quality perspective on evaluation and feedback. We added additional elements that we believed (and that the literature suggested) were missing (e.g., resources, interactions, and organizational slack). The completed ACT included eight domains of context: leadership, culture, evaluation (feedback of information), formal interactions, informal interactions, social capital, structural resources, and organizational slack (staff, time, and space). With the three "slack" elements included, the ACT contained ten elements. Using a "variance" approach, we argued that context could be decomposed into measurable and modifiable variables reflecting the eight domains. We required our context tool to meet three criteria: have a basis in theory, measure modifiable elements of context, and be parsimonious. Brevity was critical for two reasons: the instrument was embedded within a larger survey, and the LTC setting is unusually resource strapped, necessitating the least amount of time possible taken from direct care.

The ACT was intended for use in examining context from the perspectives of health care aides, registered nurses/licensed practical nurses, physicians, allied health care providers, specialists (e.g., educators), and managers. However, the tool is not designed to be congruent with the work model of physicians, and we no longer use it with them. Extensive psychometric testing of the ACT provides evidence of its reliability and validity in the other care provider populations (Estabrooks et al., 2009b; Estabrooks et al., 2011a; Estabrooks et al., 2011b; Mallidou et al., 2011; Squires et al., 2015c).

The LTC care aide version of the ACT is a cornerstone of our research program (Estabrooks et al., 2009b; Estabrooks et al., 2011a). We aggregate care aides' responses to develop our context "scores" at the care-unit and facility levels, for two reasons. First, care aides are closest to residents, spending the most time with them. We want to capture context that is as close as possible to resident experience. Second, care aides are the only work group in LTC with sufficient numbers for stable aggregate unit and facility estimates of context. The ACT is designed primarily as a unit (clinical microsystem) tool because we believe, consistent with others, that quality is made most importantly at the unit level (Nelson et al., 2002; Nelson et al., 2008; Williams et al., 2009). Our aggregation of care aide responses at the unit level is consistent with our conceptualization of context as a feature of the organization and not the individual care aide.

Making Context Understandable and Useful to System Managers

We have approached our empirical examination of context in two ways. First, we have developed and run traditional multilevel models to assess the contributions of each of the ten elements in the ACT. Second, we have developed and used context classifications that are more meaningful to our decision makers, and that make our models more parsimonious. Until recently, we used k-means clustering to dichotomize ACT scores on the ten elements, representing each LTC facility and its units as having a lower (less favorable) context (red in bar charts) or a higher (more favorable) context (green in bar charts) (Estabrooks et al., 2016). Clustering facilities and units as higher or lower context, and generating visualizations of associations reveals general patterns in data. We have published a report on this "red–green heuristic" that simplifies the complex ten-domain context data (Estabrooks et al., 2016). We discovered that the red–green heuristic is incredibly useful and easy for our decision makers to interpret. Though we lose specific information through the dichotomizing of continuous scale variables, we gain an immediate understanding from our senior-level policy partners by using the red–green classification.

One drawback to a binary classification is the difficulty in understanding where a facility or unit should work to improve its context: to become "more green," an aspiration expressed by our facility managers and directors. To address this issue, when we undertake tailored feedback to facilities after each wave of primary data collection, we decompose their red–green profile by unit into the specific ACT elements. We can thus work with them on both why change matters and how to find the best "value for effort" locations on their profiles.

Despite conducting significant psychometric testing of our measure of context, elements of the measure do not always perform well in empirical modeling (e.g., leadership or culture) or perform better when we examine specific sub-groups of residents (e.g., a 12-months-before-death cohort). Measurement is imperfect. While we could undoubtedly make improvements to the ACT and to our conceptualization of context, we believe we have a "good enough" tool, and one with which we have 10 years of longitudinal experience. We are thus reluctant to modify it and lose that longitudinal comparability. Any we lack in measurement or conceptual precision we believe we gain in being able to identify modifiable elements of context that can be addressed by LTC facilities and by regional health systems. With these elements, we are able to design pragmatic intervention studies that lead to change.

Translating Research in Elder Care: A Longitudinal Study of the Long-Term Care Sector

Translating Research in Elder Care (TREC) is a longitudinal, pan-Canadian research program in applied health services that aims to improve the quality of care and of life for residents, and the quality of work life for caregivers in long-term care (LTC) settings. Our goal is to advance KT science regarding the effects of context, facilitation, and their interaction on the use of knowledge in LTC. Our mission is to develop practical solutions that will contribute to (i) improvements in quality of care, quality of life, and quality of end of life for frail, vulnerable older adults in LTC, and (ii) improvements in quality of work life for staff. Over time, we have focused increasingly on QI interventions as a major tool for implementing evidence and creating change in context, which influences KT and QI efforts and has a direct effect on staff and resident outcomes. While our team composition has changed and we have shifted toward QI interventions, our mission to develop practical solutions that improve quality in LTC has remained constant.

Our focus on LTC is motivated by the significant and sometimes-overwhelming needs in this setting for both staff and residents. Recent emphasis has been on services to help older adults remain in their own homes, communities, and "assisted living" settings as long as possible. One consequence of this, however, is that many people now enter LTC facilities with more a severe chronic disease burden, including age-related dementias, higher dependency levels, and more advanced levels of frailty (Doupe et al., 2006; Doupe et al., 2011; Doupe et al., 2012; Kojima, 2015; Muscedere et al., 2016). In our TREC cohort, the median length of LTC stay ranges from 1.6 to 3.1 years. An analysis of our sample in 2016 showed that average resident's age is 85 years; 78 percent of residents need assistance with almost all activities of daily living; 64 percent have moderate-to-severe age-related dementia; and more than 21 percent meet criteria for marked frailty (as measured by the Resident Assessment Instrument–Minimum Data Set 2.0 [RAI-MDS 2.0] Changes in Health, End-Stage Disease and Signs and Symptoms Scale) (Armstrong et al., 2010; Hogan et al., 2012).

Early on, we realized the potential, and the necessity, of longitudinal data in tracking change over time to assess the effects of secular trends, policy changes, and interventions to influence context. We built a longitudinal platform that enables us to monitor these changes over time. As an example, we used our platform to identify a trend in Alberta toward sharply reduced lengths of LTC stay in response to policy changes some years ago. We launch all our projects from this platform, including two pragmatic cluster-randomized trials currently in the field. Our longitudinal platform incorporates and links routinely collected resident administrative data (RAI-MDS 2.0) (Hutchinson et al., 2010; Poss et al., 2008) and primary data collected from facilities and care units, regarding resources, services, staffing, ownership, and other structural components. Our platform also includes data collected from several groups of front-line staff: on organizational context (using the ACT) and staff health, well-being, engagement, empowerment, organizational citizenship, and use of best practices (Estabrooks et al., 2009b; Estabrooks et al., 2015b; Estabrooks et al., 2009c).

Our longitudinal system of measurement provides pre-, post-, and between-group measures for our clinical trials and context assessments, and the ability to: (i) identify performance gaps and QI opportunities, (ii) identify trends in quality of care over time, (iii) inform stakeholders of key situations and conditions, and(iv) inform regional and provincial policy.

Lessons Learned: Context Matters

Since 2007, we established that a more favorable context is associated positively with staff outcomes such as the use of best practice (Estabrooks et al., 2015b); lower levels of burnout (Chamberlain et al., 2017; Estabrooks et al., 2012); higher job satisfaction (Chamberlain et al., 2016); and fewer tasks rushed or left undone (Knopp-Sihota et al., 2015). A more favorable context is also associated positively with a better trajectory of symptom burden for residents in their last 12 months of life (Estabrooks et al., 2015a). We used multivariable and multilevel analytical methods to examine associations between individual elements of context (e.g., leadership, culture, and evaluation), high/low context (k-means clustering), and staff work life and resident outcomes. Using these methods, we have furthered our understanding of context, reinforcing our belief that there are complex relationships between individual elements of context and staff who work on the units. Using data collected from 1,194 care aides in 2009–2010, and mixed-effects modeling techniques, we examined individual elements of context and their associations with care aide burnout (emotional exhaustion, cynicism, and professional efficacy) (Chamberlain et al., 2017). Care aides who reported supportive work cultures, received feedback on their work, and were engaged in formal team activities had lower levels of cynicism. This analytical approach demonstrated the usefulness of examining individual elements of the ACT and their influence on the quality of work life for staff in LTC. Examining individual elements offers a targeted approach to improvements on the unit. We used a similar analytical approach to examine care aide use of best practices (instrumental and conceptual research use) (Estabrooks et al., 2015b). At the unit level, significant predictors of instrumental research use were social capital, organizational slack (staffing and time), number of informal interactions, and unit type. Significant predictors of conceptual research use were evaluation (feedback mechanisms), structural resources, and organizational slack (time).

We have found that individual concepts in our measurement of context can affect staff work life and resident outcomes. As a result, we have developed interventions to target these elements of context using QI initiatives. Even though our conceptual foundations remain in KT, our focus on QI, and to improve staff and resident outcomes, has meant that we have expanded our theoretical repertoire. We now include complex adaptive systems (Anderson, Issel, & McDaniel Jr, 2003; Anderson et al., 2014); the Institute of Healthcare Improvement's QI collaborative model (Cranley et al., 2012; Cranley et al., 2011); organizational learning (Argote, 1999; Argote & Miron-Spektor, 2011; Berta et al., 2010; Nonaka, 1994); and designing for diffusion derived from

Rogers's classic Diffusion of Innovation theory, which remains a mainstay in all of our work (Dearing et al., 2013; Rogers, 2003).

In the first phase of TREC (2007–2012), we focused almost exclusively on the "context domain" of the PARiHS framework—ensuring that we measured this domain (as we conceived it) adequately, and trying to ensure that we captured sufficient covariates to enrich our statistical models. We did not focus on the "mechanisms" by which context exerted influence. These mechanisms are not clear, nor are they described well in the literature, although they are believed to be complex and multilevel (Harvey, Jas, & Walshe, 2015; Nielsen & Abildgaard, 2013; Phaneuf et al., 2016; Yamada et al., 2017). Rather than focus on mechanisms of change, we chose to understand the elements of context that influence staff and resident outcomes, and then tried to modify those elements. In the second phase of TREC (2014–2019), we have begun to focus on mechanisms. As we undertake clinical effectiveness trials, we include robust qualitative process evaluations to better understand the mechanisms of influence. Once mechanisms are better understood, we can construct and test causal models.

Clinical Trials: Early Insights about Context and Facilitation

Engaging Care Aides

Once we began to establish a pattern of association between context and staff and resident outcomes, we developed interventions to improve quality of care and work life. Our observational work identified care aide efficacy as being surprisingly high, given their emotional exhaustion and cynicism, signaling a potential area for intervention. We adapted the Institute of Healthcare Improvement's collaborative model for achieving measurable, sustained QI, which integrates QI activities into daily practice at the front line or microlevel of a system (Cranley et al., 2012; Cranley et al., 2011). Our adaptation targets the engagement of care aides with senior leadership support and sponsorship. The result has been Safer Care for Older Persons in (Residential) Environments (SCOPE), a multisite pragmatic randomized clinical trial launched in 2018, following feasibility and pilot studies. Specific SCOPE activities include in-person learning sessions, phone meetings, data reporting, leadership involvement, and training in QI methods based around "Plan–Do–Study–Act cycles" (Institute for Healthcare Improvement, 2003). The successful feasibility project took place in ten LTC units in British Columbia and Alberta, and showed both feasibility and a significant impact (Cranley et al., 2012; Cranley et al., 2011; Norton et al., 2013). A robust pilot study took place in the province of Manitoba. Feasibility work demonstrated reductions in resident responsive behaviors, pressure ulcers, and daily pain. Some facilities reported improvements in their work environment and in use of best practices. All intervention sites in the feasibility project participated in a 1-year follow-up project for proof of principle, aimed at measuring sustainability of the SCOPE intervention. In both intervention and control groups, care aides reported decreased empowerment and job satisfaction over time. However, this decrease was less pronounced in the intervention group than in the control group. We believe that SCOPE has tapped a rich reservoir of tacit, experiential care aide knowledge and harnessed care aide capacity to achieve change. SCOPE also clearly raised care aides' sense of empowerment and brought senior leaders into a new model for change.

Engaging Managers

Participating TREC LTC facilities receive feedback reports following each wave of primary data collection (Boström et al., 2012; Estabrooks, Teare, & Norton, 2012; Hutchinson et al., 2012). Feedback of performance data to facilities is important, both to our enduring relationships with the facilities and to research use and changes that will lead to better context and better outcomes. However, little evidence exists on the most effective and efficient ways to provide ongoing performance data, or how to tailor context data to improve performance. INFORM (Improving Nursing Home Care through Feedback on Performance Data) is a pragmatic cluster-randomized trial that ran over 12 months in sixty-seven TREC facilities (Hoben et al., 2017). INFORM is based on theory and evidence related to audit and feedback, goal setting, complex adaptive systems, and empirical work on feeding back research results. INFORM targets care managers and their teams, with the intent of feeding back context data and facilitating changes that lead to improved unit context performance.

Early results from detailed process evaluation (e.g., examining implementation fidelity of the intervention by LTC teams) were promising. Data fed back to teams within the intervention successfully motivated team leaders to improve care aide involvement in elements of unit context, specifically formal interactions on resident care (e.g., care conferences, team conferences, and reports). Early process analyses suggest that teams were able to improve the context in their facility. Teams often redesigned work processes in scheduling, timing, and structure of resident care conferences to increase care aide involvement. These preliminary results suggested this may be a promising strategy for modifying contextual elements such as formal interactions, and that these modifications may improve quality of work life for LTC facility staff. Findings of the INFORM trail will soon be published.

Future Directions

In 2011, we began to work actively on the second major PARiHS construct: facilitation. In the updated i-PARiHS framework, context remains a core construct, but "facilitation is the active ingredient" in successful implementation (Harvey & Kitson, 2016; Kitson & Harvey, 2016). Harvey and Kitson propose that facilitation is the active ingredient because it initiates implementation by "assessing and responding to characteristics of the innovation and the recipients within their contextual setting" (2016 p. 6). The framework's influence on the facilitation literature is evident. Recently, Dogherty, Harrison, and Graham (2010) identified several elements of facilitation: project management, leadership, and the tailoring of facilitation efforts to the local context, plus a growing emphasis on evaluation. Baskerville, Liddy, and Hogg (2012) concurred, and identified key components as an emphasis on processes and organization of care, with less of a focus on content knowledge. This facilitation literature has two major gaps: (i) absence of empirical evidence for effectiveness of facilitation (as role or process) on KT, and (ii) consideration of operating mechanisms of facilitation. Our team recently published a theoretical paper on facilitation, proposing that an understanding of facilitation should be situated within organizational learning theory (Berta et al., 2015). Berta et al. (2005) conceptualized facilitation as a meta-routine that supports the acquisition of research evidence, and learning about applying it to improve care processes. We are now using our longitudinal database to explore opportunities to understand more about the role of facilitation, and facilitation is a core intervention component of both our clinical trials (Cranley et al., 2012; Cranley et al., 2011; Hoben et al., 2017; Norton et al., 2013).

Based on the past decade of quantitative, empirical work, we conclude that context—as we conceptualize it—matters for LTC residents, staff, and system managers. Using our conceptualization of context, many elements of context are modifiable. We deliberately do not capture elements such as funding models, which are difficult or impossible to modify for a research team such as ours. We have learned to design and execute interventions using the most robust designs possible in the LTC setting and real-world effectiveness trials. Robust evidence will increase attention to optimizing context in LTC, and to the importance of appropriate facilitation. The goal of both researchers and knowledge users at all levels is the same: to improve quality of care, quality of life, and quality of end of life for LTC residents, and quality of work life for staff. Our team views context as one major improvement pathway.

Quantitative Approaches to Monitor Change

Our work is largely quantitative, although early forays were made into qualitative case studies (Cammer et al., 2014; Rycroft-Malone et al., 2009). Quantitative approaches are valuable, both in generating the sorts of evidence that system leaders often demand and in tracking improvement. If a system is unable to measure something, it will be unable to manage it, so our motivations are strong for continuing this quantitative approach. We urge much more longitudinal work, because measurement over time is a powerful tool for change (Berwick, 1989, 2004).

With our 10 years of data, we now begin to observe secular trends, monitor disparate trends (e.g., increasing complexity of resident health issues combined with static staffing levels), and examine intended and unintended consequences of policy decisions. We continue to use our longitudinal monitoring system to leverage clinical trials. We obtain pre- and post measures from it, and follow long-term outcomes post trial to see if changes are sustained, come later, fade, or increase.

However, quantitative data are not sufficient for the understanding of mechanisms of context influence. Our trials and some studies now include extensive process evaluation work. We understood—much more than a decade ago—that only deeply embedded and high-quality mixed-methods approaches can offer a fuller picture of the nature, parameters, meaning, and impact of context on relevant outcomes. Once we have a more comprehensive understanding of influence mechanisms, we can construct causal models to test theories.

Conclusion

Our past 10 years of work show rich reservoirs of untapped opportunity for examining context, its modifiability, and its deeper impact in creating change and optimizing LTC. Tapping into these opportunities requires the assembling and maintaining of a large and diverse team from disparate academic disciplines, government, health regions, nongovernmental organizations, and engaged citizens. We have a vigorous advisory group of individuals with dementia, and family/friend caregivers of residents in LTC. Our team is international, with over fifty active members.

In our gestalt approach to context, we work between the knowledge-discovery approaches of Mode 1 (traditional science) and Mode 2 (more contextually bound and socially responsible science in partnership with end users) (Gibbons, 1994; Nowotny, Scott, & Gibbons, 2003). This Mode 3 approach (Carayannis, Campbell, & Rehman, 2016) encourages working productively between Modes 1 and 2, and it places a far greater emphasis on knowledge democratization. Our large, diverse team and our knowledge-discovery approach are necessary for our capacity for creating meaningful change in modifiable aspects of LTC context. Mode 3 often generates opportunities and new knowledge we would never have expected or seen with rigid Mode 1–like protocols for TREC. However, working in this "integrated KT" model is more difficult.

While our agendas do not always converge, large team efforts are worthwhile. Our team's success has relied on a number of interdependent factors. We are adaptable, using our database to address questions raised by partners that might otherwise be outside our focus. We are realistic. As with any large research program, there are many opportunities to expand and move into different areas. We look within our collective capacities and focus on areas where we can make realistic contributions. We take care of our relationships with all levels of stakeholders, from government health organizations to LTC owner-operators. Relationships are critical to our partnered mode of research. These relationships and time have created a transactional space to support genuine dialogue and collaborative work. Our stakeholders have learned the importance of high-quality science, thus increasing our credibility among our partners.

However, even these things combined are insufficient, because the work is difficult and, at times, discouraging, and relationship building in a complex team is demanding. We believe the fundamental requirement for a successful large team is a clear, common mission and a common core set of values. In our case, those values can be best summarized in the statement: *"A life that has been lived should not be valued less than a life that is going to be lived."*

References

Aiken, L. H. et al. (2011). Importance of work environments on hospital outcomes in nine countries. *International Journal for Quality in Health Care, 23*(4), 357–64.

Anderson, R. A., Issel, L. M., & McDaniel Jr., R. R. (2003). Nursing homes as complex adaptive systems: Relationship between management practice and resident outcomes. *Nursing Research, 52*(1), 12–21.

Anderson, R. A., Toles, M. P., Corazzini, K., McDaniel, R. R., & Colon-Emeric, C. (2014). Local interaction strategies and capacity for better care in nursing homes: A multiple case study. *BMC Health Services Research, 14*, 244.

Argote, L. (1999). *Organizational learning: Creating, retaining, and transferring knowledge.* Boston: Kluwer Academic.

Argote, L. & Miron-Spektor, E. (2011). Organizational learning: From experience to knowledge. *Organization Science, 22*(5), 1123–37.

Armstrong, J. J., Stolee, P., Hirdes, J. P., & Poss, J. W. (2010). Examining three frailty conceptualizations in their ability to predict negative outcomes for home-care clients. *Age and Ageing, 39*(6), 755–8.

Barnett, J., Vasileiou, K., Djemil, F., Brooks, L., & Young, T. (2011). Understanding innovators' experiences of barriers and facilitators in implementation and diffusion of healthcare service innovations: A qualitative study. *BMC Health Services Research, 11*(1), 342.

Baskerville, N. B., Liddy, C., & Hogg, W. (2012). Systematic review and meta-analysis of practice facilitation within primary care settings. *Annals of Family Medicine, 10*(1), 63–74.

Berta, W., Cranley, L., Dearing, J. W., Dogherty, E. J., Squires, J. E., and Estabrooks, C. A. (2015). Why (we think) facilitation works: Insights from organizational learning theory. *Implementation Science, 10*(1), 141.

Berta, W., et al. (2005). The contingencies of organizational learning in long-term care: Factors That affect innovation adoption. *Health Care Management Review, 30*(4), 282–92.

Berta, W. et al. (2010). Spanning the know–do gap: Understanding knowledge application and capacity in long-term care homes. *Social Science and Medicine, 70*(9), 1326–34.

Berwick, D. M. (1989). Continuous improvement as an ideal in health care. *The New England Journal of Medicine, 320*(1), 53–6.

Berwick, D. M. (2004). *Escape fire: Designs for the future of health care*. San Francisco: Jossey-Bass.

Boström, A. M., Cranley, L., Hutchinson, A. M., Cummings, G. G., Norton, P. G., & Estabrooks, C. A. (2012). Nursing home administrators' perspectives on a study feedback report: A cross sectional survey. *Implementation Science, 13*(7), 88.

Cammer, A. et al. (2014). The hidden complexity of long-term care: How context mediates knowledge translation and use of best practices. *Gerontologist, 54*(6), 1013–23.

Carayannis, E., Campbell, D., & Rehman, S. (2016). Mode 3 knowledge production: Systems and systems theory, clusters and networks. *Journal of Innovation and Entrepreneurship, 5*(1), 5–17.

Chamberlain, S. A., Gruneir, A., Hoben, M., Squires, J. E., Cummings, G. G., & Estabrooks, C. A. (2017). Influence of organizational context on nursing home staff burnout: A cross-sectional survey of care aides in Western Canada. *International Journal of Nursing Studies, 71*, 60–9.

Chamberlain, S. A., Hoben, M., Squires, J. E., & Estabrooks, C. A. (2016). Individual and organizational predictors of health care aide job satisfaction in long term care. *BMC Health Services Research, 16*(1), 577.

Choi, J., Flynn, L., & Aiken, L. H. (2012). Nursing practice environment and registered nurses' job satisfaction in nursing homes. *Gerontologist, 52*(4), 484–92.

Cranley, L., Norton, P. G., Cummings, G. G., Barnard, D., Batra-Garga, N., & Estabrooks, C. A. (2012). Identifying resident care areas for a quality improvement intervention in long-term care. *BMC Geriatrics, 12*, 59.

Cranley, L., Norton, P. G., Cummings, G. G., Barnard, D. & Estabrooks, C. A. (2011). SCOPE: Safer care for older persons (in residential) environments: A study protocol. *Implementation Science, 6*, 71.

Cummings, G. G., Estabrooks, C. A., Midodzi, W. K., Wallin, L., & Hayduk, L. (2007). Influence of organizational characteristics and context on research utilization. *Nursing Research, 56*(4), S24–S39.

Damschroder, L., Aron, D., Keith, R., Kirsh, S., Alexander, J., & Lowery, J. (2009). Fostering implementation of health services research findings into practice: A consolidated framework for advancing implementation science. *Implementation Science, 4*(1), 50.

Dearing, J. W., Smith, D. K., Larson, R. S., & Estabrooks, C. A. (2013). Designing for diffusion of a biomedical intervention. *American Journal of Preventative Medicine, 44*(1, Suppl 2), S70–S76.

Dogherty, E. J., Harrison, M. B., & Graham, I. D. (2010). Facilitation as a role and process in achieving evidence-based practice in nursing: A focused review of concept and meaning. *Worldviews on Evidence-Based Nursing, 7*(2), 76–89.

Dopson, S. & Fitzgerald, L. (eds). (2005). *Knowledge to action? Evidence-based health care in context*. Oxford: Oxford University Press.

Doupe, M. et al. (2006). *Using administrative data to develop indicators of quality care in personal care homes*. http://mchp-appserv.cpe.umanitoba.ca/reference/pch.qi.pdf.

Doupe, M., Brownell, M., St John, P., Strang, D. G., Chateau, D., & Dik, N. (2011). Nursing home adverse events: Further insight into highest risk periods. *Journal of the American Medical Directors Association, 12*(6), 467–74.

Doupe, M. et al. (2012). Profiling the multidimensional needs of new nursing home residents: Evidence to support planning. *Journal of the American Medical Directors Association, 13*(5), e9–e17.

Estabrooks, C. A. (2003). Translating research into practice: Implications for organizations and administrators. *Canadian Journal of Nursing Research, 35*(3), 53–68.

Estabrooks, C. A. et al. (2015a). Dying in a nursing home: Treatable symptom burden and its link to modifiable features of work context. *Journal of the American Medical Directors Association, 16*(6), 515–20.

Estabrooks, C. A. et al. (2009a). Translating research in elder care: An introduction to a study protocol series. *Implementation Science, 4*, 51.

Estabrooks, C. A., Knopp-Sihota, J. A., Cummings, G. G., & Norton, P. G. (2016). Making research results relevant and useable: Presenting complex organizational context data to nonresearch stakeholders in the nursing home setting. *Worldviews on Evidence-Based Nursing, 13*(4), 270–6.

Estabrooks, C. A., Midodzi, W. K., Cummings, G. G., & Wallin, L. (2007). Predicting research use in nursing organizations: A multilevel analysis. *Nursing Research, 56*(4 Suppl), S7–S23.

Estabrooks, C. A., Niehaus, L., Doiron, J., Squires, J. E., Cummings, G. G., & Norton, P. G. (2012). *Translating research in elder care (TREC): Technical report*. Report No. 12-03-TR. Edmonton: Faculty of Nursing, University of Alberta.

Estabrooks, C. A. et al. (2008). Patterns of research utilization on patient care units. *Implementation Science, 3*, 31.

Estabrooks, C. A., Squires, J. E., Cummings, G. G., Birdsell, J. M., & Norton, P. G. (2009b). Development and assessment of the Alberta Context Tool. *BMC Health Services Research, 9*, 234.

Estabrooks, C. A., Squires, J. E., Cummings, G. G., Teare, G. F., & Norton, P. G. (2009c). Study protocol for the translating research in elder care (TREC): Building context—An organizational monitoring program in long-term care project (project one). *Implementation Science, 4*, 52.

Estabrooks, C. A., Squires, J. E., Hayduk, L., Cummings, G. G., & Norton, P. G. (2011a). Advancing the argument for validity of the Alberta Context Tool with healthcare aides in residential long-term care. *BMC Medical Research Methodology, 11*, 107.

Estabrooks, C. A. et al. (2015b). The influence of organizational context on best practice use by care aides in residential long-term care settings. *Journal of the American Medical Directors Association, 16*(6), 537; e531–7, e510.

Estabrooks, C. A. et al. (2011b). Assessment of variation in the Alberta Context Tool: The contribution of unit level contextual factors and specialty in Canadian pediatric acute care settings. *BMC Health Services Research, 11*, 251.

Estabrooks, C. A., Teare, G. F., & Norton, P. G. (2012). Should we feed back research results in the midst of a study? *Implementation Science, 13*(7), 87.

French, B., Thomas, L., Baker, P., Burton, C., Pennington, L., & Roddam, H. (2009). What can management theories offer evidence-based practice? A comparative analysis of measurement tools for organisational context. *Implementation Science, 4*(1), 28.

Gibbons, M. (1994). *The new production of knowledge: The dynamics of science and research in contemporary societies.* Los Angeles: Sage.

Glisson, C. (2002). The organizational context of children's mental health services. *Clinical Child and Family Psychology Review, 5*(4), 233–53.

Glisson, C. (2007). Assessing and changing organizational culture and climate for effective services. *Research on Social Work Practice, 17*(6), 736–47.

Glisson, C. (2015). The role of organizational culture and climate in innovation and effectiveness. *Human Service Organizations, Management, Leadership and Governance, 39*(4), 245–50.

Glisson, C. & Hemmelgarn, A. (1998). The effects of organizational climate and interorganizational coordination on the quality and outcomes of children's service systems. *Child Abuse and Neglect, 22*(5), 401–21.

Glisson, C. & Williams, N. J. (2015). Assessing and changing organizational social contexts for effective mental health services. *Annual Review of Public Health, 36*, 507–23.

Greenhalgh, T., Robert, G., Macfarlane, F., Bate, P., & Kyriakidou, O. (2004). Diffusion of innovations in service organizations: Systematic review and recommendations. *Milbank Quarterly, 82*(4), 581–629.

Grol, R. P., Bosch, M. C., Hulscher, M. E., Eccles, M. P., & Wensing, M. (2007). Planning and studying improvement in patient care: The use of theoretical perspectives. *Milbank Quarterly, 85*(1), 93–138.

Harvey, G., Jas, P., & Walshe, K. (2015). Analysing organisational context: Case studies on the contribution of absorptive capacity theory to understanding inter-organisational variation in performance improvement. *BMJ Quality Safety, 24*(1), 48–55.

Harvey, G. & Kitson, A. (2016). PARiHS revisited: From heuristic to integrated framework for the successful implementation of knowledge into practice. *Implementation Science, 11*(1), 33.

Harvey, G. & Kitson, A. L. (2015). *Implementing evidence-based practice in healthcare: A facilitation guide*. New York: Routledge.

Harvey, G. et al. (2002). Getting evidence into practice: The role and function of facilitation. *Journal of Advanced Nursing, 37*(6), 577–88.

Helfrich, C. D. et al. (2010). A critical synthesis of literature on the promoting action on research implementation in health services (PARiHS) framework. *Implementation Science, 5*(1), 82.

Hoben, M. et al. (2017). Improving nursing home care through feedback on performance data (INFORM): Protocol for a cluster-randomized trial. *Trials, 18,* 9.

Hogan, D. B. et al. (2012). Comparing frailty measures in their ability to predict adverse outcome among older residents of assisted living. *BMC Geriatrics, 12,* 56.

Hutchinson, A. M. et al. (2012). Feedback reporting of survey data to healthcare aides. *Implementation Science, 13*(7), 87.

Hutchinson, A. M. et al. (2010). The resident assessment instrument-minimum data set 2.0 quality indicators: A systematic review. *BMC Health Services Research, 10,* 166.

Institute for Healthcare Improvement (2003). *The breakthrough series: IHI's collaborative model for achieving breakthrough improvement*. IHI Innovation Series white paper. Boston: Institute for Healthcare Improvement.

Janssen, M. A. P., van Achterberg, T., Adriaansen, M. J. M., Kampshoff, C. S., Schalk, D. M. J., & Mintjes-de Groot, J. (2012). Factors influencing the implementation of the guideline triage in emergency departments: A qualitative study. *Journal of Clinical Nursing, 21*(3–4), 437–47.

Kaplan, H. C. et al. (2010). The influence of context on quality improvement success in health care: A systematic review of the literature. *Milbank Quarterly, 88*(4), 500–59.

Kaplan, H. C., Provost, L. P., Froehle, C. M., & Margolis, P. A. (2012). The model for understanding success in quality (MUSIQ): Building a theory of context in healthcare quality improvement. *BMJ Quality & Safety, 21*(1), 13–20.

Kitson, A. L. & Harvey, G. (2016). Methods to succeed in effective knowledge translation in clinical practice. *Journal of Nursing Scholarship, 48*(3), 294–302.

Kitson, A. L., Harvey, G., & McCormack, B. (1998). Enabling the implementation of evidence based practice: A conceptual framework. *Quality in Health Care, 7*(3), 149–58.

Kitson, A. L., Rycroft-Malone, J., Harvey, G., McCormack, B., Seers, K., & Titchen, A. (2008). Evaluating the successful implementation of evidence into practice using the PARiHS framework: Theoretical and practical challenges. *Implementation Science, 3,* 1.

Knopp-Sihota, J. A., Niehaus, L., Squires, J. E., Norton, P. G., & Estabrooks, C. A. (2015). Factors associated with rushed and missed resident care in Western Canadian nursing homes: A cross-sectional survey of health care aides. *Journal of Clinical Nursing, 24*(19–20), 2815–25.

Kojima, G. (2015). Prevalence of frailty in nursing homes: A systematic review and meta-analysis. *Journal of the American Medical Directors Association, 16*(11), 940–5.

Mallidou, A. A. et al. (2011). Staff, space, and time as dimensions of organizational slack: A psychometric assessment. *Health Care Management Review, 36*(3), 252–64.

Martin, J. (1995). The style and structure of cultures in organizations: Three perspectives. *Organization Science, 6*(2), 230–2.

Martin, J. (2002). *Organizational culture: Mapping the terrain*. Thousand Oaks, CA: Sage.

McCormack, B., McCarthy, G., Wright, J., & Coffey, A. (2009). Development and testing of the Context Assessment Index (CAI). *Worldviews on Evidence-Based Nursing, 6*(1), 27–35.

McCullough, M. B. et al. (2015). The interplay of contextual elements in implementation: An ethnographic case study. *BMC Health Services Research, 15*(1).

Muscedere, J. et al. (2016). Screening for frailty in the Canadian health care system. *Canadian Journal on Aging, 35*(3), 281–97.

Nelson, E. C. et al. (2002). Microsystems in health care: Part 1. Learning from high-performing front-line clinical units. *Joint Commission Journal on Quality and Patient Safety, 28*(9), 472–93.

Nelson, E. C. et al. (2008). Clinical microsystems, part 1: The building blocks of health systems. *Joint Commission Journal on Quality and Patient Safety, 34*(7), 367–78.

Nielsen, K. & Abildgaard, J. (2013). Organizational interventions: A research-based framework for the evaluation of both process and effects. *Work & Stress, 27*(3), 278–97.

Nonaka, I. (1994). A dynamic theory of organizational knowledge creation. *Organization Science, 5*(1), 14–37.

Norton, P. G., Cranley, L., Cummings, G. G., & Estabrooks, C. A. (2013). Report of a pilot study of quality improvement in nursing homes led by healthcare aides. *European Journal for Person Centered Healthcare, 1*(1), 255–64.

Nowotny, H., Scott, P., & Gibbons, M. (2003). "Mode 2" revisited: The new production of knowledge. *Minerva, 41*(3), 179–94.

Pepler, C. J. et al. (2005). Unit culture and research-based nursing practice in acute care. *Canadian Journal of Nursing Research, 37*(3), 66–85.

Pettigrew, A. M. (1979). On studying organizational cultures. *Administrative Science Quarterly, 24*(4), 570–81.

Phaneuf, J.-É., Boudrias, J.-S., Rousseau, V., & Brunelle, É. (2016). Personality and transformational leadership: The moderating effect of organizational context. *Personality and Individual Differences, 102*, 30–5.

Poss, J. W. et al. (2008). A review of evidence on the reliability and validity of minimum data set data. *Healthcare Management Forum, 21*(1), 33–9.

Rogers, E. M. (2003). *Diffusion of innovations* (5th ed.). New York: Free Press.

Rycroft-Malone, J. et al. (2009). Study protocol for the translating research in elder care (TREC): Building context through case studies in long-term care project (project two). *Implementation Science, 4*, 53.

Rycroft-Malone, J., Harvey, G., Kitson, A. L., McCormack, B., & Titchen, A. (2002). Getting evidence into practice: Ingredients for change. *Nursing Standard, 16*(37), 38–43.

Schein, E. H. (1983). The role of the founder in creating organizational culture. *Organizational Dynamics, 12*(1), 13–28.

Schein, E. H. (1986). What you need to know about organizational culture. *Training and Development Journal, 40*(1), 30–3.

Schneider, B., Gonzalez-Roma, V., Ostroff, C., & West, M. A. (2017). Organizational climate and culture: Reflections on the history of the constructs in the *Journal of Applied Psychology*. *Journal of Applied Psychology, 102*(3), 468–82.

Scott, S. D., Estabrooks, C. A., Allen, M., & Pollock, C. (2008). A context of uncertainty: How context shapes nurses' research utilization behaviors. *Qualitative Health Research, 18*(3), 347–57.

Shojania, K. G. & Grimshaw (2005). Evidence-based quality improvement: The state of the science. *Health Affairs, 24*(1), 138–50.

Smircich, L. (1983a). Concepts of culture and organizational analysis. *Administrative Science Quarterly, 28*(3), 339.

Smircich, L. (1983b). Studying organizations as cultures. In G. Morgan (ed.), *Beyond method: Strategies for social research*. Beverly Hills, CA: Sage, pp. 339–58.

Squires, J. E. et al. (2015a). Understanding context in knowledge translation: A concept analysis study protocol. *Journal of Advanced Nursing, 71*(5), 1146–55.

Squires, J. E. et al. (2015b). Identifying the domains of context important to implementation science: A study protocol. *Implementation Science, 10*(1), 135.

Squires, J. E. et al. (2015c). Reliability and validity of the Alberta Context Tool (ACT) with professional nurses: Findings from a multi-study analysis. *PLoS One, 10*(6), e0127405.

Stalpers, D., de Brouwer, B. J., Kaljouw, M. J., & Schuurmans, M. J. (2015). Associations between characteristics of the nurse work environment and five nurse-sensitive patient outcomes in hospitals: A systematic review of literature. *International Journal of Nursing Studies, 52*(4), 817–35.

Stalpers, D., van der Linden, D., Kaljouw, M. J., & Schuurmans, M. J. (2017). Nurse-perceived quality of care in intensive care units and associations with work environment characteristics: A multicentre survey study. *Journal of Advanced Nursing, 73*(6), 1482–90.

Ward, V., Smith, S., House, A., & Hamer, S. (2012). Exploring knowledge exchange: A useful framework for practice and policy. *Social Science and Medicine, 74*(3), 297–304.

Williams, I., Dickinson, H., Robinson, S., & Allen, C. (2009). Clinical microsystems and the NHS: A sustainable method for improvement? *Journal of Health Organization Management, 23*(1), 119–32.

Yamada, J., Squires, J. E., Estabrooks, C. A., Victor, C., Stevens, B., & CIHR Team in Children's Pain. (2017). The role of organizational context in moderating the effect of research use on pain outcomes in hospitalized children: A cross sectional study. *BMC Health Services Research, 17*(1), 68.

Zúñiga, F., Ausserhofer, D., Hamers, J. P. H., Engberg, S., Simon, M., & Schwendimann, R. (2015). Are staffing, work environment, work stressors, and rationing of care related to care workers' perception of quality of care? A cross-sectional study. *Journal of the American Medical Directors Association, 16*(10), 860–6.

15

Context in Action

A Research Agenda

Ninna Meier and Sue Dopson

The basic premise of this book, built on an interpretive approach, acknowledges that there is no such thing as "the (right/objective) context": any "context" in a piece of research is the result of the work of the researcher and/or the people being studied. The important point here is that it is wise for researchers to reflect on and explicitly state how they understand the construct of context applied in their work and whether or not "context" refers to a shared/common context or an idiosyncratic/individual context, or both. For both theoretical and methodological reflections, the crucial question is not what context *is*, as a stable phenomenon "out there," rather it is *how* we theorize, operationalize, study and analyze context in action, and the consequences of these choices for the research we can produce.

In the process of editing this book, we have sought to work collaboratively with the contributors of the different chapters. To support coherence across the chapters, we asked all contributors to reflect on how they understand context theoretically, and to share reflections on their approach to the process of research and understanding of context when relevant. Additionally, our assumption was that, in order to achieve our goal and produce a contribution to the debate on context, which was multidisciplinary, we needed to organize a process that facilitated this. In essence, we created a new context for the process of creating an edited book, and the discussions and choices within it. We began with a seminar, presenting the outline of the book and our preliminary theory and methods chapter. The contributors then put forward the basic ideas for their chapters, and each was discussed in relation to the rest of the book. Our OUP editor also participated, offering input on both formalities and our discussions. At the seminar, we decided to meet for a further seminar,

Context in Action: A Research Agenda

to be held after all of the first drafts of chapters had been submitted for review. As preparation for this meeting, we asked contributors to reflect on their conceptual contribution to context and the methodological considerations and lessons learned that they could share in the book. At the seminar, we again presented each chapter and discussed the concept of context and its relationship to action, to tease out the different nuances of how the contributors approached context in their work, as well as discussing similarities and the questions that the authors struggled with across the range of approaches. The seminars facilitated a discussion of context and its relationship to action across the very different approaches contributors have taken. Moreover, our attention to certain issues—for example, the question of representation (Whose context is it?) and visibility (Who are included/excluded by the contexts we construct?)—were products of these shared discussions. As editors and authors of several chapters, this was a valuable and inspiring process for us.

As the chapters in this book demonstrate, context can be conceptualized and studied in a variety of ways, and, as certain elements are included, others are necessarily excluded. Naturally, this issue applies to us as editors and authors in producing this book. The choices we have made to focus on and write about specific topics have downplayed a myriad of other important issues, both within the health care field and in organization and management scholarship in general. Examples of such relevant issues are, for example, questions of inequality in relation to class, race, gender, sexuality, or types of work and organizing often neglected. We would like to acknowledge this exclusion and we hope the book has inspired other scholars to remedy this through future work.

Throughout this book, our ambition has been to raise some important issues about context and its relationship to action and change, and to underscore our responsibility to be mindful of how we as researchers bound context in our research, and the consequences that such specific constructions of context may have for others. This responsibility is not only a matter of quality criteria for research; it is also a matter of acknowledging the potential world-making character of research. The call for research that bridges the theory–practice gap is not new (see, e.g., the discussion in Van de Ven, 2007), but what we understand as the institutional context for academia, in general, and in particular, for the research we do, is changing. Different regulators and backers call for research that will yield impact in practice *beyond* academia. Under programs such as Open Science or the Research Excellence Framework, scholars are asked increasingly to plan for and document impact beyond academia: to specify how academic work is expected to make a difference for society. We agree with the overall idea and ambition behind such calls[1] and hope that the contributions of this book help to shift the perspective on context in action in a way that highlights the scope for future sources of impact.

Where Do We Go from Here? Furthering Contextual Research in Organization and Management

We have argued that contexts are constructed by people as they individually and socially make sense of and engage with their social worlds. Such processes happen in the present, even when they draw on past events or connect to projections of possible futures (Hernes, 2014). Thus we expect research into such "contextualization processes" to be able to benefit from prior research into the embodied, embedded, material, and emotional nature of sensemaking (Helpap & Bekmeier-Feuerhahn, 2016; Maitlis, Vogus, & Lawrence, 2013; Meier, Ingerslev, & Bjoern, 2017; Steigenberger, 2015). Moreover, because people interact increasingly with and through technology in their social worlds, we expect that the integration of contributions from science and technology studies, actor–network theory, and computer-supported cooperative work will further our understanding of how technology and people act, as well as interact, to enact certain contexts and actions/interactions.

Another potentially fruitful stream of future research lies, in our view, in integrating the contributions of this book with the important work done on materiality, work, and organizing (see, e.g., Carlile et al., 2013; Orlikowski, 2007). Moreover, when analyzing multisite and multilevel phenomena, situated analysis (Clarke, 2005; Clarke, Friese, & Washburn, 2015) offers a way forward. This type of analysis draws on interpretive approaches and symbolic interactionism, and highlights the importance of contextualization and the situated nature of actions. We would like to see, in particular, a nuanced and systematic approach to context foregrounded in the analysis of material artifacts, spaces, and interactions as they come to matter significantly, when actors engage with and change contexts for actions.

One avenue for future research that has emerged in our discussions with the contributors to this book is the exploration of the influence past events and decisions can have on current actions—specifically events or decisions not included by the researcher in "relevant context." An example of this could be how actors draw on experiences and events from their past personal life, and how these, in turn, come to matter for current organizational events in important ways. This avenue of research into the context–action relationship might draw on narrative approaches to methods and analysis; see, for example, the work of Czarniawska (1997, 2004) in this area.

In short, several key areas in organization and management have seen calls for approaches that are more contextualized: organizational behavior, organizational change, research into managerial work, leadership as practice, and implementation processes, to name just a few. It is our hope that colleagues working in these and related fields will find the contributions of this book helpful in their work to advance the understanding of these important research areas.

Further developments will be needed for social science researchers, in general, and health care researchers, in particular, to progress from the post hoc analysis of events (which is useful) toward the capacity to critically assess alternative scenarios. Such developments will require better methods for understanding complex interactions as they unfold, and while progress once achieved might not enable precise prediction, it will ensure an improved assessment of larger trends.

Additionally, work to develop further multilevel-process study designs, which allow us to study how dynamic change processes unfold unpredictably in multiorganizational systems, needs to be done with the specific focus of analyzing how configurations of contextual forces are shaped by, and shape, participants' actions over time. Here, defining and operationalizing a clear unit of analysis and focal phenomenon will prove valuable to the complex task of tracing change processes over time and across multiple sites and analytical levels. Multilevel research is growing and expanding our knowledge of issues central to organization and management theory, but theoretical and methodological challenges remain (Paruchuri et al., 2018). A systematic approach to what is constructed as a relevant context for a phenomenon, and why, will aid comparative studies across organizations, sectors, or national settings, provided the researcher tackles the challenges inherent in multilevel approaches. This will not only add to a solid, empirical knowledge base for future research but also further develop context as a theoretical construct.

A Call for Action for Contextual Research

We anticipate issues about who would undertake new, large-scale, multilevel research projects. Where would they be based academically? The former Centre for Corporate Strategy and Change, launched in 1985 and discussed in Ferlie's Chapter 12, was a freestanding and self-funded research center at the Warwick Business School. Given the changes in the research-funding climate considered above, one question is: Could these research agendas generate significant health management research contracts now? A wider institutional question for many current business schools is whether they indeed wish to champion such health/public management research as part of their research mission, or whether they have since become too narrow and "siloed" (Currie et al., 2016). A major change in many business schools since the 1980s has been the rise of large finance groups, with their own, and distinctive, research concerns and common use of quantitative and technical methods. Many business schools now appear to be narrowly orientated to the study of a relatively restricted range of private-sector settings (notably shareholder-owned public limited companies (PLCs)), despite the political, economic, and societal importance of public service organizations, certainly including the health care sector. While there is growing public and academic disquiet about the role and future of private corporations, such important concerns have too infrequently influenced the research agendas of many business schools. So finding an academic and institutional base for progressing theoretically informed contextualist research in the UK and other health care organizations may not be easy.

Existing writing networks and learned societies (e.g., the Society for the Study of Organizing in Health Care) may have an important facilitating role to play in forming supportive links across the relevant academic community. A pressing question is how to incentivize and support the multidisciplinary work that is needed to make progress on the complex set of challenges facing those delivering health and social care. The current research-funding context makes this challenging despite efforts to bring social science and medical sciences together (e.g., CLAHRCs and Academic health science centers in the UK). A review of these efforts to ascertain learning about the impact of attempts to shift the context of research and knowledge sharing is urgently needed, not least to inform policy makers about options to facilitate the construction of a context for collaboration.

Implications for Practice

Universities face similar challenges to those of business schools: sources of independent research funding are decreasing; competition for funding is increasing; and researchers spend vast amounts of time writing grant proposals to funding bodies, which have rejection rates as high as 90 percent. The larger the scale and complexity of the research proposed, the more time researchers need to put together a short text displaying the relevance of the research questions, the theoretical contribution, the design and methods choices, the composition of the team, and the expected outcomes for theory and practice. Calls for impact beyond academia are both a welcome reminder of the relationship between research and society and a tricky issue to address in a few lines. This is because some elements of impact often have a "long tail" (they may only show themselves long after the research is over); others are notoriously hard to identify and measure because of the methodological challenges with which causal relationships can be unequivocally established in human affairs. Within academia, these issues are debated intensely as policy makers and funders call increasingly for "proof of impact" before funding and after the research project is over. In terms of the task of receiving funding for and carrying out the kinds of research projects we advocate in this book, such institutional changes in academia are potentially challenging because of the many other performance measures a researcher faces. Indeed, such performance measures may de-incentivize researchers from spending time and energy on "more risky" work within emerging fields, on large-scale projects, or collaborations across organizational or national borders. The issue of what interventions and changes to the current research-funding and academic-career context would facilitate high-quality impact work in health care studies is beyond the scope of this book, but it remains an important wicked problem worthy of reflection by policy makers and academic leaders.

Note

1. We would also like to note that the question of impact is not easy or straightforward. In particular, requirements to measure and document impact bring with them a range of methodological and practical challenges. As always, large-scale implementation of top-down institutional change initiatives may bring about unintended consequences, which has the potential to change the conditions for research in ways that may not yet be fully understood. These issues are outside the scope of this book, and are already subjects for debate within academia (see, e.g., the ongoing discussion on the London School of Economics and Political Science Impact Blog http://blogs.lse.ac.uk/impactofsocialsciences/all-posts/, where references to further discussions and publications can also be found).

References

Carlile, P. R., Nicolini, D., Langley, A., & Tsoukas, H. (2013). *How matter matters: Objects, artifacts, and materiality in organization studies*. Oxford: Oxford University Press.

Clarke, A. (2005). *Situational analysis: Grounded theory after the postmodern turn*. Thousand Oaks, CA: Sage.

Clarke, A., Friese, C., & Washburn, R. (2015). *Situational analysis in practice: Mapping research with grounded theory*. Walnut Creek, CA: Left Coast Press.

Currie, G. & Spyridondis, D. (2016). Interpretation of multiple institutional logics on the ground: actors position, their agency and situational constraints in professionalised contexts. *Organisation Studies, 37*(1), 77–97.

Czarniawska, B. (1997). *Narrating the organization: Dramas of institutional identity*. Chicago: University of Chicago Press.

Czarniawska, B. (2004). *Narratives in social science research*. London: Sage Publications.

Helpap, S. & Bekmeier-Feuerhahn, S. (2016). Employees' emotions in change: Advancing the sensemaking approach. *Journal of Organizational Change Management, 29*(6), 903–16.

Hernes, T. (2014). *A process theory of organization*. Oxford: Oxford University Press.

Maitlis, S., Vogus, J. T., & Lawrence, B. T. (2013). Sensemaking and emotion in organizations. *Journal of Organizational Psychology Review, 3*(3), 222–47.

Meier, N., Ingerslev, K., & Bjoern, K. (2017). Longing for future organisation: Embodied, material, and emotional aspects of prospective sensemaking. Paper presented at the *33rd EGOS Colloquium 2017: The good organization: aspirations, interventions, struggles*, Copenhagen Business School, Copenhagen, Denmark.

Orlikowski, W. J. (2007). Sociomaterial practices: Exploring technology at work. *Organization Studies, 28*(9), 1435–48.

Paruchuri, S., Perry-Smith, J. E., Chattopadhyay, P., & Shaw, J. D. (2018). From the editors. New ways of seeing: Pitfalls and opportunities in mulitlevel research. *Academy of Management Journal, 61*(3), 797–801.

Steigenberger, N. (2015). Emotions in sensemaking: A change management perspective. *Journal of Organizational Change Management, 28*(3), 432–51.

Van de Ven, A. H. (2007). *Engaged scholarship. A guide for organizational and social research*. Oxford: Oxford University Press.

Index

Note: Tables and figures are indicated by an italic "*t*" and "*f*" following the page number.

Aarons, Greg 95
accident and emergency (A&E) medicine 45, 46*t*, 47–8
action 28
 definition of term 1–2
 embodied 28–9
activity theory 17*t*, 57–8, 138–40
actor-network theory (ANT) 104, 107–8, 115, 252
actors
 blending of contextual elements 82
 bodily experience 28–9
 change processes and 21
 coherence of care and 44
 comparison across 59–60
 comparisons across 162–3
 context as actor 51, 75
 contextual change and 21, 192
 enacting context 14–15, 22–3, 53–4
 enactment of context 16, 82
 exploring context 20–1
 external personal experiences 51, 252
 heterogeneity of viewpoints 47, 50–1, 59, 175–6, 178
 identity of 104
 improving coherence 43–4
 inclusion criteria 52
 interactions with context 2–3, 14, 44–5, 71, 75–6, 80, 104, 155–6
 liminality and 60, 183, 186–7, 190–1
 policy context and 74
 process and 5, 7
 relationships and interactions between 15, 28–9, 75, 77
 relevance and bounds of context 79
 role in change processes 16, 52
 rules and norms for action 9
 sensemaking 53–4, 71
 shaping context 184–5
 social roles and group membership 185–7
 social roles and group memberships 18–19, 50–1, 185–6
 variation of viewpoint 18–19

acute care 75, 78–9, 111, 158, 220–1
addiction *see* substance abuse
Advisory Group on Genetics Research (AGGR) 39–40
Affordable Care Act 92
Alberta Context Tool (ACT) 63, 234–8
all-rounders 224
anthropology 17*t*, 52, 71–2, 207–8
Arendt, Hannah 1–2
asthma 160
Aston Studies 73, 207–8

bedside technicians 224, 226
bodies 28–9
 as instruments of action 28–9
 as source of knowledge 178
 as centres of knowledge 175–8
 as condition for action 28–9
 interactions between 110–11
 knowledge centres separated from 59
 patient knowledge of 177–8
 place and 176
 size of 109–11
 spatial location and movement 114–15, 166–7, 172, 176–9
boundary-drawing 19–20, 51–2, 190, 216–17
 organizational 73, 187–8, 205–6
 researcher as boundary constructor 60, 183, 187–9, 191
 temporal 26–7
building design 55, 78, 104, 115–18
 as context 115
 research implications 117
 kitchens 112–16
 patient engagement and 158
 patient room size 108–9, 111, 115–16
 projection devices 105–6, 110, 117–18
 temporality 114–15

cancer *see* oncology
care aides 239

Index

Center for User Driven Innovation 110
Centre for Corporate Strategy and Change 198–9, 213, 253–4
change processes, strategic 100, 184, 204, 206
Chicago School 107
chief executives 56–7
  contextual awareness and monitoring 129
  contextual levels 131–2
  orientation and connection work 129
  see also leadership; management
child abuse 18–20
childbirth 78, 155, 221
chronic conditions 48–9, 58–9, 93, 96–7, 161–4, 168
chronic pulmonary obstructive disease 22
citizen role 224
clinical areas 226
  see also operating rooms
clinical trials 239
coherence (of care) 9–10, 43–5, 47–9, 168–70, 173–4, 202
commerce 97
configurational analysis 26
conjectural causation 74
Consolidated Framework for Implementation Research (CFIR) 94–6, 234
consultations 48–9, 171–4
context
  agency and 217–18
  analytical layers 14–15, 26
    chief executives working across 131–2
  analytical levels 1–2, 6–7, 20–1, 26–7, 50, 139–40, 187, 253
  building design as 115
  causal vs interactive conceptions 123–4
  comparisons between 43
  defined 24, 123, 183–4, 216–18
  definition of term 1–2
  dynamic nature of 155–6
  as efficient cause 124
  as empirical concept 34
  external 73
  as external environment 16
  health care as 8
  individuals' influence on 50
  inner 51, 53–4, 61–2, 73–4, 82, 95, 123–4, 200, 206, 211–12
  interactionist view 72
  language and 2–3
  layers of 14–15, 82
  liminality and 192
  measurement standards 99, 234
  methodological approach 3
  receptive and nonreceptive 73–4
  as relational construct 24
  representational vs pragmatic approaches 124–5
  scope and boundaries 25–7, 54, 183
    for comparison 49
    methodological considerations 187
    researcher-set 183, 185, 189
  as sensemaking 82
  temporal 41
  stability 33
  theoretical 3
  as theoretical construct 14, 24, 138
    coherence 27
    conceptual clarity 24
    unboundedness 2
    unidirectional view 50, 184
contextual analysis 5–6, 15–16, 20, 22–3, 28–9, 218
contextual variables 109–10, 123–4
contextualism 61–2, 184, 197–8, 208–10, 212–13, 253–4
correctional systems 93
critical realism 217–19
  emphasis on social stratification 217
  generative causal mechanisms 218
  institutional dualism 217–19
  research design 219
cultural context 204

dementia 155, 159, 242
Denmark 9–10, 45, 108–10, 116–17, 139–40
  hospital-building 108
  national health care policy 41
Department of Health (UK) 38
Department of Trade and Industry (UK) 38–9
depression 96–7
Depression Improvement across Minnesota-Offering a New Direction (DIAMOND) 96–7
DH (Department of Health) 39–41
diabetes 159–62, 206
Diffusion of Innovations model 94–5
District Health Authorities (DHA) 61–2, 199–201, 204, 206, 211–12

engagement 125
EPIS (Exploration, Planning, Implementation, Sustainment) model 95–6
error 26
ethnography 57–8, 72–3, 98, 128, 139–41, 167–8
evidence-based medicine 14–15, 78–9, 90, 96–7, 99–100
exogenous context 124
external context see outer context
extrapreneurs 79–80

factory floor 106–7
families 159–61
Food and Drug Administration 97

Index

Framework for Studying Context in Action
  Question 1 (what constitutes context?) 20, 52
  Question 2 (how do actors engage with context) 21, 55

general practitioners (GPs) 45–7, 159–60, 169, 177
genetics 35–8, 41–2
genetics knowledge parks (GKPs) 35–42

healing hospital concept 107–8, 114, 116
healthcare support workers (HSW) 223
  all-rounder 224
  bedside technicians 224, 226
  citizens 224
  distribution and performance of tasks 225*t*
  management 227
  nurses and 228
  pay banding 223*t*
  roles 225*t*
  shift patterns 227
  ward teams 228
Heraclitus 91
hospital buildings 104–6, 109–13, 116–18, 198
  building projects 108
  design competitions 112
  patient room size 109
  size 113–14
housing policy 91–2

implementation strategies 96
information and communication technologies (ICT) 61, 151–2, 209–10
  vulnerability and 139
inner context 61–2, 73, 206, 211–12
  defined 200
  outer context and 51, 53–4, 73–4, 82, 95
  over-reliance on 200
innovation-adoption processes 75–6
inscriptions 104, 108, 111, 114–15
institutional perspective 9
institutional theory 17*t*, 184–5
integration programs 188
interactionism 53–4, 58, 71–5, 80–2
  data analysis 80–1
  emerging developments 82
  evidence-based medicine 78
  extrapreneurial responses 79
  history and development 72
  influence of national and cultural elements 77
  metholodological implications 80
internal medicine 43, 45–9, 46*t*

job context 123–4

knowing and knowledge 139–40, 142, 174–6, 178–9,
  defined 14–15
knowledge-transfer models 168–9
Kvalitetsfonden programme 108–9

laparoscopy 148–9
leadership 44, 160–1, 184, 233–4
  coherence creation and 47–8
  distributed and collective 76–7
  as domain of context 234–6, 238
  facilitation and 241
  from clinical professionals 208
  service change and 203–4
  transformational model 207–8, 234–5
  see also chief executives; management
learning health care system 55, 99–100
liminal space 60, 182–3, 185
liminality
  boundary objects 190
  boundary spanners 190
  defined 182–3
  delineation of contextual spaces 189
liminars 186–7, 190–1
linkman role 132–3
long-term care (LTC) 63, 236–43
long-term conditions *see* chronic conditions

management 126–7, 133–4
  clinical relations 205
  coherence creation and 43
  context comprehensibility 235
  context relevance to 126
  as element of context 28
  engagement 240
  functional vs interpretive nature of work 132–3
  general management role 199–200, 203–6, 208
  healthcare support workers 227
  of healthcare support workers 225, 227–8
  oncology 172
  use of research findings in practice 232–3
  as vantage point 125
  see also chief executives; leadership
managerial work 28, 125–6, 132–4, 252–3
maternity care 78, 155, 201
Medicaid 92, 96–7
Mental Health Parity and Addiction Equity Act (MHPAEA) 90
mental illness 97
microarrays 40–1
midwives 78–9, 221, 228
mixed methods 98
multimorbidity 43, 48–9

259

Index

network analysis 81
New North Zealand Hospital 112
New Public Management 8, 61, 77–8, 126, 201, 208, 211
NHS England 216, 220
NHS Internal Market 74, 90
NHS Labs 36, 38–41
NHS Trusts 209, 211–12, 219
nurse practitioners (NP) 217
nurses
   coordinator 47–8
   healthcare support workers and 220–3, 227–8, 235
   observation of 139–40
   oncology 171–3, 176–7
   patient interactions 156
   student 222–3
   surgical 142–5, 150–2
   wellbeing 157
nursing homes 155

obesity 55, 99–100, 206
oncology 45–7, 46t, 50, 139–40, 172
   cancer as chronic condition 168
   choice as case study 48
   distribution and fragmentation of care 59
   elements of care 170
   failure to adhere to treatment 174
   fragmentation of care 169, 178–9
   challenges and problems 170
   patient experiences 171–2
   patient vigilance of own bodies 177
   side effects 170–1
   unpredictability 48
   ward specialization 169
operation rooms 139
   action programmes 140
   patient safety 141
   support work 142
   see also clinical areas
Oregon 97–8
organizational change 1–2, 7, 15–16, 28, 43, 47, 51, 61, 73, 107–8, 157, 183–4, 198, 200, 208
   bounding context 183
   comparisons across organizations 41
   future research challenges 210
   Pettigrew Triangle 200
   receptive and nonreceptive contexts 202
      cultural 204
      environmental 204
      goals and priorities 206
      interorganizational networks 205
      leadership 203
      policy 202
   vantage point and 44
organizational change theory 17t

outer context 61, 82, 94–5, 184, 197, 200–1, 207–8, 210, 217
outpatient care 21–2, 48, 59, 112, 168

patients
   accommodation
      hospital room design 105–6, 108–13, 115–16
      shared 158–9
      single rooms 159
   body size 109–11
   criticism of care organization 158
   experience of care 171
   home self-care 159–61
   information comprehension and retention 168–9, 171, 174–5
   involvement in care 45–7, 59, 166–79
      body as source of knowledge 178
      as collaborative and integrative 173
      as compensation mechanism 173
      as compliance tool 173
      location and experience of context 176
      self-monitoring 176–7
   observation of other patients 156
   physical location and movement 167
   reflection on own care 157
   safety during surgery 142
   social interactions 158
   staff interactions 160–2, 178
   suggestions for process improvements 157–8
performance 210
personal context see inner context
PESTELI trends analysis 61, 210
Pettigrew Triangle 200
   change process 201–2
   content 200
   context 200–1
philosophy 14–15, 25, 27
philosophy of science 22–3
policy context 7, 35, 54–5, 87, 91, 93–100, 202
   dynamism 91, 94t
   external impacts 93, 94t
   as external influence 86–7
   extrapreneurial responses 79
   implementation and 96
   levels of analysis 87
   ongoing learning 99
   operationalization 97
   policy framing 93, 94t
   policy implementation 94
      as implementation strategy 96
   research context and 97
   short termism 92
   socio-ecological model 88
   temporal focus 92, 94t
   uncertainty 91, 94t
practice theory 14, 17t
primary care trust 77–8
prisons 93

Index

private finance initiative 209
process theory 24–5
professional networks 75

qualitative methods 18, 20–1, 59, 163

race 34
radiology 47–8, 149–50, 170
representation 3–5, 16, 52, 57, 167–8, 179, 250–1,
   selectivity of 57
   transparency of 52
research context 34
research design
   context multidimensionality and 51
   context representation 51–2
   context underdescribed in 33
   multi-method case studies 219
   Shaping Strategic Change 198
research perspective 51–2
Resident Assessment Instrument-Minimum Data Set, 2.0 237
residual categories 123–4, 173–4, 176–7
Rogers, Everett 94–5
Royal College of Nursing (RCN) 220–1

sensegiving 53–4, 71, 75–6, 82
sensemaking 4, 54, 133, 183–4, 252
   change and 75–6
   context as integral to 18–19
   context-bounding as 82
   contextualization and 20, 54
   directed attention 19–20, 54, 75–6, 82
   during surgery 145
   leading to action 53–4, 71, 78
   motivations for 76
   nonverbal 20
   policy 93–4
   power relations 75–6
   sensegiving and 76
   as social process 25, 75–6
   visual 145
shadowing 59, 123, 125, 127–8, 163
shaper role 132–3
Shaping Strategic Change 198, 207
   background and research design 198
   change context model 202
   gaps in analysis 209
shift patterns 227
situational context 123–4
smoking 91, 97
social workers 19
socio-ecological model 88
sociology 17t, 41, 52, 55, 57–8, 106–7, 138–9, 199, 207–8
State Health Practice Database for Research (SHPDR) 97–9
sterile zones 141

strategic change 100, 184, 204, 206
substance abuse 48–9, 90, 97
super hospitals 117–18
surgery 57–8
   abdominal 139–40, 149
   distributed attention and interaction 143
   efficiency 146
   endoscopic 142–3, 149
   gastrointestinal 148–9
   imaging technologies 150
   interruptions
      changes of approach 149
      equipment failure 148
      inaccessible information systems 149
   operating team 142–3
   orthopedic 139–40
   patient participation 150
   patient safety during 139
   postoperational phase 145
   preoperative coordination 142
   safety procedures 141, 146
   support workers 143–4
   surgeon's attention 145
   surgical instruments 142–3
   vascular 139–40, 150, 152
   wordless communication 144

technology 57–8, 148–9, 252
telemedicine 22
theoretical discussions of context 4–5, 14
time 41, 57–8, 60–1, 138–9, 197
   temporal reordering and fragmentation 168
tobacco 91, 97
Translating Research in Elder Care 236
transparency 4, 21–3, 34, 71–2, 80–1
transparency regarding 21–2, 34, 51–2

vaccination 93–4
vantage point 3–4, 16, 162, 167, 179
   importance of 45–7
   liminality and 186
   as outsider position 21–2, 50
   practitioner's 177
   researcher's 18
venous access catheter 150–2
vocational training 226, 229
voices 58–9, 81, 143–4
vulnerability 57–8, 139, 143–4, 149–50, 161

welfare 168–9
wicked problems 212
Willowtown Primary Care Trust 77–8
work organization 215–16
   heathcare support workers 220
   layered context 217
   workplace context 226

X-ray images 152